Death, detention and disappearance

David Smuts

Death, detention and disappearance

A lawyer's battle to hold power to account in 1980s Namibia

Tafelberg

Tafelberg
An imprint of NB Publishers
A division of Media24 Boeke (Pty) Ltd
40 Heerengracht, Cape Town, 8000
www.tafelberg.com

Cover photos by Tony Fiqueira
Cover design by Doret Ferreira
Book design by Nazli Jacobs
Map by Marguerite Rankin
Set in Dante

Originally printed in South Africa
ISBN: 978-0-624-08879-0 (First edition, first impression 2019)

LSiPOD: 978-0-624-08986-5 (Second edition, first impression 2019)
ISBN: 978-0-624-08880-6 (epub)
ISBN: 978-0-624-08881-3 (mobi)

To the memory of my parents.
And to the many who courageously resisted.

'The struggle of [people] against power is the struggle of memory against forgetting.'

Milan Kundera, *The Book of Laughter and Forgetting*[1]

CONTENTS

Ring the bells that still can ring
Forget your perfect offering.
There is a crack, a crack in everything
That's how the light gets in.

Leonard Cohen
'Anthem', 1992

ANGOLA

Tsumeb

NAMIBIA

Swakopmund

WINDHOEK

Walvis Bay

BOTSWANA

ATLANTIC
OCEAN

Mariental

SOUTH AFRICA

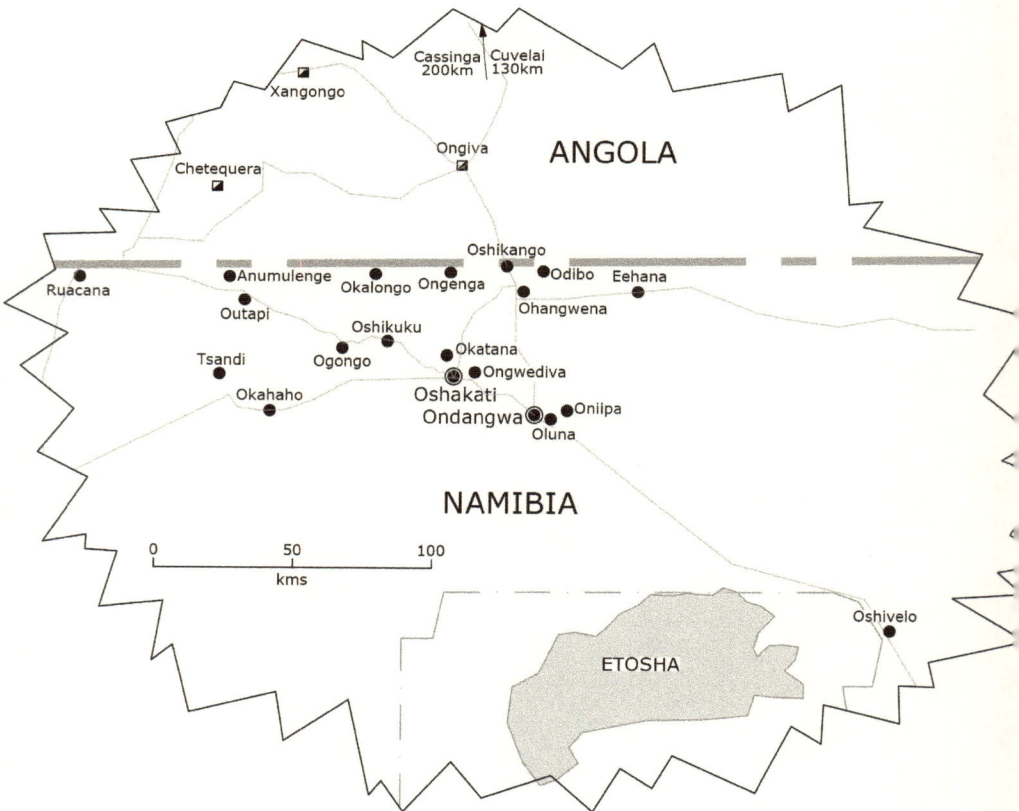

Cassinga
200km

Cuvelai
130km

Xangongo

Ongiva

ANGOLA

Chetequera

Oshikango

Ruacana

Anumulenge

Okalongo

Ongenga

Odibo

Eehana

Outapi

Ohangwena

Oshikuku

Tsandi

Okatana

Ogongo

Ongwediva

Okahaho

Oshakati
Ondangwa

Oniipa

Oluna

NAMIBIA

0   50   100

kms

Oshivelo

ETOSHA

The historical setting

Colonialism came late to Namibia. The country's rugged coastline, aptly called the Skeleton Coast, is littered with shipwrecks. Stretching inland for some distance from this uninviting shoreline is the world's oldest desert, the sublime Namib, which gives the country its name. On the eastern side of Namibia lies the vast expanse of the Kalahari Desert, which extends deep into neighbouring Botswana. These two deserts cover much of Namibia's territory, making it the most arid country in sub-Saharan Africa. This geography may have discouraged colonial powers until the late nineteenth century. But the discovery of diamonds and other minerals changed that.

Imperial Germany was the first to stake a colonial claim by proclaiming a protectorate around the port of Angra Pequena on the southern coast in 1884 at the behest of a trader, Lüderitz. The harbour settlement was later called Lüderitzbucht after him. The German colonial area was expanded and the boundaries of German South West Africa became settled after treaties with Portugal in 1886 and Great Britain in 1890.

The land policy of the German colonial period was directed not only at depriving the indigenous population of land for colonial settlement, but also – according to leading historian André du Pisani[2] – at destroying the political autonomous structures of the indigenous people. This was perpetrated by removing people from land and then dumping them on reserves of crown land as an effective way of exercising political and economic control over them. In this way, groups were fragmented and their leadership undermined. This approach was essentially followed and became intensified by the successive South African governments that replaced German colonial rule in 1915.

German policies of land deprivation and other abuses led to uprisings from 1904 to 1907. These were brutally put down, culminating in the infamous proclamation of extermination of the Herero by Governor Von Trotha (the 'Vernichtungsbefehl') and the genocide that followed. War crimes were also perpetrated against the Nama and Damara communities, which had revolted against German rule in the uprisings of 1904–1907.

Although German colonial rule is primarily remembered for the genocide and war crimes perpetrated against Namibia's people, the legal system imposed on the territory was also oppressive and operated against the indigenous people. German colonial rule did not, however, interfere with land tenure north of the 'red line'. Owamboland was instead to provide a pool of cheap labour. A migrant labour system was introduced which would, subject to refinements and adaptations, remain enforced until the 1970s. A pass law regime was rigidly enforced upon black inhabitants over the age of fourteen from 1907. The Germans passed a law that prevented blacks from owning title to property, or even horses or cattle, without the governor's consent. According to Pakenham,[3] those found guilty of stock theft

---

2   Du Pisani, A. 1986. *SWA/Namibia: The Politics of Continuity and Change.* Jonathan Ball Publishers: Johannesburg.

3   Pakenham, T. 1991. *The Scramble for Africa 1876–1912.* Jonathan Ball Publishers: Johannesburg.

under German law could be (and frequently were) sentenced to death after trials by all-white settler juries.

This was the nature of the legal system inherited by the South African government when it invaded the territory in 1915 following the outbreak of the First World War, marking the end of German rule. The territory was governed under military rule by South Africa until 1920.

The League of Nations was established after the end of the First World War and, under the Treaty of Versailles, the territory became a class C mandate entrusted to South Africa as mandatory power as a 'sacred trust of civilisation' with 'full powers of administration and legislation' over the territory 'in the best interests of the indigenous population'. The South African parliament passed legislation to formalise the mandate in 1919 and military rule formally came to an end with the appointment of an administrator in 1920. German law ceased to apply and Roman-Dutch common law as applied in South Africa became the legal system in the territory, together with statutes enacted for or applied to Namibia.

From the outset of the mandate, South Africa's government proceeded to rule the territory as a fifth province of South Africa. The influx of Afrikaners from the Boer republics during German times increased after South Africa took control. Large tracts of land were allocated to these white settlers for farming.

Native reserves continued and were expanded in size after South African rule, especially after the National Party won power in 1948 and implemented its far more rigid racial segregation policy of apartheid in Namibia as well. The native reserves were controlled through selected tribal leaders who acted under the control and supervision of white officials of the South African government. The reserves under German rule were pockets of mostly small pieces of land for the Nama, Damara and Herero people. This system became more formalised and consolidated under South African rule after the

Odendaal Commission, which, in 1964 recommended the imposition of its homeland policy of ethnically separated homelands, implemented in 1968. Apartheid by then affected every facet of life in Namibia.

The highly regulated and resented migrant labour system, the lack of access to land (after the initial deprivation) except in reserves without tenure, and massively inferior spending on public services on racial and ethnic lines meant that the profound level of inequality inherited from German colonial times became more entrenched and was further compounded by apartheid policies. The huge inequality in education and other public spending continued right up to independence in 1990, despite the installation of two interim governments with limited powers during the 1980s.

After the end of World War II, the United Nations organisation (UN) was established in 1945 and the League of Nations was formally dissolved the following year. The UN Charter did not, however, deal directly with former mandate territories, although the expectation was that these would form part of the system of trusteeship envisaged in the Charter. South Africa resisted trusteeship, however, and preferred incorporation of the territory into South Africa, a move supported by the all-white legislative assembly established for the territory. Thus began years of dispute over the territory between the UN and South Africa.

The National Party government furthered a policy of incorporation by providing for representation in the South African parliament to white inhabitants of the territory in 1949 and became more and more defiant in its dealings with the UN and the international community after 1948.

As decolonisation elsewhere in Africa and Asia led to new members of the UN adopting a more militant position against South Africa, there was a rise in black political movements and resistance within Namibia. The OPO (Ovamboland People's Organisation) was set up in 1958 (as the Ovamboland People's Congress), primarily directing its focus upon the detested system of contract labour although also espousing wider nationalist and economic objectives. The South West African National Union (Swanu) was formed in 1959 and was initially closely aligned with the OPO in opposition to the apartheid regime's policies – as was Chief Kutako's Herero Chiefs' Council. These three organisations headed a defiance campaign against the forced removal of black residents from what was known as the Old Location in Windhoek to Katutura. At least 11 people were killed in the clash between protestors and the South African police on 10 and 11 December 1959. The South West Africa People's Organisation (Swapo) was formed in 1959 from the OPO into a national organisation. Both Swapo and Swanu directed petitions to the UN.

Two UN members, Liberia and Ethiopia, brought a case against South Africa to the International Court of Justice (ICJ), demanding South Africa's accountability to the UN for its administration of the territory and also declaring that, by imposing apartheid upon the territory, South Africa was violating the mandate. The ICJ decided in 1962 by a close margin that the two states, the only two sub-Saharan members of the League of Nations, had standing to raise the dispute. The merits of the dispute later returned to the ICJ in 1966. The court instead revisited the jurisdiction issue and decided by a majority of one to reject the standing of the two states. It did not address the merits in a ruling that shocked international lawyers with its narrow and formalistic approach, as the court had dealt with that issue previously and avoided the merits.

Following the controversial 1966 ruling, Swapo decided to take up arms against South Africa's occupation, commencing a guerrilla war on 26 August 1966 at Ongulumbashe in Owambo. Most of the initial group of guerrillas were captured and tried under the new Terrorism Act of 1967, which was backdated to prosecute them. The defendants included Andimba Toivo ya Toivo. They were all sentenced to lengthy terms of imprisonment on Robben Island.

In the wake of the ICJ ruling in 1966, the General Assembly, in July of that year, revoked South Africa's mandate and declared the territory to be the direct responsibility of the UN. In 1968 it adopted 'Namibia' as the name for the territory, hence the use of that name in this book for the period after 1968. The UN Security Council in 1969 recognised the General Assembly's right to administer Namibia and requested South Africa to end its administration immediately. South Africa contested the validity of the resolution and refused to vacate Namibia. The Security Council referred the dispute back to the ICJ in 1970. The ICJ returned an advisory opinion in 1971, ruling that the mandate had been lawfully terminated, that South Africa's continued occupation was illegal, and that South Africa was under an obligation to withdraw from the territory. Swapo welcomed the ruling and called for immediate independence for Namibia.

In the years that followed, international pressure mounted upon South Africa over its continued occupation of Namibia. There was also growing resistance to its rule from Namibians, both inside the country and through the guerrilla war, which escalated after the collapse of the Portuguese empire in April 1974.

Within the country, workers mostly from Owamboland downed tools in 1971 in a crippling strike over the inhuman South West African Native Labour Association (SWANLA) migrant labour system. The massive mobilisation of workers compelled the authorities to abandon SWANLA. Not only did the workforce become more politicised as a result of the strike – the youth, who began to leave the country in droves to join Swapo to take up arms or to study, given the poor prospects for them in Namibia under the system of Bantu education, also became politicised.

Under diplomatic and internal pressure, the South African government embarked upon a policy of détente with countries to its north by promising action upon Namibia and Zimbabwe, then Rhodesia under Smith's Unilateral Declaration of Independence (UDI) regime.

There was even a commitment made by the then South African Prime Minister Vorster in 1976 that 'the peoples of South West Africa be allowed to decide their own future without being hampered or disturbed'. Pretoria convened a constitutional initiative in 1974, through its National Party leaders in Namibia. Dirk Mudge, then a prominent member of the National Party, announced invitations to separate ethnic groups with the emphasis on group rights and representation and excluding political parties. This became known as the Turnhalle conference, which was based upon ethnic fragmentation with white control of the economy. After months of deliberations, the Turnhalle conference reached agreement in 1976 upon an interim government from the beginning of 1977 for a two-year period while a constitution for an independent Namibia was to be developed, with independence envisaged for 31 December 1978. The prospect of sharing power – even on an ethnically fragmented basis – was too much for many within the all-white National Party, which split soon afterwards. A breakaway faction under the more enlightened Mudge formed the Republican Party.

While these South Africa-sponsored efforts were taking place, the UN Security Council passed Resolution 385 in 1976, which called for 'free elections under the supervision and control of the UN'. South Africa rejected the resolution. The five western members of the Security Council at the time formed a contact group and began a process of mediation with the South African government to break the international deadlock. They made considerable progress, with South Africa announcing the appointment of an Administrator-General for the territory in 1977 as a precursor to independence and an end to white representation in the South African parliament from the territory. Further diplomatic talks resulted in a compromise proposal, which would mean that South Africa would administer the elections subject to UN supervision and control. This resulted in the adoption of Resolution 435 by the Security Council in 1978. Other features

7

were that the process of elections to independence should be completed within twelve months. The resolution also required the repeal of repressive and discriminatory laws, the release of political prisoners, the phased withdrawal of South African forces from Namibia, and the demobilisation of ethnic and citizen forces, which fell under the South African Defence Force (SADF).

The South African government agreed to the terms of the compromise embodied in Resolution 435 in April 1978. Within days, however, it mounted a massive military raid on Swapo bases in Angola. Within months, it had reneged on its undertakings and, on 20 September 1978, decided instead to go ahead with a constituent assembly election pursuant to the Turnhalle initiative in defiance of the international community. That election proceeded in December 1978 amid international condemnation; the Democratic Turnhalle Alliance (DTA), a coalition of ethnically based parties led by Mudge, won 41 of the 50 seats. Swapo boycotted the election, as did moderate political parties or groupings that were not based on ethnic allegiance. The South African government installed a council of ministers and an assembly in May 1979. That assembly approved an ethnically based governmental structure the following year, called AG 8 of 1980, providing for eleven separate ethnic legislative and executive authorities for each 'population group'. The South Africa-sponsored internal initiative was roundly rejected internationally. A dispute between the Administrator-General and the council of ministers about public holidays led to the former dissolving the assembly and resuming direct rule.

There were sporadic diplomatic efforts aimed at persuading South Africa to implement Resolution 435. These invariably stalled, with the South African government linking Cuban troop withdrawals from Angola to the implementation of Resolution 435. By doing so, South Africa was latching onto a precondition set by the Reagan Administration, which had raised the issue of linkage as from 1981.

Not all diplomatic efforts came to naught. In 1982, the western contact group was able to secure the agreement of South Africa and Namibian political parties to a set of principles that would govern the constitution adopted by the Constituent Assembly elected pursuant to Resolution 435. As international diplomacy otherwise failed to make further headway, South Africa embarked on another internal initiative in 1983 by convening the Multi-Party Conference which, in June 1985, led to the installation of another interim government involving those who had participated in this initiative. The DTA was the dominant group, and Swapo was again excluded.

During these developments in the 1980s, there was an escalation in the guerrilla war in northern Namibia, which was under effective martial law. During 1988, renewed diplomatic efforts made progress in the wake of bruising battles in Angola for all protagonists. At the end of that year, an accord was reached, providing for the implementation of Resolution 435 on 1 April 1989.

A harsh and
hostile environment

Politicians are often fickle and feckless in the promises they make. Sooner or later, a promise solemnly undertaken is deviously denied or undermined to avoid or delay fulfilment. South Africa's Prime Minister John Vorster was no different. The undertaking made by the South African government in April 1978 to implement the UN peace plan for Namibia was soon in tatters.

The prospect of self-determination and justice for Namibia, so long denied, promised by the UN peace plan (later embodied in Security Council Resolution 435), entailed free and fair elections and inde-pendence under UN supervision. The South African cabinet was said to be divided when Vorster made that promise on 25 April 1978,[4] with the military balking at the idea. Its decisive response was swift and came nine days later: Operation Reindeer, a massive military incursion into Angola on 4 May 1978, the intended body blow to the implementation of the UN peace plan. It was a deadly two-pronged assault – on a Swapo base at Cassinga some 250 km into Angola, and on Chetequera some distance away, a cluster of Swapo forward base

---

4   Giliomee, H. 2003. *The Afrikaners*. Expanded edition. Tafelberg: Cape Town.

camps between 8 km and 20 km inside Angola, just north of the Omba-lantu area of western Owambo. Swapo casualties – mostly refugees – were heavy. This operation not only succeeded in scuppering the UN peace plan, but also signalled that the military had gained the upper hand in policy and decision making for Namibia at the expense of the diplomats supported by Hendrik van den Bergh, the head of the Bureau of State Security, known as BOSS.[5] Later that year, this mili-tary dominance was cemented when Vorster was to resign over the information scandal, bringing P.W. Botha to power.

The ensuing militarisation of South African rule in Namibia was to have a profound impact upon human rights and the law in the decade which followed. This book is about that impact over that period, starting with a case that arose from Operation Reindeer. It is about the assertion of rights and the law in a harsh and hostile environment against the backdrop of increasing lawlessness, includ-ing extrajudicial killings and criminal conduct by the military and security establishment, a descent into a darkness in which the mili-tary ultimately discarded the law and even suborned when it did not suit them.

The repressive legal landscape in Namibia at that time shared sev-eral similarities with the system in place within South Africa. Apart-heid policies were, after all, also applied to Namibia. They were scrupulously defined by law that was central to their rigid enforce-ment. Law was also used to deal with dissent. Several of the most oppressive laws were applied to Namibia, such as the Terrorism Act,[6] an earlier version of the Internal Security Act,[7] and the Police Act[8] and Defence Act.[9] There were, however, some significant differences

---

5   Giliomee, H. *The Afrikaners.*

6   Act 83 of 1967.

7   Act 44 of 1950 (Previously called the Suppression of Communism Act).

8   Act 7 of 1958.

9   Act 44 of 1957.

too. Unlike the ANC and PAC in South Africa, Swapo was not a pro-hibited organisation. Following the adoption of UN Security Council Resolution 385 (the forerunner to Resolution 435), a number of dis-criminatory laws were repealed when the first Administrator-General (South Africa's supreme representative) was appointed in 1977. These included the Prohibition of Mixed Marriages Act,[10] the Immorality Act,[11] separate amenities and segregated areas legislation. But the fundamental basis of apartheid through its separate ethnically based administrations with their profound inequality, especially in educa-tion, as well as access to land, remained in place until independence. Even the installation of the two interim governments by the apartheid regime did nothing of substance to change or even ameliorate that.

Another distinguishing feature was that the northern areas were under effective martial law, having been declared security districts under the notorious Security Districts Proclamation, 1977.[12] These areas were previously collectively referred to as the Police Zone (Owambo, Kavango and Caprivi), where more than half the popula-tion lived. A ruthlessly enforced curfew was in place in Owambo. That proclamation also gave the security forces (both the police and military) wide powers of arrest and detention. Any security force member of any rank had the power to detain for up to 96 hours. That was soon extended to 30 days. Later, the AG gave himself the power to extend those detentions indefinitely. Detainees were denied access to family and lawyers. They were also denied the ability to receive letters and have any contact at all with the outside world.

The enforcement of martial law in the northern areas was primari-ly in the hands of the SADF, an occupying army that had military bases of varying sizes spread across the entire area. Military check-points were set up on most major and several minor routes in the

---

10   Act 55 of 1949.
11   Act 23 of 1957.
12   AG 9 of 1977.

area, to be negotiated by local residents with varying degrees of indignity, depending on the disposition of those manning those points. Military patrols would search for and sometimes pursue insurgents without regard for people's homes and livelihoods. The sheer terror and lawlessness in the northern areas escalated even further and took a more sinister turn with the establishment of the soon to be feared paramilitary police unit called Koevoet (the Afrikaans word for 'crowbar') in January 1979.

Those living south of the northern war zone were able to live their lives largely unaffected by these military activities, although this was to change towards the end of the 1970s as remote white farms and some urban areas were also sporadically targeted by insurgents.

This legal setting and growing militarisation held little promise of a smooth and comfortable professional journey for a new entrant to the legal profession at the beginning of 1980 whose prime purpose was to defend those who had come into conflict with the apartheid state. It was instead to be a bumpy yet buoyant ride, unpredictable for the most part and mired by an incremental descent to lawlessness coupled with covert criminal conduct on the part of the military and security establishment.

During my very early teens growing up in South Africa, I recall becoming vehemently opposed to apartheid at a very young age. By my early high school days I had become determined to study law to defend people who challenged the apartheid state. Although my parents were not politically active, they were unambiguously against apartheid and encouraged an enquiring mind. I read widely and, from a young age, developed an intense interest in politics.

My ideal to represent clients charged for political offences by the regime was powerfully reinforced by an experience in my second-last year at high-school in 1971. I had been able to attend a single day of the celebrated political trial of the Dean of Johannesburg on charges under the Terrorism Act, which took place in Pretoria, where I spent my high-school days.[13] In a dramatic afternoon session, I observed the illustrious senior counsel, Sydney Kentridge, demolish a security police brigadier in a carefully constructed cross-examination, ensnaring the brigadier in his own web of deceit and contradictions until his version seemed to collapse. It was riveting. I was inspired and would be hooked.

I wanted to become a defence lawyer.

But my life was to take a new turn the following year. I was still in high school when my father was transferred to Windhoek to take up the position of Surveyor-General of the then South West Africa. (The name 'Namibia' was adopted by the General Assembly of the UN in 1969 and had been used increasingly since then. I used the term 'Namibia' in my practice in the years covered by this book, hence my use of the term).

I instantly took to my new home. The downtown area of Windhoek had a distinctly different feel from Pretoria. It was more racially mixed. Black citizens were not effectively excluded from Windhoek's central shopping area and made to feel as unwelcome as I felt was the case in downtown Pretoria at that time, even though white political attitudes were very similar in both places in support of apartheid policies. Namibia's unique status in international law added to its allure.

During my university years, it was my good fortune to attend a master class in cross-examination by another eminent South African senior counsel, Issy Maisels, which also had a profound impact on me. It was during my mid-year university break in 1976 and the setting was the Windhoek High Court.

At the end of a lengthy trial of Swapo activists under the Terrorism Act earlier in 1976, it was discovered that the Windhoek law firm defending them had been infiltrated by the security police. A part-

---

13   Reported as *State v Ffrench-Beytagh* 1972 (1) SA 828 (T).

ner called Anton Smit and Mrs Ellis, a secretary, had been recruited as security police informers and had, throughout the trial, deliberately and actively leaked key elements of the defence case to the security police who would in turn inform the prosecution. The firm applied for a special entry in the trial record to reflect this.

Issy Maisels was brought in to lead the legal team in the application to place evidence to this effect on record. It entailed cross-examining a security police captain named Nel and his co-conspirators, who had so fundamentally undermined the justice system. The defendants in that trial included Aaron Mushimba, a prominent Swapo member and brother-in-law to then Swapo president Sam Nujoma. He and three of his co-accused had been convicted under the Terrorism Act. Mushimba and a co-accused had been sentenced to death, and the others to terms of imprisonment. (Mushimba had been sentenced to death for allegedly providing a Land Rover vehicle to Swapo activists for transporting persons intending to undermine and overthrow the administration in Namibia. To make matters worse, leave to appeal was refused by the presiding judge but later granted on petition to the Chief Justice of South Africa.)

After conviction and sentencing, suspicions – and, later, evidence – emerged of security police interference with the defence, hence the application to enter evidence to that effect on the appeal record. Maisels was magnificent in exposing the conduct of Capt. Nel (who, despite this, was subsequently promoted and later became a brigadier in the security police in the late 1980s). Such disgraceful conduct was rewarded in the security police. To them, the end justified the means, as this book will demonstrate.

The appeal succeeded the following year.[14] The Appeal Court in Bloemfontein, the highest court of appeal at the time for cases from Namibia, cast aside the convictions and sentences in March 1977

---

14   Reported as *S v Mushimba en andere* 1977 (2) SA 829 (A).

because the infiltration of the defence amounted to such a gross violation of the principle of attorney–client privilege that lies at the heart of a fair trial. That court rightly found that this gross irregularity resulted in a failure of justice.

The forensic skills of Maisels were compelling to observe. But the context of the trial and the surrounding events made even more of an impression upon me. It was my introduction, even if vicariously, to defending dissidents in Namibia. But there was an enforced two-year delay before I could do so in person, caused by compulsory military conscription.

I had been in the first group to be called up for two years of compulsory conscription at the end of my law studies in November 1977 – a very grim prospect. I thought about leaving the country, but decided this was not viable as it would exclude any future involvement for me at home. I reported in January 1978, completed basic training and a short officer's course, and became a law officer in May of that year. As the only LLB with a Windhoek home address, I was posted to Windhoek, to appear in courts martial and review disciplinary proceedings.

One of my first duties was to defend a corporal who had absented himself from a newly established mixed-race battalion. He was a former foot soldier for the FNLA faction who had fought in Angola's civil war. The FNLA had been backed by the CIA and SADF and, by then, was all but crushed. He had been recruited by the SADF and allocated to 911 Battalion – a unit comprising mostly Namibian volunteers and conscripts of colour, and a few Angolans, led by white SADF officers. My client was repelled by the discriminatory practices within this battalion and had stayed away, but was caught. Charged with being absent without leave, he could not dispute his absence – but he decided to give evidence describing the racially abusive treatment he had experienced at hands of his white superiors, which had offended his dignity. This did not go down well with the colonel in charge of the legal department in Windhoek. He was the presiding officer and soon adjourned the proceedings to call me aside.

'What do you think you're doing?'

'I'm defending this person to the best of my ability.'

'Se gat, man! [Like hell, man!] You can't be serious with this kind of evidence. You're looking for shit. I've adjourned for you to reconsider.'

'Colonel, my instructions are to place this on record as it is all relevant for sentence.'

'You have one last chance to reconsider and drop this line of questions.'

'There is nothing to reconsider. It's my client's choice and I find it relevant.'

He stormed off to resume his presiding position. My client was punished and his sentence was reduced on appeal to a dishonourable discharge – his preferred outcome.

Within a week or so, my own punishment was also determined. The colonel summarily announced to me that I had been transferred to Owambo and instructed me to report to the officer commanding 1 Military Area at Oshakati, Colonel Kat Liebenberg. A few days later I sat in Liebenberg's office. He was blunt: 'I have no need for another law officer and didn't ask for one. There are two at my headquarters and no need for any more. I don't know what to do with you. But I've got a meeting with my four battalion commanders later this morning and one may have some use for you. Otherwise, I'll have to send you back.'

I hung around and was later called in again. A commandant was in Liebenberg's office. 'This is Cmdt Benade, OC of 53 Battalion. He says he can use you for disciplinary issues and boards of inquiry. Get your things and go with him to Ondangwa.'

It was an infantry battalion, a fighting unit with an armoured column attached to it. I did not fit in. One of my first boards of inquiry concerned the death of an unarmed civilian shot in his car by soldiers manning a temporary checkpoint. They had opened fire because the vehicle had been moving very soon after sunset. It had not got dark yet. The driver had not been challenged, nor had there been any attempt to fire warning shots. He had been struck by more than one bullet. The shots had all been clustered around the driver's position he occupied. I was required to meet the bereaved family members and soon understood their profound and justified grievance with the senseless killing. In stark contrast, there was an arrogant sense of entitlement and justification on the part of the military. Their stance was that he had, strictly speaking, contravened the curfew and could have been a terrorist. Attitudes to local civilians on their part (varying only in degrees between deadly indifference that negated their humanity to more intense race-based enmity) were to be a recurring theme in my next few months there, and later in my years of practice. I later investigated other instances of abuse of local residents and recommended that some officers be prosecuted by court martial. Although my OC, Cmdt Benade, generally backed me up and did not approve of abusive behaviour towards local residents, I became unpopular with the other officers in the unit and soon became regarded as a nuisance. Liebenberg was later promoted to brigadier and, I suspect, suggested to my colonel that I should be returned to Windhoek. And so I was recalled to Windhoek, not to be replaced.

A few months after my return, and while my colonel was on leave, the commanding general (Geldenhuys) called for an inquiry from the colonel's office. In searching for the file, I came across another, marked 'top secret'. A cursory glance showed that it concerned the summary execution of four unarmed civilians in northwest Owambo. They had been approached about the movements of insurgents and seriously injured in the assaults that accompanied the questioning. The captain in charge of the platoon decided that they should be executed and buried in a shallow grave a few kilometres north, just over the Angolan border. The platoon members were sworn to secrecy.

These appalling events would take their toll on a young conscripted member of the platoon, however. Deeply distressed by this bloodbath, he broke down to the visiting Chaplain General when he was touring the operational area. The chaplain sought an inquiry from Gen. Geldenhuys, which my colonel was appointed to conduct. The colonel recommended no disciplinary action, and a cover-up. His reason for this was to avoid the political fallout that would result from the exposure of the cold-blooded killings of those civilians. The general signed off on that. This so shocked me that I immediately reported the matter to the SADF's chief legal officer, Brig. Pretorius at SADF headquarters in Pretoria. I simultaneously decided that I would fly to Cape Town over the following weekend to raise this case with an opposition figure I respected in South Africa, Frederik van Zyl Slabbert, if Brig. Pretorius did nothing. My concerns on that score were soon dispelled. He caught the first available flight to Windhoek. When I fetched him at the airport, we proceeded straight to the Attorney-General, Donald Brunette. Both Brunette and Pretorius agreed that prosecutions must proceed. They agreed on a general court martial for murder in Pretoria, because part of the crime had been committed in Angola. The captain, a lieutenant and two non-commissioned officers were charged and convicted of murder in the court marital. The officers received lengthy terms of imprisonment. They later had some success on appeal, which was presided over by a judge.

My colonel never returned to his office. He was boarded on health grounds and retired early. Brig. Pretorius told me he could not trust such terrible judgement. I was to hold the fort until a replacement was found. In the next few months, and prior to a new colonel's appointment, another serious board of inquiry into military excesses was to pass my desk for me to advise the general on a recommendation. My advice was not accepted by the military command, which again preferred a cover-up. Again, I contacted Brig. Pretorius. Again, he flew to Windhoek urgently to meet the second-in-command about the matter and insisted that my advice be accepted. It had his full backing, and was begrudgingly accepted. My standing within the command increased. I was even invited to travel by air with the head of operations, Colonel Eddie Webb, to the northern zones so that I could attend to a board of inquiry while he attended to some meetings of his own there. En route, we stayed overnight at the same suite in Grootfontein and played several hands of bridge well into the early hours of the next morning with his second-in-command and the head of air force operations in Windhoek. Webb's name was to crop up just over ten years later as the SADF general in charge of special operations, which included command over a covert group curiously called the Civil Cooperation Bureau (CCB) that was responsible for my friend Anton Lubowski's assassination in September 1989.

Possibly because I had stood up to the command, at the end of my two-year period of national service I was promoted to the substantive rank of captain. I was made to understand that I was the only conscript in my intake to have received such a promotion. There still remained the obligation to do eight 30-day camps, to be served annually, which was to make life and practice more complicated than things already were.

My two-year stint had seen my political views undergo a change from liberal to a radical rejection of the status quo. I was firmly against the war and considered South Africa's presence in Namibia illegal.

The firm that had defended Mushimba and his fellow defendants was Lorentz and Bone. It was the only firm that defended political activists at the time. They had a vacancy in January 1980, which arose following the departure of Anton Lubowski, a university friend since 1973. Unlike me, he had put his compulsory military conscription behind him before going to university. While I had been caught up in mine, he had completed his two years of articles of clerkship (the training period to qualify as an attorney) at the firm, but had not passed the attorneys' admission exam within those two years. He decided to do pupillage as an advocate instead. He later became a prominent member of Swapo, although he was then very active within the Namibia National Front (NNF), which was also firmly opposed to the apartheid regime, its policies and its favoured politicians who formed part of the ethnic and homeland structures. Anton strongly recommended articles at the firm because of the political work being done there and its potential. Our friendship grew stronger in the years that followed.

On 1 March 1980, I started my two years of articles with Lorentz and Bone, articled to the senior partner, John Kirkpatrick, the leading commercial lawyer of his time in the country. He ably represented the leading transnational mining concerns operating in Namibia. The firm was hierarchical but liberal. The partners all opposed the apartheid policies imposed upon Namibia and believed in defending those who opposed the system. That was exceptional during those times. The overwhelming majority of the white community, then comprising about 8 per cent of the total population, strongly supported the apartheid state and the imposition of its policies on Namibia. The partners in Lorentz and Bone paid for their principles as many conservative white clients took away their business and caused their institutions to do so as well. For instance, the municipality of Windhoek, then dominated by white Afrikaners, took away much of its lucrative property work from the firm as a consequence of our representation of Swapo insurgents and activists in political trials.

During my initial two and a half years with this firm, I represented Swapo activists in their brushes with the law. I had developed a special interest in detention without trial and the myriad laws that facilitated indefinite detention, typically without any access to lawyers or family. I had seen that opponents of the apartheid state in Namibia were seldom put on trial. Instead, the authorities detained the regime's opponents for lengthy periods. No major political trials took place during this period or during in the following year while I was pursuing postgraduate studies on scholarship in the United States. There was, I suppose, hardly any need or incentive to put people on trial if they could be neutralised by detaining them indefinitely. As John Dugard explains in his seminal work *Human Rights and the South African Legal Order,*[15] the South African state would resort to trials of dissidents primarily for propaganda purposes – for internal as well as external consumption. This was also the approach in Namibia (by the self-same security apparatus) – a fastidiousness in going to great lengths to employ the powerful array of punitive measures at their disposal and to be seen to be relying upon the law in dealing with dissidents.

The distance from the immediacy of practice that a year's postgraduate study in the US had afforded me (in 1982/3) gradually gave rise to a realisation that I should shift my focus towards finding ways to mount assertive challenges to detentions and oppressive practices, seeing that my clients would seldom face trial. Intense critical discourse with my fellow students from diverse legal systems and backgrounds assisted in crystallising my ideas.

Trials under the Terrorism Act were heavily weighted against defendants (and justice). The accused were invariably detained for several months without access to lawyers or their families. This meant that torture and ill treatment, then routine, could and would mostly go undetected. Witnesses, often accomplices or informants, were also detained and promised release if their testimony satisfied their incarcerators. The statutory offence of terrorism was framed

---

15   Princeton University Press, 1978.

widely and also included an inverted burden of proof. The effect was that defendants would need to prove their innocence, instead of the universally accepted standard of guilt being established beyond reasonable doubt.

The composition of the courts also undermined notions of fairness. Some, but not all, of the judges who were selected to preside in these earlier cases in Namibia had been ardent supporters of apartheid, rewarded for their loyalty with appointments as judges to the court in Windhoek.

There would be little prospect of a fair trial under these circumstances. This was to change in the 1980s, however, with judicial appointments increasingly made from the ranks of local lawyers, making a significant difference.

The inherent unfairness of political trials did not mean that defendants should go unrepresented. As long as they and their families wanted representation, which they did, there was no doubt in my mind that they should have it. Their defence was to be seen within the overall context of an unjust legal system, and the need to expose this. Necessary as it was, defence work in infrequent trials was not enough.

My focus was to shift away from defence work to finding ways to tackle detentions head-on instead of waiting for the unlikely occurrence of our clients being charged.

I no longer saw my role as primarily a defence lawyer. It was rather the pernicious system that should be put on its defence, in its various facets, by seeking to use the law to bring about accountability. A more assertive stance was required against detention laws and those stifling dissent and delaying progress to self-determination.

This book concerns some of the cases and work I was privileged to become involved in over the years, in this context of pursuing a more assertive approach, which would require adapting at times to meet the impact upon the law of increasing militarisation and the authorities' increasing subversion of the law. This despite the attempt to mask this trend by packaging it in the veneer of a more benevolent multiracial front under the Interim Government (IG) installed by Pretoria in mid-1985. The inclusion of a bill of rights in its empowering proclamation promised much, but delivered no real change in human rights abuses and the fundamental inequality that apartheid policies brought about and whose core remained firmly in place with the separate ethnic administrations and structures until the eventual implementation of the UN peace plan in 1989, which coincided with the demise of P.W. Botha and, eventually, of the malevolent military edifice that surrounded him. The cases illustrate how the ultimate control in Namibia remained with the security establishment, whose abuses intensified and later became more sinister, resorting to covert criminal conduct. The first of these cases following my return from the US concerned uncovering the secret internment without trial for some six years of over 100 Swapo cadres captured in Angola in the course of Operation Reindeer. It was to be a watershed, and an ominous portent of what was to come.

1

Secret – and indefinite – internment

Late one night in mid-February 1984, there was a quiet yet persistent knock at the door of the small garden cottage I rented in suburban Windhoek, a creatively converted double garage at a discreet distance from the main house. My friend and colleague, Hosea Angula, and Samson Ndeikwila of the Council of Churches in Namibia (CCN) quickly entered, accompanied by another man, introduced as Bennie Shilongo, who slid in behind them. He looked around uneasily. His eyes continually shifted their gaze, alternating between the surroundings and my interaction with Hosea and Samson. He seemed intrigued by Hosea's familiarity with the surroundings: Hosea made his way straight to the fridge, and took out and opened a few beers, while Samson, with equal ease, engaged in casual small talk with me.

By the time we sat down, Bennie, with beer in hand, was discernibly more comfortable. After Samson amplified his introduction, hinting that crucial linking evidence was at last at hand, Bennie soon began to speak freely about going into exile and his capture by the SADF on 4 May 1978 at a Swapo transit refugee camp called Vietnam at Chetequera in southern Angola. He said that the camp had been pulverised by a powerful attack by an armoured column, preceded by aerial bombardment. Heavy fighting had ensued. Several people had been killed. After about four hours of intense fighting, resistance had finally been quashed and an eerie stillness had descended. Along with about 200 other refugees, he was rounded up, taken prisoner by the SADF and brought back to Namibia.

The official accounts differ about the number of people killed in this attack.[16] The network of camps around Chetequera constituted Target Bravo of the SADF's Operation Reindeer. Target Alpha, the primary target, was a Swapo base at Cassinga. The accounts of numbers of those slain at Cassinga do not differ as much as those at Chetequera. According to the Swapo reports at the time, 615 Swapo refugees were killed at Cassinga and 100 at Chetequera.[17] The official South African account puts those figures at 600 and 248 respectively. This mass slaughter is annually commemorated as a public holiday in independent Namibia, although the focus is mainly on the Cassinga massacre, with little said about those slain and captured at Chetequera.

It would appear that no one was taken prisoner at Cassinga. Several hundred Swapo refugees were left there, injured. The South African troops were ferried back by helicopter from a point near Cassinga to their bases close to the Namibian border. There was no space on board the helicopters for prisoners.

According to the South African account, 202 Swapo members were captured at Chetequera. Sixty-three of them were said to have been released on 29 May 1978 and 118 were transferred to a rudimentary internment camp at Mariental.[18] These figures roughly accord with

---

16 Usefully collected in Annemarie Heywood's *The Cassinga Event* (National Archives of Namibia, Windhoek, 1994), quoting from official statements made and the accounts by Willem Steenkamp in *South Africa's Border War, 1966–1989* (Helion and Company, 2014); Richard Dicker in *Accountability in Namibia: Human Rights and the Transition to Democracy* (Human Rights Watch, 1992); and *The Combatant* (PLAN's monthly organ).

17 Heywood, pp. 118–119.

18 Heywood, pp. 118–119.

those provided to me by former detainees. I have not encountered an explanation for the 21 persons unaccounted for in this version. It is possible that some died, while others may have been released even earlier. The official Swapo version is that 270 refugees were taken prisoner.[19] Most detainees put the figure at about 200, however. Presumably, several refugees were unaccounted for in the turmoil that followed the attack. Some may have been able to flee, and may even have got back home again. Others may have died; these facts were not known by Swapo at the time.

Bennie had left northern Namibia along with several other young Namibians from his area about a week before the attack on Chetequera and their capture. After crossing the border, they had made their way to the Vietnam base at Chetequera where they had met up with other refugees and been welcomed by Swapo cadres. This base, some 20 km inside Angola, formed part of a network of forward bases of varying sizes in the area, ranging from 6 km to 28 km inside Angola as supply points and as reception or transit centres for Namibians going into exile.[20]

Bennie had gone into exile in the hope of studying further and bettering himself. Prospects in Namibia for him at that time were bleak. He had left school early and migrated to Windhoek in search of employment. The best he could do was to become an ice cream vendor, on a bicycle, ringing his bell to offer his wares in the small city centre, the more affluent areas and at sporting events. His exile was short-lived, however, with the SADF attack on the Vietnam base occurring within a week of his arriving there. Bennie was released in the group of 63 captives on 29 May 1978. Presumably the remaining detainees were considered more hard-line; one can only speculate about the motivation, as no reasons have ever been given. Some time after his release, Bennie was employed as a driver at the Otjihase

19   Heywood, pp. 118–119.
20   Heywood, p. 49.

copper mine near Windhoek, a position he occupied at the time of our meeting.

Bennie dispelled the myth repeatedly put out by the South African propaganda machine and slavishly disseminated by the local media that youngsters in Owambo were violently abducted and taken away at gunpoint by People's Liberation Army of Namibia (PLAN) fighters every time they left in droves to join Swapo. Most of those perpetrating and perpetuating this distortion (assuming they believed it) failed to understand or even consider the deep disillusionment felt by young people at massive inequality along racial lines and the lack of opportunities facing them, let alone the rapidly growing political consciousness that motivated these departures. Political consciousness had risen sharply following the national strike in 1971 directed at the hated SWANLA contract labour system, which denigrated people to mere labour units and severely restricted their mobility.

Resentment at the discriminatory education system and the regime also escalated dramatically among young people after the 1976 Soweto uprising in neighbouring South Africa. Namibians were subjected to fundamentally the same form of Bantu education that continued until independence, despite the installation of the IG by the apartheid regime in 1985. Indeed, despite its professed commitment to doing away with racism and racial inequality, the IG was party to its perpetuation by maintaining the racial and ethnic segregation in schools and the profound disparity on education spending. Ten times more was spent on the education of children in segregated white schools compared to children in Owambo in 1986.[21] The discrepancy was probably considerably worse when Bennie left school in the mid- to late 1970s.

---

21 *Ex parte Cabinet for South West Africa: In re advisory opinion* 1988 (2) SA 832 (SWA) at
    864H-J.

Bennie had a friendly and open disposition and spoke with ease and coherence about the events. He confirmed the capture of those in the original list of thirteen names of detainees I had obtained the previous November, initiating my inquiries, which started the case. He wanted these friends to be released, as well as the others captured with him at Chetequera. He was now prepared to come forward, assist with the challenge and make an affidavit in support of an application for the release of the remaining 118 detainees captured with him and secretly held near Mariental. He confirmed that the detainees mentioned in my November letter to the military had, in fact, been captured with him at the Vietnam base. They had been brought back to Namibia and held in a makeshift tented internment camp adjacent to the Oshakati military headquarters, surrounded by high barbed wire fences with watchtowers at intervals. Later, corrugated iron structures, which the military called the 'hokke' (cages), had been erected there.

Most of his fellow captives had not been released with him on 29 May 1978. He had recently heard from some of their families that they were being held at a military internment camp near Mariental after some had been permitted visits. He also said that, during his detention, he and other detainees had been tortured, including by way of electric shock treatment. He had been blindfolded for most of his detention but at one point had managed to see that one of his fellow detainees, Nikodemus Katofa, had been suspended for long periods by his arms, which were tied with wire above his head, his legs unable to touch the ground. He also spoke of frequently hearing screaming from his fellow captives as they cried out during torture sessions.

Bennie's account represented a breakthrough in unearthing evidence of the secret detention of the remaining captives from Chetequera – then held for almost six years without charge.

The idea of challenging their secret detention had come to me while I was doing postgraduate studies in Cambridge, Massachusetts, in the US spring of 1983 – some nine to ten months before. I had been invited to a seminar organised by the UN Council on Namibia at Columbia Law School in New York to speak on a panel about Namibia's position in international law. My task was to make a brief presentation on the repressive legal framework and how it operated against those who pressed for self-determination, and to speak about legal practice there. I provided damning details on the former and a few brief remarks on the latter. I had only recently qualified as a lawyer.

Preparing for my talk afforded me the opportunity to look at detention laws afresh from afar. This was a fruitful exercise. The detention power principally invoked by the South African security forces was in Security Districts Proclamation AG 9 of 1977 (AG 9) enacted by the first Administrator-General (AG) shortly after his appointment in 1977. It authorised any member of the security forces (both SADF and police) of any rank to detain people without trial. They could initially do so for up to 96 hours, soon extended to 30 days. In 1979 AG 9 was amended by the AG to authorise himself to order the further and indefinite detention of detainees already in custody. This amendment was embodied in section 5 bis.

It struck me that this amendment had probably been included in a bid to legalise the incarceration of the Mariental detainees captured in Angola, who became known as the Cassinga detainees – a slight misnomer as they were captured at Chetequera but as part of Operation Reindeer, which was primarily directed at Cassinga.

Rumours of their capture and subsequent detention had circulated for some time. But these were not confirmed by the SADF or the authorities. Indeed, the detainees were held at a secret location. Shortly before I left for my studies in the US in 1982, there was some talk of them being held in an internment camp near Mariental, about 270 km south of Windhoek. These accounts started surfacing after family contact with detainees was eventually permitted, at first by letter in 1981 and later in the form of visits in 1982. I later discovered that these forms of contact had been brokered by the good offices of the International Committee of the Red Cross (ICRC). But I had not received any direct corroboration of this when I left Namibia for my studies in mid-1982.

Attendance at the New York seminar was rewarded with refreshments afterwards. That was the best part, as I suppose it usually is at events like these. I did not need much persuasion to loiter a little over the tepid American beer on offer – not just because I was putting off braving the cold, grey spring afternoon to make my way back by subway to Penn Station to catch my train back to Boston. I was missing home and enjoyed the friendly reinforcement from a group of exiled Swapo members and officials. Their longing for home was understandably much stronger than mine. I could, after all, go home on completion of my studies; their homecoming seemed an incomparably remote and distant prospect. One of their number in particular stood out. He was Swapo's then United Nations representative, Theo-Ben Gurirab, a charming and erudite man, who had spoken earlier.

Exiled Swapo members were eager for news and more recent impressions of the situation at home. Their generous encouragement in my human rights work was unequivocal, their acceptance re-affirming. But my commute back to Boston beckoned.

In the course of extended farewells and exchanging contact details, a striking African-American woman purposefully joined our circle and introduced herself in a discernible southern drawl as Gay Mc-Dougall. She wanted a quick word. Gay, too, needed to travel, but in the opposite direction – back to Washington, DC, where she worked for a respected civil rights organisation, the Lawyers' Committee for Civil Rights under Law. Gay directed its Southern African Project, which supported those engaging in legal challenges to the South

African regime. She came quickly to the point and offered her collaboration and financial support to defend those on trial. She invited me to visit her office before returning home after my studies. I spoke of my growing interest in making challenges to detentions and the laws that facilitated them, given that so few people were put on trial. I updated her on the breakdown of law in the northern areas of Namibia, with security forces acting with impunity there. Her eyes lit up when I spoke of the need to bring about some accountability for the deaths, detentions and disappearances that regularly occurred in those areas.

Our frenetic chatter continued as we strode together towards the nearby subway station. I referred to the 1979 amendment to AG 9 enacted after the Mariental detainees were already in detention, and thus questionable. I suggested to Gay that her organisation may wish to support investigating a challenge to the legality of their detention financially. It seemed viable; Gay enthusiastically agreed.

I would only return to Namibia after the summer, however, as I had landed a position of summer associate with Ropes and Gray, a leading law firm in Boston. Before eventually returning to practice at Lorentz and Bone in Windhoek in October 1983, I had a final conversation with Gay about the logistics of investigating a challenge. Gay understood that communication with her after my return home would of necessity be minimal until an application had been served. This was because telephone lines were invariably tapped and correspondence intercepted of those engaged in work against the apartheid regime. We had always suspected this and were to receive proof a few years later when my friend and fellow activist, Gwen Lister, discovered a letter in her postbox, marked 'top secret', from the head of the South African Police to notify the Postmaster of Windhoek of the authorisation to intercept her mail. When Gwen made this public, she was arrested and detained over a weekend on charges of contravening the Official Secrets Act for making known a classified communication.[22] It seemed like something straight out of Kafka. The bizarre charges were dropped six weeks later.

Upon my return, I set about making enquiries, seeking the names of detainees who had been captured in Angola and the whereabouts of their relatives. An activist Catholic priest, Father Stegmann – who consistently provided staunch and invaluable support in detainee work – declined to give any information. He had become aware of the detentions and the location and even knew some of the names of detainees and their relatives. His church was assisting the ICRC in putting relatives in contact with the detainees. Some had even visited their detained relatives through the church's intermediation. He had been sworn to confidentiality on the issue. It had been a condition of the church's participation in arranging the visits. He was concerned that the privileges and the improved conditions that the ICRC had painstakingly negotiated over a long period may be withdrawn and future visits refused if I were to start stirring. A highly principled person, he considered himself bound by the oath of confidentiality he had taken. Through my work for detainees, I had also come to know the ICRC's representative well. He confirmed the detentions too, but could not divulge any further information or provide any leads because of his position.

A close colleague on matters of this nature at the firm and a very good friend, Hartmut Ruppel, also voiced his concern that my enquiries and activism on the issue may have adverse consequences for the detainees themselves along the lines put forward by Father Stegmann, who had obviously enlisted Hartmut's support to prevail upon me to drop my enquiries in the best interests of the detainees.

I understood why they felt this way. The security forces were often vindictive to detainees when efforts were made to obtain access to them or when there were petitions for their release. Detainees

---

22   *The Cape Times*, 31 January 1985.

were also appallingly treated, especially in the outlying areas where there was little or no supervision and often no restraint. Conditions there were frequently makeshift and routinely subhuman. This was also the case, as I later discovered, for the detainees in Mariental. The conditions were grim for the first few years but were vastly improved from 1981 when they were moved to a new camp nearby with better facilities. This coincided with the involvement of the ICRC.

Although I respected their concerns about jeopardising the gains in detainee access and treatment, the risk of setbacks was, I believed, well worth the reward of the resultant exposure – and a possibility, even, of success. Their detention was indefinite, without even the remotest prospect of release after more than five and a half years of secret incarceration. The issue of their release would not, in my view, receive attention unless their plight was exposed and pressure generated on the issue. The detentions would also need to be justified as a matter of law.

My colleague Hosea Angula, who was doing his articles with us at the time and was later to make history as the first Oshiwambo-speaking person to be admitted as a lawyer in Namibia, was, in contrast, unqualified in his support of a challenge to the detentions. From then on, we drove the legal action together. We had become close friends from his first year at university when he had worked in my office as a student assistant during his long vacation at the end of that year. This was in the first year of my articles. He had applied for vacation work. He was interviewed by one of the partners, a well-meaning liberal man who told him to return for the outcome of that interview in the afternoon. In the meantime, the partner approached me to avoid some personal discomfort in turning Hosea down, and preferred me to do so. Sensing this, I asked for his reason. He said we had no space. Upon my further enquiry, he confirmed to me that this was the only impediment, and reiterated, 'Yes, unfortunately you must turn him away as a result.'

It was true that there were no spare offices. I felt at the time that some sort of makeshift plan would have been fashioned for the child of a well-connected client in a similar position. When Hosea came back in the afternoon, I instantly got on with him. We first chatted about the work I was doing and his studies and the student unrest at his university. We turned to the matter at hand. I informed him that there was no space and that the firm was minded not to make him an offer for that reason. But if he cared to share my office, there would be work for him. That was the start of an enduring friendship and close working relationship. He returned to the firm each long holiday after that and joined to do his articles upon completing his studies. I was in the US with my graduate studies at the time and informed the firm that my decision to return to them could be affected if he were not to be offered a position. I did so because there was some doubt expressed by the firm to me on that score. I was told that other (white) applicants had approached the firm and had LLBs – a five-year degree course, as opposed to the four-year BProc that Hosea was then about to complete. I greatly admired Hosea's tenacity in completing his studies at the University of the North in South Africa in what were very turbulent times at segregated black South African universities. Boycotts and unrest frequently interrupted lectures and exams. Completing a course in the designated duration was no mean feat, and took very special qualities. I expressed this to John Kirkpatrick in my correspondence with him about my own future with the firm, urging him to adopt a wider view about qualifications and the qualities of applicants. Fortunately he was persuaded.

My enquiries to my usual church and other sources in my work for information about the Mariental detainees and their relatives drew a blank. I then turned to Dan Tjongarero, a prominent Swapo leadership figure. At the time, he was Director of Communications at the CCN. He said he needed some time to follow up, and would get back to me. He, too, was excited about the idea of a challenge and promised to do what he could. About ten days later he brought his CCN colleague, Samson Ndeikwila, to see me.

Samson originally hailed from the Ombalantu area in the western part of Owambo. He had gone into exile several years before and received military training, but was later detained in Tanzania at Swapo's instance. On his release he travelled to Kenya where he furthered his studies. He had returned to Namibia some three years previously[23] and obtained employment from the CCN after its recent establishment. Samson had heard that some of the detainees were from his area. He knew someone who would possibly be prepared to assist us. He, too, needed time to make his enquiries. They would be discreetly done in person when he next travelled to the northern areas. As the detentions were secret, and not publicly acknowledged, we needed not only the names of the detainees to enquire about the legal basis of their incarceration, but also witnesses who could confirm the detentions themselves in case this was denied, seeing that the detainees were being held in secret. A witness to attest to the circumstances of their capture was also essential to provide evidence of their seizure in Angola and that they had already been incarcerated in 1979, before the amendment to AG 9 had been passed and their further detentions presumably ordered – no doubt a legislative attempt to legitimate an existing state of unlawful detention.

Within a week or two, Samson returned with a list of thirteen names of detainees. I addressed a letter on 16 November 1983 to the General Officer Commanding the SADF in Namibia, seeking confirmation of their detentions and enquiring as to the legal basis. The reply was swift. In a letter dated 23 November 1983, the military acknowledged that they had been detained under the 1979 amendment (section 5 bis), upon an order of further detention by the AG.

We now had evidence that the people on Samson's list were, in

---

23   His autobiography *The Agony of Truth* (Kuiseb Publishers, Windhoek) was published in 2014.

fact, being detained. But we still had no evidence about the circumstances of their capture. Samson did not know anyone who could attest to that. He undertook to extend his enquiries over the Christmas holiday period at the end of 1983 when he visited his family home in northern Namibia. During that holiday period, I called upon a friend in Cape Town – Jeremy Gauntlett, an advocate practising there – to seek advice about bringing the case. He had been the top final-year student at Stellenbosch University in my first year and had tutored a small group of us in our first year. In 1983, he was fast becoming an exceptionally fine barrister, combining his formidable intellect with a capacity for focused hard work. I had already briefed him in a political case. He had been impressive. He gave advice about building the case to challenge the detentions. The lawfulness of orders to extend detentions of people who had previously been unlawfully captured was highly questionable; he would be comfortable arguing that case.

The breakthrough, however, only came in mid-February 1984, with Samson and Hosea bringing Bennie to meet me at my house that evening.

The next day yielded more progress. In the morning, Samson brought Josef Katofa to my office. Two of his brothers, including Nikodemus mentioned by Bennie, were among the detainees at the Mariental camp. I was to learn later that Katofa was Samson's key contact person in establishing the names of detainees, getting in touch with their relatives and Bennie, and subsequently persuading them to make affidavits in support of the case. This he did at considerable personal sacrifice, as subsequently emerged. Unbeknown to me, he was covertly picked up by the military and detained just before the case came to court.

Josef Katofa cut a very colourful figure as he entered my office, with his confident air and exuding charisma. His flashy sunglasses were ostentatiously tucked into his thick and bushy hair on one side, just below the brim of the cream Stetson hat he sported at a slight angle to accommodate the position of his sunglasses. His brightly coloured tie competed with a shirt of even more gaudy, clashing shades. He needed no persuasion to make an affidavit. He quickly cut to the point as he had other business to complete in Windhoek before returning the next day to his small cuca shop business at Eengolo not far from Outapi, in the Ombalantu area. (These shops were called cuca shops in northern Namibia after the Portuguese beer sold at them in earlier days, when it was sourced from nearby Angola.)

Katofa confirmed that he had heard of his brothers' capture at the hands of the South African military from Bennie. He had more recently heard from fellow members of the Uukwaluudhi community who had visited their relatives at the camp near Mariental that his two brothers were also being held there. He also made more enquiries at Samson's request.

I promised to prepare an affidavit that same day and requested him to return by no later than 4 pm so that I could accompany him to a commissioner of oaths for him to formally depose to it. He responded by undertaking to return to my office later, but that it would be 'past four'. Despite my repeated entreaties, he would not be tied to a more exact time. I left it at that.

True to his word, at 4.25 pm and to my relief, his flamboyant figure appeared in my doorway. We were able to have the affidavit signed before a fellow attorney in a different firm. (Affidavits must be signed and sworn before a commissioner of oaths not connected to the case. Court officials, lawyers, bank managers and police officers are commissioners of oaths. The banks had already closed by then. Court officials were no longer available for this purpose after 3 pm. If he were to have come later, it would have meant going to the police station. This we clearly wanted to avoid. It was critical to keep the application under wraps so as to avoid interference with and intimidation of other witnesses.)

Samson, Hosea and I then planned to go to the northern war zone area of Owambo urgently to take affidavits from the other detainees' relatives. Hosea and I would stay at the Roman Catholic mission at Okatana, near Oshakati. Owing to the very sensitive nature of the case, Father Stegmann requested that we consult witnesses elsewhere, given his church's role in arranging visits of relatives to detainees, fearing that this facilitating role would be terminated and visits ended if they were seen to be assisting with this application. We respected that.

Hosea came up with a solution. His sister and brother-in-law owned a service station at Ongwediva, some 10 km from Oshakati. It was a convenient location. It had a small back office usually used on a weekly basis for consultations by a medical practitioner who was away pursuing a specialisation. It was available for us to use. No questions would be asked of us; it was perfect for our purpose. And the presence of people waiting outside to consult with us would not attract undue attention as people often gathered at the service station to secure lifts in minibus taxis to Oshakati. These were the only form of public transport in the area.

Samson would need to bring the witnesses from the Uukwaluudhi area to the service station, a distance of about 120 km. Hiring a minibus from a car rental company to do this may have aroused suspicion and attracted attention. We decided to approach the General Secretary of the CCN, Dr Abisai Shejavali, to permit Samson to use one of their vehicles. This meeting was hastily set up by my friend, Nora Chase, who had a senior position at the CCN at the time. A church organisation minibus conveying people within the area would not be out of the ordinary. The churches had a strong hold on their members. Meetings and synods were well attended. It would be commonplace for a church organisation to transport congregants or members to a synod or a funeral or the like.

I explained to Dr Shejavali that our hiring a vehicle would no doubt invite unwanted attention, which could result in interference and harassment and may even thwart our purpose. Dr Shejavali, a courageous and greatly respected opponent to the South African occupation and its policies in Namibia, had not been in his position very long by then and was widely regarded as a stickler for correct procedures. Highly principled, he would not permit the unauthorised use of CCN vehicles or funds under any circumstances. He pointedly responded: 'But my brother, you are not engaged in CCN work. That precludes the use of a CCN vehicle.'

I respectfully urged him to adopt a wider view of CCN work and its mandate, and gave a detailed overview of the issues raised in the case.

Dr Shejavali listened attentively. He was persuaded, and relented in the generous spirit that has characterised all my interactions with him. A CCN vehicle could be used. He went further and gave the case his blessing and his warm support, as he did to my subsequent cases and work.

Samson was to leave the next day for the area. He would spend the weekend tracking down relatives and then bring them to the service station on the following Tuesday morning. Hosea would also proceed separately, obtaining a lift to the north and arriving a day ahead of me so that he could start consultations very early on the Tuesday morning before my arrival. He could, at that stage, still travel without being under observation from the authorities. My arrival would be noticed, however. I would stick out starkly: a white civilian in a non-military vehicle, a very rare phenomenon. It was too risky for me to be observed before witnesses were already at our consultation venue.

I left my office late on the Monday afternoon and stayed over at the mining town of Tsumeb, some 450 km from Windhoek and about 250 km from Ongwediva. I arrived at the Minen Hotel at about sunset. The northern areas were declared security districts, under proclamation AG 9. Those areas were previously referred to as the police zone. You entered the Owambo area through a military and police checkpoint and gate in the veterinary fence at Oshivelo some 90 km north of Tsumeb into a military zone where martial law was effectively in place.

The curfew was rigidly and relentlessly enforced, without regard for human life. No movements other than those of security force members were permitted between sunset and sunrise. Vehicles could be – and were, in fact – shot at for a breach of the curfew, at times with fatal or severe consequences. Everyone travelling to and from Owambo would need to pass through the permanent military checkpoint at Oshivelo. There were also several other checkpoints within Owambo, some permanent and others temporary, the latter dependent upon recent insurgency in specific areas. These checkpoints caused considerable resentment for those living in the area. People were not only questioned in a disrespectful and often aggressive manner. Body searches were also routinely conducted, without regard to the dignity of those being searched. Vehicles were also searched, again mostly with contempt or at best indifference for the dignity of the occupants.

There was an all-pervasive military presence in the area, characterised by the constant movement of convoys of large mine-protected vehicles carrying heavily armed SADF troops or members of the notorious paramilitary police counterinsurgency unit known as Koevoet. At least three different variants of these vehicles were used: Casspirs, Hippos and Buffels (buffaloes). They were ever present. There were also others – mostly named after wild animals – which were encountered less frequently. Occasionally, more ferocious-looking armoured columns of highly mobile light tanks and armoured personnel carriers called Ratels (the Afrikaans word for honey badgers, very resilient, aggressive mammals) could also be encountered.

Before leaving Windhoek, I had prepared a number of draft

affidavits with different permutations in typed form. This was done so that I could, for the large part, merely type in the relevant personal and other details. Of course, this was well before the advent of personal computers. I had taken along an electric IBM golf ball typewriter to make the necessary insertions and for typing other affidavits, as may be required and when I was able to do so. The mission where we would stay (like most places in Owambo) was not on any grid and dependent upon a generator for power.

After I checked in at the Minen Hotel, I took a table on the open veranda beer garden area where meals were served as well as thirst-quenching beers. I had barely placed my supper order when I recognised a familiar figure striding to the hotel's reception area. A warrant officer in the security police. I could see from my vantage point not far off that he was checking the hotel register and speaking to the receptionist. Within minutes, he swung around to scan the dining area on the veranda. Seconds later his gaze settled upon me. He immediately made his way over to my table and greeted me by my first name with forced familiarity which irked me – a security police custom I made a point of never reciprocating. He awkwardly attempted small talk by pointing out that we were both out of town and asked where I was proceeding or whether I was in Tsumeb for a case. I was taken aback at his directness. I did not want to appear too defensive in my response. Maintaining my composure, I merely said off-hand that I had some work in the area and expected to be back in Windhoek very soon, by the night after the next, at the latest – being very vague but at the same time accurate in the sparse detail I provided. He could see that I would not be drawn further into discussion, and left as quickly as he had arrived. This came as a surprise to me. Very few people knew of my movements. Only Hosea and my trusted secretary, Anita Witt, knew that I would be staying at that hotel that evening. Neither would have readily divulged this information. I subsequently found out from Anita that a close friend with whom I had studied in the US had called from Mexico City late that afternoon. When she was informed that I was out of town, she insisted on a telephone number from Anita where she could reach me that evening. After some persistence, Anita had reluctantly given my friend the hotel's phone number, which was no doubt picked up by the security police in their eavesdropping and then easily traced to the hotel.

I left early the next morning so that I could reach the military checkpoint at Oshivelo shortly after it opened. There were a few extra temporary checkpoints that day in Ovambo. About halfway to Ongwediva, a gaping hole in the bitumen-surfaced national road bore testimony to the low-intensity war in the area. A landmine must have been detonated there a day or two before. There was a heavy military presence in evidence for much of the way, especially from about 60 km south of Ondangwa following a checkpoint at Okatope, which was home to a Koevoet base as well as an SADF base on opposite sides of the national road.

I arrived at the service station by mid-morning to find Hosea immersed in consultation. Some twenty people were sitting in the ample shade afforded by a huge, indigenous sycamore fig tree on the premises of the service station. Hosea had been at it since quite early. Progress, he said, had been very slow, however. It had taken some time to win the trust of the people and explain what information we needed.

Our consulting room was tiny. We shared a table. At one end, I typed in the details supplied by Hosea, who made his notes at the other end while consulting the people in their shared vernacular. February falls at the peak of the summer raining season. It was hot and humid. The small fan in that cramped office was strained at its optimum speed, struggling to make any discernible difference. After some time, I became concerned at our rate of progress. Each person spoke at considerable length to Hosea. Sometimes it would eventually turn out that they were not related to a detainee – or, if they were, they had not visited their relative. But all this took time to establish. We had decided to take affidavits only from those who had actually visited detainees or from relatives of those detainees whose detention had been admitted by the military in correspondence with me.

We both felt that it was crucial to have at least three duly signed affidavits that afternoon and to complete the rest the next day after typing them overnight. We were concerned that the military or the security police – or, worse still, Koevoet – may become aware of our work and that witnesses may be interfered with overnight. Other practical difficulties also stood in our way. There were no lawyers in full-time practice in that area. The only commissioners of oath whom we could approach with some degree of confidence were the branch managers of the two major banks in Oshakati. It was, of course, out of the question to have affidavits commissioned at the Oshakati Police Station. But the banks closed early – at 3:30 pm. The only alternative was the Postmaster at the Oshakati Post Office. We would have to get there by 4.30 pm, before it closed to the public. There was also the curfew to consider – we would have to stop our work well in advance of sunset to enable us all to get safely to where we would spend the night.

I noted at one stage that one particular woman of advanced years was speaking at great length in a slow and deliberate manner. Hosea had at one point even stopped taking notes while she did so. I could discern that she had earlier also asked him several questions. It was equally clear to me that this discourse went outside what we required for the affidavits: Hosea was no longer writing anything down. I turned to him and urged him to find a way to cut her short and get to the point, unnecessarily adding that we did not have time to canvass all sorts of other issues as well. He patiently explained that it would simply not be possible for him to cut her short and that the same applied to many of the other people there. She was, he said, entirely unused to consulting lawyers, and would not and could not be rushed. She would get to the point in her own good time and would certainly not be confined to the specific questions we had raised. In fact, he said it was taking time to get anywhere near the issues at hand. Some of her questions were directed at ascertaining more about Hosea's and my backgrounds before Hosea could even broach the subject matter.

The shame I felt at my own insensitivity and impatience was compounded by the tactful way in which Hosea had administered this fundamental lesson. It was one that proved invaluable in the years which followed. It was also reinforced a few years later when learning the language myself, and coming to a more rounded understanding of culture and discourse in the area. You simply could not hurry people, especially older people, in any meaningful consultation as a general rule, but most certainly not when it concerned sensitive matters of this nature – matters in which a lack of trust and confidence could lead to reprisals and compromise others.

It turned out that the old woman would not be a witness. She had not visited a relative in detention. Nor was her relative among those listed in our enquiries. But we took down the name of her son and undertook to enquire about his detention and revert to her. Hosea also assured her that, if the case were to be successful, her son would also be released. This more than satisfied her. The unconditional warmth in her gratitude to us for seeing her and taking up the issue of her son's detention at the end of the extended consultation only served to drive home the lesson I had learnt even harder.

As the 4.30 pm deadline approached, we agreed that I would go to the post office with three witnesses and an interpreter while Hosea would continue to consult. I covered the 10 km to Oshakati at high speed along the near-deserted road, populated only by a few military vehicles – a far cry from the steady stream of congested traffic along that stretch in today's Namibia. We just managed to reach the post office before closing time.

I asked at the counter if I could see the Postmaster. Within a few moments a middle-aged Afrikaans man appeared. He looked quizzically at this unusual group of people seeking his assistance. I politely apprised him in Afrikaans of the purpose of our presence at his post office. I explained that I was a lawyer with three witnesses in a court case who needed to depose to affidavits, while the fourth would act as their interpreter from English or Afrikaans to Oshiwambo. It seemed that he was seldom called upon to commission affidavits. He asked to see the affidavits. I handed them to him.

After quickly perusing them, he dismissively discarded them on the counter and looked up sharply. His air of almost benign indifference had in an instant turned to open animosity. He continued in Afrikaans, with an edge to his slightly raised, high-pitched voice: 'I can't commission affidavits to that effect because I'm not satisfied that the affidavits are true. I don't know that the people referred to in the statements are in fact detained and where and for that long.'

I was at pains to point out with all the courtesy I could muster that this was not his function. His task was to satisfy himself that the witnesses knew and understood the nature of the oath and swore that their statements were true and correct. Despite this explanation, he remained reluctant. This spurred me on to assert that he was required by law as a commissioner of oaths to perform this function when it was requested of him and that he could be acting in breach of his statutory duty if he declined to do so. His increased displeasure at our presence and purpose there was palpable. He paused and eventually responded: 'All right. I'll do it. But I refuse to use the interpreter you have brought with you.'

Without even looking at our interpreter or awaiting my response, he looked over his shoulder and raised his voice to an even higher pitch and yelled, 'Paulus!'

Within seconds, the middle-aged Oshiwambo-speaking man who had been summoned appeared from one of the back rooms of the post office. The Postmaster turned towards him and, with increased vehemence, commanded him in Afrikaans: 'Paulus, find out from this old man if these are really his words and that they are in fact the truth according to him or whether these words were put into his mouth by this lawyer or others.'

His manner was overbearing and intimidating. It would also have become obvious to our witnesses that he was being dismissive and openly aggressive towards both them and me.

His employee, whom he addressed only by his first name in a deeply demeaning tone, then turned to the ageing, white-haired Dominic Amutenya and explained this question in some detail in the vernacular. Dominic Amutenya paused plaintively for what seemed an eternity as he considered his answer, which was then delivered in a carefully measured manner, with manifest gravitas. The instant he finished his answer and before there was time for its translation to commence, the Postmaster, possibly sniffing my blood, impatiently snapped at his subordinate in Afrikaans: 'Come, come, Paulus, what is he saying, man?'

The atmosphere, already heavy due to the oppressive humidity, thickened appreciably. I had visions of the case collapsing calamitously before getting out of the starting blocks and of my potential disbarment on grounds of putting words in witnesses' mouths to subvert justice. I suddenly regretted not foreseeing the real risk of such a hostile commissioner of oaths and not taking the time to prepare Dominic Amutenya for this eventuality in our excessive haste to make it to the post office on time.

The post office employee, with his eyes gazing ahead to avoid the Postmaster's persistent stare, unhurriedly delivered the translated answer: 'Baas, the old man says that he is an old man in years. He has already lived for many years. He has seen and experienced many raining seasons and many other things in his lengthy life. But in his whole lifetime, he has never spoken a truer word than that contained in that very document. He furthermore says that it is a very great privilege for him to make this true statement officially in a court document. In fact, it is very true and has been true for nearly six years now and still remains the truth. He finally also says that the injustice and suffering must cease.'

The postmaster then snatched at his official stamp and hastily did the necessary with all too obvious irritation. While his head was bent over officiously applying his stamps and signature, Dominic Amutenya – for the first time since giving his telling answer – turned to me, flashed a smile and simultaneously gave an exaggerated conspiratorial wink of the eye. This gesture has remained with me ever since and is one I shall never forget.

When the Postmaster had completed the task of commissioning the other two affidavits, he grabbed his stamps and hurriedly retreated, storming off in the direction of his office without saying another word. A discreet departing nod in our direction from his employee, known to us only as Paulus, meaningfully spoke of solidarity and respect.

Our shared relief when leaving the post office was echoed, by strange coincidence, by a heavy downpour. It provided a welcome release from the overbearing humidity that had been building up incrementally all day, reaching its climax during the encounter with the Postmaster. I bade my farewells to Dominic Amutenya, the interpreter and the other witnesses. I thanked them all warmly, particularly Dominic. He responded that it was for him to thank me for enabling him to support a case he felt so strongly about. He was grateful to be able to do something about his son Willy's detention during his lifetime. He added that he would not want to die without doing so. I subsequently learnt that Willy had been injured during the aerial bombardment that had preceded the assault on the base and had consequently had an arm amputated. Willy became a leading figure in the group and has published an account of his capture and his time in detention.[24]

I returned to the service station to collect Hosea, still studiously consulting, for us to make our way to Okatana where we would stay overnight before the curfew would take effect.

Okatana is a Catholic mission station and school nestled in a grove of huge indigenous fig, leadwood and acacia trees, lending it an air of tranquillity amid the prevailing turbulence in the area. A warm welcome from Father Hubrecht was followed by a hearty dinner. Upon my enquiry, he said that the generator would stay on until 9.30 pm. Hosea and I continued to work on the affidavits until then. The generator was switched on again at 5.30 am the next morning, in time for the mission station to prepare for morning mass. We continued our work on the affidavits from then until breakfast time. Hosea dictated details while I typed as quickly as I could.

As we left the mission station, schoolchildren of varying ages were converging upon it from all directions. The energy in their approach may have had something to do with the morning's freshness following the rain of the previous late afternoon and evening. This energy was also no doubt because of how strictly the impending school starting time was presumably enforced, given the influence of German Catholicism. We continued to encounter them for some distance, demonstrating how far away some of the children lived from the school, with latecomers scurrying with even more urgency towards the mission station.

We returned to finalise the remaining affidavits and spent some time going through them with the various deponents. We also noticed that the numbers of people had begun to swell in the course of

---

24 Amutenya, WM. 2011. *Brave Unyielding Comrades: The Untold Story of Vietnam (Chetequera) Prisoners of War in the Liberation Struggle of Namibia.* Macmillan Education Namibia: Windhoek.

the morning while we were carefully checking details and contents with deponents. Samson explained that they also wanted to consult with us. Some of them had a relative detained at Mariental; others knew of people who had a relative detained there; still others wanted to discuss disappearances or detentions unrelated to the Mariental detentions. All said that they had received word of the case and had come to support it.

Hosea and I tried our best to explain in a respectful manner that affidavits from everybody would not be neither necessary nor possible in the time available to us. But we assured them that, if the case were to succeed, all the detainees at Mariental would have to be released. We agreed to take down their details and those of their relatives who were in detention or who had gone missing, and promised to do what we could. We also thanked them all for their support and willingness to come forward, expressing our appreciation and respect for their courage in doing so in difficult times. An elderly man in the group stepped forward as a spokesperson and movingly thanked us on behalf of all present. We then went to the Oshakati branch of Standard Bank where the manager commissioned all the remaining affidavits without demur. In all, 21 affidavits had been completed since the day before.

A light lunch awaited us at Okatana. As we approached the mission station, the children toiled homeward in small groups mostly defined by their size, their languid movements no doubt the consequence of the heat and humidity that had long since replaced the day's early freshness.

The fast pace of our progress back to Windhoek was only temporarily interrupted by the frequent military and police checkpoints which were negotiated without incident. We encountered a few showers along the way. At sunset, we stopped to stretch our limbs alongside the road near the Omatako mountains midway between Otjiwarongo and Okahandja.

The presence of some clouds in the west served to accentuate the range of colours of the sky as the sun set to spectacular effect and disappeared behind those near-symmetrical mountains, which stood out dramatically from the seemingly endless plains of surrounding farmland. The sight was so splendid that we stood there for some moments, marvelling at the timeless beauty of the scene and reflecting on the past 36 hours. The serenity of this spectacle combined with sheer exhaustion stirred our emotions, which ranged from relief to a sense of elation at eventually having secured sufficient evidence to take the case to court. But we also had a deep sense of uncertainty and foreboding about what was to come, not knowing what the consequences would be for our clients and witnesses, and what would happen in the case. We spoke briefly about our thoughts – which were strikingly similar, our having worked together on the case for some time. For most of that time, we had not made much progress, and then this flurry of developments. We travelled the remaining hour and a half mostly without speaking as we each contemplated these themes to the strains of Bob Dylan, Ry Cooder and Bob Marley playing on some tired cassette tapes in the background. We were both physically and emotionally drained on our return to Windhoek that night.

I spent time the next day preparing a draft of my own affidavit. I also approached the Anglican Bishop of Namibia, James Kauluma, to join the application as an applicant to apply for the release of those detainees whom it had been admitted were in Mariental and for whom we had not been able to trace any relatives. He was the serving president of the CCN, whose member churches represented some 85 per cent of the Christians in the country and over 95 per cent of those living in Owambo. He enthusiastically embraced the idea. It was the start of an enduring partnership in human rights work. As he was about to head for Owambo, he agreed to approach the bishop of the Evangelical Lutheran Church in Namibia (ELCIN), Kleopas

Dumeni, to do so as well. I was to speak to the Catholic bishop, Bonifatius Haushiku, on the Monday after the ensuing weekend as he was out of town at the time.

Our approach was to argue that the three bishops would have standing to apply for the release of those for whom family could not be found. The courts had acknowledged about ten years before in a leading case that the Anglican Bishop of Namibia had standing to interdict the flogging of activists by state-supported tribal leaders in the north because of their political activism.[25]

I travelled that weekend to Cape Town to consult Jeremy Gauntlett. He agreed to spend Saturday settling my own and Bishop Kauluma's affidavits and the terms of the notice of motion. My own affidavit essentially set the background and the enquiries I had made, and the responses from the military. It also dealt with the further steps taken to obtain affidavits. Jeremy excellently embellished upon my rather ordinary draft for Bishop Kauluma, dealing with the question of standing in the following way:

> During the course of the tragic hostilities in South West Africa, and notably Owamboland, I have often been approached by members of the civilian population who have asked me to assist them in their search for lost family and friends, caught up in the war, some of whom have been held by the South African Defence Force (the SADF) or the South West African Territory Force (SWATF). By the nature of my vocation as a bishop, the vows I have taken to serve God and man in the dictates of the Christian Gospel, I have sought to assist where I can . . . I consider it my duty to coordinate and consolidate the activities of member churches and to promote and protect the several interests of member churches, the membership of such member

---

25   *Wood v Ondangwa Tribal Authority* 1975 (2) SA 294 (A).

churches representing 85% of the population of South West Africa, and to act on their behalf . . .

I have read the Notice of Motion and all other supporting affidavits filed herein. I am personally aware of the circumstances at present prevailing in Owamboland which make it most difficult to find family or friends of the abovementioned detainees; the fact that some of the areas concerned fall within the war zone, the great distance, the lack of means of communication and the general atmosphere of fear.

After careful reflection, I consider it my duty to join in this application on behalf of the aforesaid detainees.

It was certainly necessary to set out the claim for standing in detail. Our experience by then, and repeatedly confirmed subsequently, was a deliberate strategy on the part of lawyers acting for the security establishment to take every conceivable procedural point they could to persuade courts to find for them without the need to go into the merits of cases. They relished making it as difficult as possible for detainees and their families to have access to the courts (and tried to avoid going anywhere near the merits of cases, given the nastiness of security force action).

I dropped off the draft affidavit for Bishop Kauluma with the Dean on my return that Sunday. He would take the draft to the Bishop in Tsumeb the next day. I then met with the Catholic bishop, Bonifatius Haushiku, the next day. His support was likewise emphatic and enthusiastic. His assistants' initial resistance to the case had in the meantime given way to wholehearted support, once they became aware of the headway we had made and the scale of case. After he and Bishop Kauluma had signed their affidavits, we decided to serve the papers before we had received Bishop Dumeni's commissioned affidavit because he would only be able to return it to us the following week.

The minister of defence was cited as the first respondent in the application as the minister in charge of the SADF. The AG was also cited because he had signed the orders for the further detention of the detainees. Hosea and I had scrambled to ensure that the papers were ready and handed to the deputy sheriff for service on Friday 5 March 1984. We provisionally set it down for hearing on 4 April in the event of no opposition. If opposed, a subsequent date would be sought.

Once service of the application was out of the way, I was at last able to telephone Gay McDougall for the first time to report on the application to her. She was ecstatic. I had written a long letter to her before our breakthrough in February and our securing the affidavits in the north. Visiting friends from the US had taken the letter back with them and mailed it to her from there on their return, to avoid its interception.

These were the days before fax machines. The best I could do was to courier a copy of the application to Gay. I met with my close friends, Tony Weaver and Gwen Lister, both journalists. Gwen worked for the *Windhoek Observer*, a fiercely independent newspaper at the time. She was its political correspondent. She also did some freelance radio work for the BBC World Service, widely listened to by Namibians who had access to shortwave radio, and who thirsted for some balance in reporting and wanted to escape the relentless propaganda of the local state-controlled radio stations and indirectly controlled newspapers. Tony was then the Windhoek-based correspondent for the erstwhile *Rand Daily Mail*, the most progressive of South Africa's daily newspapers, and the other morning newspapers in its group, including the *Cape Times*. They both provided extensive coverage to the launching of the application.

For the first time, the plight of the Mariental detainees had received media attention – some six weeks short of the sixth anniversary of their capture and incarceration. While details of the Cassinga and

Chetequera raids had been sketchy, the local media heralded the military operation as a body blow to Swapo. In contrast, the international community condemned it as a major atrocity. It was long thought that prisoners had been taken, and now at last there was some official confirmation of their circumstances.

Gay, a seasoned activist, ensured that the detentions and the application secured considerable publicity in the US and elsewhere.

The government respondents in the application had a few weeks to file a response. On the last day for doing so, they dropped a bombshell.

Instead of filing a notice to oppose the application and opposing affidavits, a terse certificate under the signature of the Minister of Justice of South Africa, Kobie Coetsee, was lodged at court and a copy served on us. Under the heading 'Certificate in terms of section 103 ter of the Defence Act, 44 of 1957', it proclaimed in the Afrikaans language:

> Whereas I, Hendrik Jacobus Coetzee, in my capacity as Minister of Justice, have been authorised by the State President in terms of section 103 ter (4) of the Defence Act, 1957 to issue a certificate directing that the civil proceedings instituted by James Hamupanda Kauluma and 22 others against the Minister of Defence and Another in the Supreme Court of South West Africa should not be continued:
>
> I hereby direct, as contemplated in section 103 ter (4), that those proceedings shall not be continued.

I was caught completely unaware by this dramatic turn. In fact, I was flabbergasted by the Orwellian phraseology and oblivious to the cited legal provision that facilitated it. This power had never before been invoked in any case of this kind. I was unaware of the existence of this power, in this obscure section, until I looked it up. At its core, it prohibited the institution or continuation of any court case (civil or criminal) against the State or the military or one of its members for any act done in good faith by the military 'for the purpose of or in connection with the prevention or suppression of terrorism in any operational area'.[26]

The provision went on to empower the minister of defence to certify that a particular act had been committed 'for the purpose of or in connection with the prevention of or suppression of terrorism'. A certificate by the Minister or the Prime Minister issued under this sub-section established conclusively that the act in question had been committed for the purposes of, or in connection with, the prevention or suppression of terrorism.

It got worse. Sub-section (4) stated that no court of law had jurisdiction to determine both the issue of whether the act had been committed for the purposes of, or in connection with, the prevention or suppression of terrorism, and whether it had been done in good faith. The effect of a certificate was to leave nothing for a court to decide. The issuing of the certificate would conclusively determine both the nature of the act (as being for that stated purpose) and the existence of good faith. Under sub-section (6), the consequence of a certificate was that the court proceedings lapsed and were 'deemed to be void'.

The final blow was administered by sub-section (7). It stated that 'no court shall have power to review, set aside or declare to be void or otherwise question the validity of any certificate issued under sub-section (3) or (4)'. This is an extreme form of what is known in the

---

26   Section 103 ter (2) states: 'No proceedings, whether civil or criminal, shall be instituted or continued in any court of law against the Minister, a member of the State, the State President, or any other person in the South African Defence Force of any act advised, service of the State by reason commanded, ordered, directed or done in good faith by the State President, the Minister, or a member of the South African Defence Force for the purpose of or in connection with the prevention or suppression of terrorism in any operational area.'

law as an ouster clause because its purpose is to oust or deprive the courts from exercising jurisdiction to determine the validity of the certificate.

I was appalled that I had not even heard of this draconian provision. It had never been referred to at law school. Nor had I read any publicity about its passage through parliament in South Africa.

No one I turned to had heard of this provision either. Jeremy was also surprised and undertook to research section 103 ter and to see if there could be a way out.

I called Tony. I said I had something to show him. We met at the nearby Café Schneider for a cup of coffee. This was our regular meeting spot after the application had been served to brainstorm follow-up angles to keep the story alive.

When I showed the certificate to him, he gasped, 'Holy shit.' After rereading it, 'This is dynamite.' A few seconds later, 'Phew, this is really big.' And after another minute or so, 'This now becomes huge. But what are you going to do?'

I had also brought a copy of the section with me and gave him a few minutes to absorb its meaning. 'Oh my God, so the court's totally excluded. This is unbelievable. I've never heard of this power before. Had you?'

I confessed that I had not. Nor had anyone else so far. The section was tucked away towards the end of the Defence Act, which most lawyers would not have much occasion to research. I said we would look into it and see if there was any possible basis of challenging the certificate, despite the explicit removal of the court's jurisdiction to pronounce upon its validity. He would run the story immediately. We agreed to meet the next morning to discuss follow-up avenues.

Tony's report made it to the front pages of all the newspapers in the morning group in South Africa. It was in fact the lead story in both the *Rand Daily Mail* and the *Cape Times*. Gwen also gave it prominence in the next edition of the weekly *Windhoek Observer* and did a detailed report on the Africa Service of the BBC. Even the local pliant pro-apartheid media reported on the banning of the case – as necessary in combatting terrorism. I was referred to in these reports. A consequence was running into an acquaintance of my parents the next week in town. 'What a disappointment you must be to your poor mother,' she lamented. I was so surprised that all I could come up with was that my mother fully supported what I was doing. Her disbelief showed as she hastily moved on. This exemplified the view of most of the white community.

Later that afternoon I phoned Gay, impatiently having to wait for much of the day for the opening time at her office because of the time difference. She was equally aghast. She fired many questions to me about section 103 ter. Like Tony, she expressed her horror at the import of the section.

'You all must see what you can do about this. I'll certainly raise all hell about this from here.'

We agreed to remain in close contact about the issue.

True to her word, the certificate banning the case received prominence in the *Washington Post*. Within a week or so, it was also raised in the House of Representatives of the US Congress. Gay also saw to it that it was raised as a question in the House of Lords in England. I contacted my friends at Ropes and Gray. One of the partners was a leading figure in the American Bar Association. Within a few days that body petitioned the US Secretary of State, George Shulz, to approach the South African state president about the issue. I put Tony in touch with Gay. He duly kept the issue alive by according all of these events considerably wide coverage in the media in South Africa, as did Gwen in the *Windhoek Observer*.

In the meantime, our research revealed that section 103 ter had been inserted in the Defence Act in 1977. The parliamentary debate in South Africa did not shed much useful light on the subject. Jeremy discovered that the wording closely followed an indemnity provision which had been enacted by the Smith regime in 1975 in what was then Rhodesia.

The senior partners in my firm were, by this stage, concerned that I was becoming obsessive about this case. The terms of the section were, they said, clear and prevented any further challenge in court. I had done my best for my clients and exposed a gross injustice. I should learn to accept it when I had been defeated. It was time to move on. But I was not ready to do so.

When Jeremy could not come up with a clear answer for a sustainable basis to challenge the certificate, I asked a few senior counsel for their views, including the local Bryan O'Linn who seldom steered clear of a scrap with the security establishment. Similar sentiments to those expressed by the senior lawyers of my firm were conveyed to me.

I sought Gay's approval to approach the great South African and later English senior counsel, Sydney Kentridge,[27] for his views. To my delight, she readily agreed. I called his Johannesburg chambers, only to be informed that he was in London, where he was increasingly practising. His secretary said he would be back in Johannesburg the following week but that he was fully engaged in a case set to run for some time after his return. After I explained the nature of the case to her, she was empathetic and said that he would be arriving over the weekend (on Saturday) and that I should phone his son Matthew, who was staying at their Johannesburg home and was in frequent contact with his parents. I could ask him to raise the issue with his father to see if he would see me. Matthew was a student and I should call that evening.

A few hours later Matthew was most enthusiastic in his support of our case. His father was due to call the next day and he would do his best to prevail upon him to see me over the weekend. He was

---

27   Later Sir Sydney Kentridge.

confident that his father would do so. I informed him that I would be in Kempton Park on Sunday and Monday. This was the nearest town to Johannesburg's international airport. I was heading there because Gwen Lister had been charged under the Internal Security Act of South Africa for being in possession of documents about banned organisations – the ANC and PAC – on arriving at that airport the previous year en route to Namibia from a UN-sponsored conference she had attended in Paris. Her trial was set down for that Monday in the Kempton Park regional court.

Her arrest had taken place during my time in the US. In my absence, she had initially been advised by a new colleague in my firm, a former prosecutor, to plead guilty to the charges because the items had, in fact, been found on her when the security police had swooped upon her as she had landed and before she could enter the arrivals hall. She told me about this on my return. I advised her to change her stance. A conviction under the Internal Security Act could have consequences. It could preclude her from starting a newspaper or it could be used to support a ban of her current newspaper. It could also form the basis of withdrawing her passport and a realm of other actions that could conceivably be taken against her. She gladly accepted my advice. I took over her defence within the firm and engaged both senior and junior counsel to defend her. Jeremy was the junior counsel and would be able to accompany me to a meeting with Sydney Kentridge.

Matthew called me back the next night. With evident delight in his voice, he reported that his father would see us at 4 pm on Sunday afternoon as he was tied up from Monday onwards.

When Sydney took us through to his study, he politely informed us that he had time constraints because he had dinner guests coming early that evening. I wasted no time in setting out the factual background to the application. Jeremy took him through the provisions of section 103 ter. Sydney had also been unaware of this provision and had been taken by surprise when he had read about the banning certificate in *The Times* in London.

When we had both finished our respective presentations, he quietly asked me how I proposed to challenge the certificate in view of the ouster clause. I suggested that the detentions were not in good faith. Nor was the certificate. His compelling counters to those propositions were unanswerable. I desperately tried to come up with a few other ideas. Each was quickly disposed of as being untenable. And each time, there was no rebuttal to his devastating logic. It now seemed to me that we had finally reached the end of the road – a cul-de-sac. Rising to my feet, I thanked him for seeing us on a Sunday afternoon and apologised for wasting his time.

'Not so quickly, young man,' he said. 'There's something you've said which could possibly be developed further.'

I sat down. He turned to Jeremy and asked him to reread the section. When he got to the part 'the proceedings were instituted by reason of an act advised, commanded, ordered, directed or done . . .', Sydney stopped him.

'This section,' Sydney said, 'concerns wrongful acts done in the past. The past tense contemplates that the acts are completed.'

This, he said, was the purpose of an indemnity provision. It dealt with something which had been done – as a finite act – in the past and afforded an indemnity for that act. It could not concern conduct in the future or an ongoing wrong such as an unlawful detention. Unlike an arrest, the act of detention was, he said, not an act done in the past tense but a continuing one, which carried on every day the detainees remained in detention. He concluded that the section could not apply to the continuing wrong of detaining my clients. The certificate would thus not be a bar to the proceedings. We should press ahead with the application.

This irrefutable logic had of course not arisen from anything I had said. I knew that I had just witnessed a level of intellectual brilliance I had not encountered before and have not since.

The next step, he advised, would be to address a letter to the Government Attorney to record this and to call upon the government respondents to file answering affidavits if they wished to do so and then set the case down for hearing.

I asked him if he would be prepared to argue the application. He was unfortunately tied up for a few weeks and would then start another case. But he did not expect his current matter to run the full course and should be free on either 25 or 28 May. It was not certain, though.

'If you want to secure the services of somebody else, you should do so,' he said.

I replied that we would certainly prefer to take our chances on his availability.

In my excitement and with my lack of experience, I had not discussed another practical matter that one customarily discusses when engaging counsel. He realised this: 'If I may be commercial for a moment, I don't know if you have funding for this matter. But you needn't be concerned if you don't have. This is a matter of such fundamental importance that I would be prepared to assist without charge.'

I assured him that there was funding available.

As we were gathering up our papers, Sydney's wife, Felicia, gently knocked and entered to announce that their dinner guests had arrived. As Sydney escorted us towards the front door, he paused at the lounge door and stuck his head into the room. 'Arthur, there is someone I'd like you to meet,' he said.

A tall, friendly figure emerged. I was introduced to Arthur Chaskalson, the brilliant senior counsel who had left a flourishing practice at the Johannesburg Bar to head the Legal Resources Centre (LRC). Meeting Arthur was the crowning moment of an exhilarating afternoon.

As we drove back to Kempton Park, Jeremy suggested that I obtain a mandate to secure Arthur's involvement as well in case Sydney would not be available. Realising what was at stake in the case, and having great respect for Arthur, Gay was quick to agree. Arthur was available and was on board.

The next day also went very well. Ian Farlam, our senior counsel, was outstanding in presenting Gwen's defence. His cross-examination of a security police officer, Derek Brune, was masterful, securing crucial concessions from this feeble and fumbling witness. We called the widely respected journalist, Allister Sparks, as an expert witness.[28] He gave evidence about pamphlets and brochures from organisations being thrust upon journalists at conferences of the kind attended by Gwen, the protagonists eager to disseminate their messages to members of the media. The regional magistrate accepted Ian's argument that it had not been established beyond reasonable doubt that Gwen had the necessary intention to possess the documents in question, and acquitted her.

On my return to Windhoek, I sent the letter, as advised by Sydney, to the Government Attorney to the effect that my clients had been advised that the certificate did not apply to the present proceedings as the minister of justice and state president had acted outside their powers in respectively signing and issuing the certificate. The Government Attorney was notified that we intended to press ahead with the application and set it down for hearing. The government respondents were called upon to file opposing affidavits if they wish to do so. I gave notice that the application would be heard on 28 May 1984.

The response from the Deputy Government Attorney, Chris Brandt, came a few days later. Its tone was threatening, as were its contents. It said that the actions contemplated in my letter were 'malicious'

---

28   Allister Sparks was a former editor of the *Rand Daily Mail,* then correspondent for the *Washington Post,* a political commentator and analyst of great ability. He is the author of *Tomorrow is Another Country* (Struik, Johannesburg, 1994) and died in 2016 shortly after his autobiography *The Sword and the Pen* (Jonathan Ball Publishers) was published.

and 'politically motivated' and that a special order of costs would be sought against me personally. This was most unusual. Cost orders are normally sought and granted against the parties to a case, and not against the lawyers who bring them. I informed Jeremy of this response and he in turn contacted Arthur. I heard years later from my friend Geoff Budlender, who worked with Arthur at the LRC, that the usually calm Arthur had been outraged by this threat.

On the following weekend, Jeremy and I met Arthur at his offices to work on the written argument that would be presented a week later. When the draft was ready, we all went to Sydney's home for his final input. The written argument was filed after my return to Windhoek.

The hearing was set for the following Monday, 28 May. Nothing was forthcoming from the Government Attorney until late on the preceding Friday afternoon when a voluminous set of papers was filed. These included answering affidavits. A colonel in the SADF admitted that the detainees had been captured in the course of a military operation in Angola. It was said that the operation was to combat terrorism in an operational area and that their capture and subsequent detention were necessary in order to do so. This had occurred on 4 May 1978. More than a year later the AG had, under section 5 bis of AG 9, issued detention orders under the 1979 amendment in respect of all of the detainees to authorise their 'further detention'.

The head of the Mariental internment camp stated in an affidavit that the detentions had been recently 'reviewed' and that release warrants in respect of 55 of the 113 detainees had been issued; 31 of the 36 detainees whose release was sought in our application were in that number and would be released together with 24 fellow detainees over that weekend (immediately preceding the application). No explanation was given about the review itself – concerning criteria, considerations and its timing. But this was a thrilling development.

I immediately called Gay with this momentous news. We would, of course, proceed for the release of the remaining five detainees in our application. Another 58 detainees also remained in detention at Mariental. If we succeeded with the application, they too would be released. I also called counsel in both Johannesburg and Cape Town to apprise them of these developments. They decided that we should argue the case on the Monday rather than seek some time to reply to the opposing papers.

The courtroom was packed to capacity well in advance of the starting time. All of the lawyers in my firm came to court and took up positions on the attorneys' bench. That was out of solidarity because of the Deputy Government Attorney's stated intention to seek a special costs order against me personally. I had become a junior partner in the firm a few months before, on 1 March 1984. The three bishops, resplendent in their purple, took up their positions in the row behind me for clients. Several clergymen were in the public gallery, together with relatives of the detainees and activists, including Samson. Every single seat was taken. All available standing room at the back and on the sides was also occupied. The registrar, Mr Peters, was a fair man and was in attendance to ensure that every possible space inside the court could be utilised. In the foyer outside the court, a throng of people gathered to wait outside.

This, I felt, sent a powerful message to the three-member bench for the case. The newly appointed Judge President, Hans Berker, presided. He was flanked by Judges Chris Mouton on his right and Johan Strydom on his left. Berker's appointment to the bench had been widely welcomed. He was drawn from the ranks of the Windhoek Bar and was from Namibia. This was a departure from the string of political appointments emanating from Pretoria and elsewhere in South Africa that had preceded his. He was also thought of as having liberal instincts. I knew him well. I had worked with him on a few cases in my first year and a half of articles until his appointment to the bench. His charming wife, Marianne, had played bridge with my mother before my parents had retired to Cape Town a year or so before. The Berkers occasionally invited me to their home for meals, which were enjoyable. He was open-minded and I felt we had more than a fair chance that he would find in our favour.

The other judges were also Namibian appointees. Their appointments had also been welcomed by the local profession. Judge Mouton, however, was a reliable supporter of the apartheid state and its policies. He had previously served as a National Party senator in the South African parliament. Until a few years before, whites in Namibia could vote for, and were represented by, six members in the South African Parliament and two senators. They were all members of the South African ruling party's local branch and thus all subscribed to apartheid policies. A few years before, in 1977, representation in the South African Parliament had been abolished as one of the first steps taken by the South African government prior to its acceptance of the western proposals to bring about Namibia's independence. Mouton then turned to practise full time in Windhoek. Although I did not hold high hopes of Mouton finding for us, given his political background, he had found against the security police in a nasty case in which a detainee client of ours, Johannes Kakuva, had gone missing and whose detention had been denied. Hartmut had succeeded with an application presuming Kakuva's death at the hands of the security police. Judge Mouton had rejected the stonewalling by the security police and granted the application.

The third member of the court, Johan Strydom, had been appointed the year before. He was born in Namibia and had run a successful practice at the Windhoek Bar for several years before taking his appointment to the bench. I had worked with him in two matters. One had been a large commercial matter where I had assisted my principal during the first year of articles. He was a humble man, extremely pleasant to work with and a very competent counsel. He was also well-known in practice for his unimpeachable integrity. He had, significantly, never acted for the government in political cases. Nor was he active in political matters, unlike Mouton. These were good signs. He had always struck me as a fair and decent man, which he more than demonstrated in his many years on the bench that culminated in his elevation to Chief Justice of Namibia in 1998 – a position he held with great distinction until his retirement. But he was new on the court then and I was not sure how he would respond to the case, which so fundamentally challenged the status quo. I thought he could be a possible swing vote on the court, however.

Shortly before the start of the proceedings, the second-most senior member of the government legal team, Louis Harms,[29] later a prominent judge in South Africa, took Arthur aside to say that the government would no longer apply for the special costs order that had been threatened against me. Arthur said he seemed to distance himself from the stance of the Government Attorney in that respect. Arthur was not surprised that he would have felt uncomfortable with the Government Attorney's approach. He had served with him on the General Council of the Bar in South Africa and respected his professionalism.

The leader of the government legal team, the well-known Pretoria senior counsel, William de Villiers, was a more regular choice for the government in political cases and was widely known for his right-wing leanings. This became more evident to us in Namibia in 1989 during the implementation of the UN peace plan (Security Council Resolution 435) when he appeared for some politicians backed by the South African regime and its security establishment in seeking

---

29 A year or so after the case, Louis Harms was appointed as a judge in what was then called the Transvaal Provincial Division and was later elevated to the Supreme Court of Appeal in South Africa, where he served until his retirement.

an injunction against political activists I represented in those cases. This and other attempted injunctions were baseless, and were politically motivated to discredit and distract our clients during the run-up to the election. Judge Strydom had no difficulty in dismissing them in 1989.

After counsel had placed themselves on record, there was complete silence in the courtroom during Sydney Kentridge's address, delivered in a measured and logical manner and with such clarity. At the outset, he first dealt with the release of 55 of the detainees – 31 of whom were no longer part of the application – over the preceding weekend and said it was no longer necessary to apply for their release. He then referred to the threat of the special order of costs against me.

> Since the papers were first filed, there have been a number of developments in the case which I should mention to your Lordships, largely in order to clear them out of the way.
>
> My Lords, the application was originally brought in respect of 37 people who were detained in a camp in the Mariental area. In fact it appears that owing to a misunderstanding, one of the names was duplicated, so that there were 36 detainees involved.
>
> Now, my Lords, since then, 31 of them, I am glad to say, have been released. My Lords, let me make it clear that the respondents say that this had nothing to do with the present application, so let us accept that it was but a happy coincidence. But be that as it may, my Lords, 31 have been released and there are 5 still in custody in respect whom which we wish to press the application.

Sydney then listed the five names of those still incarcerated and proceeded:

Now, my Lords, the other development which took place in this case, was that the Minister of Justice issued a certificate purporting to have been issued in terms of section 103 ter of the Defence Act . . . [I]n terms of this certificate the Minister purported to order that these proceedings should terminate. Now, my Lords, the applicants acting on legal advice, are submitting to your Lordships that this certificate is bad in law; it is a nullity, it is issued without jurisdiction on the ground, shortly, if I may give it in its shortest form, that s 103 ter does not relate to or cover proceedings of this nature, this is to say, *habeas corpus* proceedings.

. . . After this certificate was issued, the attorney for the applicants wrote a letter to the State Attorney, who was acting for all the respondents, in which it was said, in the second paragraph, 'it is our view that the issue of such certificate in the present application is an act of *ultra vires* Act 44 of 1957 and void in law', and the respondents were ultimately called on to file answering affidavits.

Sydney turned to the letter from the Government Attorney to me, threatening costs against me on a special scale and stating that he regarded the proceedings as malicious.

Now, my Lords, in my respectful submission, that is an astonishing and indeed, most improper method for one attorney to write to the other. It is a threat made against the applicants' attorney to attempt to deter him from proceeding with the case. It verges in our submission on contempt of court and my Lords all I need say about it is that this attitude is not persisted in any longer by the respondents . . .

As your Lordship will see from page 97, a further point was taken . . . that the Minister of Justice had to be cited as a party to this matter. My Lords, that point, although not as offensive as the other point taken by the State Attorney, is equally without substance and I am glad to tell your Lordships that this point is also not persisted in by the respondents, so that your Lordships may deal with the merits of the certificate and the merits of the application.

His understated irony in referring to the timing of the release of 55 detainees as a 'happy coincidence' was met with much semi-stifled mirth in court. It even evinced smiles from two of the three judges. Mouton remained stern-faced, and William de Villiers' body language spoke of despair.

Using simple and plain language, Sydney proceeded to set out the argument against the certificate and the detentions in an easy, logical progression. Everyone could follow and appreciate the weight and sheer sense of the arguments. During both the tea break and the lunch adjournment, many of the clergy and activists in court felt there could be no answer to his compelling arguments.

The two senior counsel for the government split the argument between themselves. Louis Harms dealt with the certificate. Upon his analysis and interpretation of section 103 ter, the certificate should be upheld. William de Villiers rambled on about the detentions, arguing that the SADF had wide powers under the Defence Act and that the capture and detentions themselves were lawful. And, he said, the AG could validly extend detentions of people even if they were initially taken unlawfully into custody.

Although different in style and delivery to Sydney, I was also struck by the simplicity of language used by Arthur in his excellent reply. He incisively deconstructed and then demolished the arguments advanced by the government lawyers. The combination of Sydney's argument and Arthur's reply had been the most impressive display of advocacy I had witnessed up to then, and ever since.

The court reserved judgment as expected. I rushed our counsel to the airport in time for their late flights out of Windhoek. In high spirits, I joined Hosea and a few friends to reflect on what had been an enthralling day. We felt that the government lawyers had no answer at all to the argument on the certificate and considered that we had a sound chance on the detention issue.

Weeks went by while we anxiously awaited the court's ruling. Eventually, on 21 June, the court registrar called to say that the ruling would be handed down the next day. Most of the lawyers in my firm trooped off to court the next morning in the company of Bishop James. On these occasions, the full judgments are not read out. Only the concluding order is read out by the judge.

I was ill prepared for what followed.

Judge President Berker announced that he had prepared a judgment which his colleague Strydom had agreed with and that Judge Mouton had written a separate judgment. My hopes suddenly skyrocketed. I had not expected Mouton to find in our favour and a division held out the promise of success. As quickly as my hopes had risen, so they were dashed. In his next breath, Berker said that the result, however, was the same on both approaches. The application had lapsed under section 103 ter and no order is made. In other words, they accepted the validity of the certificate, resulting in the case lapsing; the application failed for that reason.

The court had rejected the powerful arguments against both the certificate and the detentions. The majority of the court (in the opinion written by the Judge President and agreed to by Strydom, J) found that it was for the state president to form an opinion not merely as to the good faith of the act in question, but also as to whether the court proceedings were instituted by reason of an act of the kind specified in section 103 ter (4). According to the court, the State President could thus form an opinion as to his own jurisdiction in deciding whether the court proceedings were by reason of an act contemplated by the section. They found that, once he had formed that opinion, the court had no power to declare his opinion invalid on the grounds that it was, objectively speaking, wrong or founded upon incorrect facts.

Judge Mouton's judgment was even more reactionary and in favour of the military. He considered that 'the act of continuously holding in custody' was, as a matter of law, an act 'contemplated and foreseen by section 103 ter'.

As for the detentions, the majority, although inclined to the view that the detainees were not in lawful custody at the time of the AG's ordering their further detention in May 1979, found that the term 'custody' used in the 1979 amendment 'does not mean lawful custody but simply refers to the factual position of a person being held in custody'. The AG could thus order the further detention of those unlawfully in custody. Judge Mouton agreed with this conclusion but went considerably further and found that the detainees had at all times, in any event, been in lawful custody. He said that the power to arrest and keep in custody flowed from the powers of the SADF to suppress 'terroristic' activities.

So much for the rule of law. The outrage I felt at the court's ruling was so intense that it felt visceral, like being winded by a blow to the stomach. When the blow was administered in court, I looked down at the blank page of the pad in front of me so as to avoid the glance of the exultant Chris Brandt who made no attempt to temper his delight at his triumph. The written judgments were handed to me. I scoured the majority judgment in my numbed state of disbelief, desperate to discern how things had gone so wrong. I got up to leave after the others had already gone so as to avoid encountering Brandt. I spoke outside to relatives of detainees and the bishop about an appeal. Without the need for any discussion on the issue, there was an instant consensus to do so.

It struck me that the court's reasoning on the certificate issue was formalistic and contrived, steering a compliant course. The appeal would be directed to the Appeal Court in Bloemfontein, South Africa. It was the highest court of appeal for cases from Namibia until independence. (It had the same status for South African appeals.) We agreed to meet formally to finalise the notice of appeal after I had also consulted counsel about the matter.

Gay was understandably also disappointed at the ruling and supported an appeal.

I was so downhearted. I decided to call Arthur that evening. His wonderful wife, Lorraine, said he was not at home and would only return late after a meeting. She was unequivocally supportive and had already become a good friend. Lorraine let me vent my anger at this injustice and then responded with coherence in her soothing tones, acknowledging that it was an awful setback. But, she said, they had also experienced setbacks in some of the outcomes of Arthur's cases. She said I was justified in feeling anger and being let down. The legal system could be fickle and nasty. Victories within it were very hard to come by. What was important, she said, was that I could hold my head high in the knowledge that I was in the right, even if the court ruling had gone against us, and had done my best for my clients. And to remember that it was important to keep believing in fighting injustice. Her warm words worked wonders.

Although I remained disillusioned about the outcome, this conversation had given me much-needed perspective. I knew that Arthur must have had many setbacks over the years of a similar kind. Yet he had tirelessly continued and had no doubt learnt from them in becoming the bastion of principle and excellence he was to us younger lawyers who aspired to do human rights work. Arthur called me the next day at work. He was also reassuring and encouraging, reminding me of the remarkable success achieved so far in the case by securing the release of 55 people after more than six years in secret detention. He quickly turned to practical matters, talking about an appeal and expediting it because of those who remained in detention. I set about putting those steps in motion at once.

There was a heavy atmosphere of gloom the next night at the Press Club where I met with my circle of friends on Friday evenings for drinks. The Press Club met on Friday evenings at the private bar of the rather sleazy Kaiserkrone Hotel in the city centre. Tony and I and a few other friends, including Hosea and Hartmut, commiserated about the outcome to the strains of Abdullah Ibrahim's iconic 'Mannenberg' – the signature song of the Press Club. The pathos and pent-up anger in that beautifully written and played jazz composition matched the mood. The locally brewed beer flowed and fuelled our vehemence in expressing our anger and frustration, and was about to give way to a sense of futility in taking on the system in the courts. I left before I became completely enveloped in despair.

My feeling of deep disillusionment about practising law continued for a few days until I realised that it was beginning to affect my colleagues as well. I recalled Arthur's words about our success in securing the freedom of 55 detainees, and exposing the injustice of the detentions and the lengths to which the regime had gone to prevent justice from being dispensed. But much more importantly, I realised that success would not be measured in court rulings in our favour. Those would not be readily forthcoming. The real outcome for our clients was, after all, what mattered most. Fifty-five detainees had been released, a serious abuse previously concealed had been exposed, and accountability on the issue had been forced, even if the court had not been receptive to our arguments. I recalled my thinking on being more assertive in the courts. That approach would not necessarily result in success in the narrow sense of the outcome of the case itself. Success was to be understood in a broader sense. My frame of mind improved. I felt I was on the right track. But the events that unfolded soon afterwards would preclude time for more introspection and rather demand that my attention be directed to more immediate concerns. This became a recurring theme in my practice during the 1980s – moving from one challenge to the next, often arising from the former, without a breather.

The case had been exhausting and I decided to take the following weekend off. I invited Hosea to join me and a visiting friend from the US at the Etosha National Park for three nights. It was the perfect antidote for the pressure of the case and the disappointment that followed it. Or so I thought.

On the second evening of our stay, one of the friendly conservation officers came to our fireside as we were about to start our braai in that magnificent setting, overlooking the floodlit waterhole at the Okaukeujo camp inside the park. He said he had an urgent telex for me. And so it was. Tony had written to tell us that my partner Hartmut, friend Anton Lubowski and other friends in the leadership of Swapo, including Dan Tjongarero and Niko Bessinger, had been arrested and were being detained without trial, apparently for breaching a law regulating meetings. A braai had been arranged by Swapo at Döbra, a Roman Catholic School just outside the capital, to welcome the newly released 55 Mariental detainees back into society. The venue had been surrounded by about 80 heavily armed security and riot police officers who had closed in on the event to arrest 37 of those there. We cut our stay at Etosha short and returned to Windhoek early the next morning.

An emergency partners' meeting was convened at the house of senior partner John Kirkpatrick that Sunday afternoon. The security police had, in the meantime, confirmed that all persons were being held without trial under security legislation (AG 9) and that charges under the meetings legislation were being investigated. They could be detained for up to 30 days on this basis.

John, always an imposing presence, spoke first: 'I've been approached by the *Beeld's* reporter [a leading South African Afrikaans daily newspaper based in Johannesburg, which supported the apartheid regime]. I've been asked what action we as a firm would be taking against Hartmut.'

Hartmut had also become a junior partner on the same day as I had, some two months before. John said that other members of the media would be approaching him and he first wanted to consult the firm about his response and which actions we would be taking against Hartmut.

The next most senior partner took his turn to speak: 'There is a need to take some form of action, and to be seen to be doing so. I suggest a suspension.'

Claus Hinrichsen was next in line to speak but first wanted to hear my views before stating his position.

I was profoundly disturbed by both the question being posed and the trend of thinking of those who preceded me, and said so. I did so as tactfully as I could. Even though distressed by what they said, I wanted to persuade them rather than have a showdown.

'I thought we'd been called together to see what we could do for Hartmut and about the other detainees and coordinate our actions,' I said. 'I'll be calling Gay at home this evening and get on to Amnesty International, Helen Suzman and some embassies in South Africa tomorrow. I'll also call my friends at Ropes and Gray [in Boston] and ask them to take it up with the US State Department. But there are also some pressing practical issues we need to discuss such as Hartmut's court work, like securing postponements and the like. I'll go in early tomorrow to look at those and ask Hosea to help with that as well. We also need to support his parents and I'll be going there straight after this. I simply can't see how we can even consider any action against Hartmut while he is detained without any access to him. We should instead be doing what we can about his detention and to support him.'

Claus firmly agreed with me and immediately offered to assist with Hartmut's files the next day.

The mood of the meeting fortunately changed and the two senior partners agreed with these steps. I proposed that the *Beeld* reporter be told that no steps of any nature could be considered without any charges and until we had been afforded the opportunity to consult Hartmut about those charges. There was consensus on this and I excused myself to visit Hartmut's parents. They were in a state of extreme anxiety. I explained to them what steps we would take. I promised to be in touch with them every day with an update until his release. If I could not get to see them every day, I would at least call. I kept my promise to them until Hartmut and the other 36 detainees were released five days later.[30]

They were never charged with any offence.[31] During his detention, I tried to have access to Hartmut on the pretext of work and the need for his input on certain of his cases, which I was then attending to. This was refused point-blank. After some negotiations, I was permitted to send him a few notes with questions about his cases. I included some gratuitously coded messages of support, which he later told me he appreciated.

The arrest and detention of the 37 at the braai received wide international media coverage and condemnation, both inside South Africa and abroad. The South African minister of police distanced himself from the arrests, given the bad timing. The arrests had been made at a Catholic church school just north of Windhoek. His state president was about to meet the Pope when this had occurred. The arrests were said to be an initiative of the police chiefs inside Namibia. Not surprisingly, the arrests went down well with the state-controlled media in Namibia, and those who supported the security forces of the apartheid state such as *Die Republikein*, the DTA mouthpiece.

The Windhoek Bar Council, led by Bryan O'Linn, issued a statement condemning the arrests and detentions. Under his leadership,

---

30   *Rand Daily Mail*, 11 June 1984, 12 June 1984; *Sunday Times*, 17 June 1984.
31   *Rand Daily Mail*, 6 July 1984.

that body, which represented practising advocates, became increasingly vocal in criticising human rights abuses.

The Law Society, the larger professional organisation representing all attorneys, was shamefully reluctant to speak out on those issues. I was then its secretary and formally asked the elected council to follow the lead of the Bar Council and condemn the arrests, which included one of their members, Hartmut. The Council conferred and declined to do so. I resigned my position, as did John Kirkpatrick, then vice president, who had consecutively served on the Council for 33 years. I respected his stance, given his initial view of the arrests. His stand came at much greater personal cost than mine. It was shortly after this that institutional work was taken away from the firm because of the work we were doing. The Law Society continued on its path of acquiescence until independence. It was, after all, the body that had failed even to discipline the lawyer from Lorentz and Bone, Anton Smit, who had been complicit with the security police in the *Mushimba* case and leaked the defence case to them. Not even a reprimand was forthcoming from the Law Society for such disgraceful conduct. (An application to strike him off the roll struck me as the more appropriate measure). He was naturally fired by Lorentz and Bone and moved to a small town in the Orange Free State in South Africa to continue practising there.

The appeal process took time. The record first had to be prepared. Although a simple task, weeks passed before it was ready to be dispatched to the Appeal Court in Bloemfontein. After a few months, these formalities were met.

In the meantime, international pressure mounted for the release of the remaining 74 Mariental detainees. (There were a few other detainees captured outside Namibia in addition to the remaining 55 seized on 4 May 1978.) The best efforts of Tony and Gwen to keep the story alive were strained as there were simply few developments of a newsworthy nature on which to hang further airing of the issue.

Without any forewarning or prior notice of any kind to us, on 18 October 1984 the rest of the detainees were transported by military aircraft to Ondangwa in northern Namibia and released at Oshakati. This was probably done to avoid another welcoming braai and an accompanying celebration by Swapo in Windhoek. Their release was announced with a flourish on the evening state-controlled television news by the authorities. I indicated to Samson that those released may wish to consult about potential claims in case we won the appeal. Despite remaining on record for five of the remaining detainees, I was never informed of their release by the authorities. I had also applied for access to all the detainees we represented at an early stage – before the court hearing. This had been refused. No reasons were ever given for that refusal. Some of the detainees arranged a meeting with Hosea and me after the final releases to thank us warmly for our efforts. Some instructed civil actions for damages, which were eventually settled.

I did not meet either of Josef Katofa's brothers who were detained at Mariental until some months later when Nikodemus Katofa called on me in early 1985. His purpose in approaching me was to enlist my help. Josef had, entirely unbeknown to me, gone missing and was thought to have been detained in May 1984 already, shortly before the case had been heard in court. The suspicion in the community was that the reason for his detention had been his active and crucial participation in preparing the application. I set about enquiries concerning him, which ultimately led to court proceedings.

The appeal still went ahead, even though everyone had been released. It could still proceed because it raised issues of great public importance about the issuing of certificates under section 103 ter, the powers of the SADF and detentions under the 1979 amendment. But the date of hearing could no longer be expedited and we had to wait for more than two years for it to be heard.

The appeal was eventually set down for hearing on 23 February

1987. The then Chief Justice of South Africa, Pieter Jacobus Rabie, was a conservative and supporter of the apartheid government. By this time, he knew to allocate his most reliable conservative colleagues to security-related appeals for the preferred outcome. He presided over a carefully selected, conservative, five-member bench. They listened attentively to Sydney's argument, asking very few questions.

The government respondents were then represented by a different team, led by a controversial figure, Piet van der Bijl. He had been a government legislative drafter who worked in the AG's office in Windhoek, having been brought in from South Africa. He had, we suspected, been the author of the 1979 amendment, as well as a range of other draconian security legislation in Namibia. The IG, installed in 1985, had astoundingly nominated him to be appointed as a judge in Namibia to preside over a constitutional council. Two members of the IG's cabinet, who were not as pliant in adhering to Pretoria's plans for Namibia as the others, opposed his appointment. A curious choice, a senior Pretoria civil servant with a murky human rights background, to preside over a council to come up with a constitution for the country. A farcical situation developed as those two cabinet members sued their cabinet colleagues and the apartheid government in a widely publicised court application to set aside his appointment. The case became settled. The South African government and AG and the compliant cabinet partners, together with Van der Bijl, agreed that his appointment be withdrawn and that he be given a handsome financial settlement. He then went to practise at the Pretoria Bar as a senior counsel. This status is usually earned by those in practice who are nominated for this distinction by their peers after a rigorous selection process. But not in his case. He had not practised at the Bar. Instead, he had worked his way up within South Africa's Justice Department, culminating in his appointment as a senior drafter specialising in security legislation. His loyal service to the apartheid state was rewarded by senior counsel status.

Getting to one's feet after what was a vintage Kentridge performance would invariably be a daunting task. The contrast between them could not have been starker. Van der Bijl's delivery was ponderous; the court repeatedly pounced upon his lack of precision in his formulation of propositions and pulverised him with a series of questions about his defence of the court's judgment on section 103 ter. He grasped in vain for answers to those questions. They did not interrupt much, however, when he turned to the legal justification for the detentions and the narrow positivist interpretation of the 1979 amendment adopted by the local court, which he enthusiastically supported.

The unanimous judgment of the court was handed down a month later on 25 March 1987. It overturned the Windhoek court's approach on section 103 ter, upholding Kentridge's argument outlined in his study at our first meeting – that the state president could not invoke that power in proceedings relating to an ongoing wrongs like detention. The court was unequivocal in doing so. But it found that a detention order under the 1979 amendment did not require preexisting lawful custody and that the further detentions were lawful after the AG had issued his orders a year after the detainees had been captured. This conservative bench had earned the reputation of seldom finding against the apartheid state in security matters. They duly delivered in this case too. Overruling the Windhoek court's executive-minded approach on section 103 ter did, however, set a significant precedent, even though we had lost the appeal itself because the detentions were found to be lawful.

2

The liberation of Josef Katofa

Three weeks before the Mariental detainee case was heard in court, a group of Buffel vehicles descended upon Josef Katofa's tiny cuca shop at its remote location at Eengolo, in the general vicinity of Outapi in Owambo. This was on 7 May 1985. His stall was a rudimentary structure, mostly of corrugated iron, without any windows and with very little ventilation. It sold anything from small radios to T-shirts to tinned and dry food products, as well as beer and locally brewed alcohol. It had been built with the modest savings he had accumulated during his six or seven years of work as a driver for a construction company in Windhoek in the 1960s. Josef was respected in his community, an active member of his local parish and a committed Swapo activist.

As often occurred on such occasions, he was blindfolded by the military and had a hessian sack shoved over his head when they came for him and took him away. His initial destination was the nearby military base at Outapi. There, he spent his first night in detention. His captors took him the next day to their battalion headquarters at Ogongo, some 60 km west of Oshakati. He was questioned there about whether insurgents had obtained food at his shop. He denied this. Later that day, he was taken to the detention barracks at the Oshakati military headquarters, called the 'hokke'. On arrival at Oshakati, he was asked whether he had transported any insurgents. This, too, he denied.

For some three weeks he faced no further questions. Towards the end of May, he underwent vigorous interrogation accompanied by torture. He was made to sit on a bench with his arms tied between his legs and to the bench itself. The method of torture was similar to the notorious practice of waterboarding used by the US more recently. A wet sack was placed over his head and water was continuously poured over the wet sack. It did not take long before he was inhaling water. As a result, he passed out on three occasions, slumping backwards on the bench but not falling over completely because his arms were tied to the bench. While the water was being poured over his head, he was repeatedly beaten with sticks and hard objects on his left shoulder and upper chest; his back bore the brunt of several further blows, all struck with considerable force. He sustained injuries particularly around his left shoulder. Scars were still visible there when I consulted him just over a year later.

It was repeatedly put to him during his interrogation that he had provided food to insurgents. He persisted with his denials. At one point, he challenged his interrogators to produce an insurgent making this allegation against him. After a short break in the interrogation, another captive with a sack over his head was dragged into the interrogation enclosure. His sack was removed and he was announced as 'Kondja' Angula. Josef subsequently recounted that Angula was in 'a most distressed state and appeared to have multiple bruise marks and was bleeding from certain wounds on the shoulders'. He was quickly removed after Josef conceded that if he had served him at the shop and if Angula had been an insurgent, he had not been aware of that.

The day after his interrogation and torture, Josef was taken to his shop under military escort. Without requesting the keys from him, the military broke the lock and searched the store. They found nothing to incriminate him. Instead, three of them helped themselves to a T-shirt each and one took a small radio from the items offered for sale in the store. His small pickup truck and an older truck were towed away by the military. They said that a landmine had been discovered hidden nearby his shop. They said it had been buried there by insurgents. He denied any knowledge of this and was taken back to the detention barracks at Oshakati. There he remained until being transferred to Windhoek in November 1984. No further questioning took place during that period, except for an occasional brief question about whether he knew the names of people who had been arrested. After his transfer to Windhoek, no one asked him anything at all for the next nine months, until his release.

When his brother Nikodemus was released from the Mariental internment camp, he learnt that Josef had been detained shortly before his own release. Months went by while the family awaited Josef's release. The remaining Mariental detainees were freed in October 1984. Josef, however, remained incarcerated. Early in the following year, Nikodemus approached Samson about Josef's continuing detention. Samson arranged for Nikodemus to travel to Windhoek to see me. This was in late February 1985. Samson strongly suspected that his detention was tied to his invaluable assistance to us in the Mariental detention case. He had, after all, obtained the names set out in the initial list and had tirelessly toiled to secure witnesses in support of the case. Most of the relatives we had consulted had been mobilised by him to meet with us. He had also persuaded Bennie Shilongo to come forward and make his affidavit. I shared Samson's sentiments and was outraged by his detention in these circumstances. I regretted only coming to hear about it when Nikodemus came to see me towards the end February 1985, some ten months after he had been picked up.

On 4 March 1985, I sent a letter to the AG, recording that Josef had not been seen since being picked up in May the previous year and enquiring whether a warrant for his detention had been issued – and, if so, seeking a copy. The response came ten days later. It revealed that he had been detained under Proclamation AG 26 of 1978 at the Windhoek Central Prison.

His detention under AG 26 was unexpected. At the time, this law was seldom invoked for detentions, and then only to detain activists south of Owambo. This was because AG 9 of 1977 (the Security Districts Proclamation) did not initially apply to areas south of Owambo. AG 9 was the preferred detention mechanism in the northern areas as its powers were so much wider. Any security force member of any rank could detain a person for up to 30 days without trial and the AG could then extend that detention indefinitely in terms of section 5 bis of AG 9, as had occurred with the Mariental detainees. Under AG 9, access to lawyers was expressly excluded during the initial 30-day period.

After contacting Nikodemus about the AG's letter, I responded on 27 March 1985 to inform the AG that Nikodemus would visit his brother. I added that, because AG 26 did not exclude access to lawyers, I intended to consult Josef and enquired about a convenient time for that consultation. I also asked for a copy of the warrant, which, despite my earlier request, had not been provided to me. Under AG 26, a detainee is entitled to receive the warrant of detention.

When I had received no response to this letter by 10 May 1985, I called upon the AG to reply. That only came on 1 June. A copy of the warrant was refused. I was told that a copy had been given to Josef, as the terms of AG 26 required. I was further told that AG 26 did not provide that anyone else was to receive a copy. As if this was not obstructive enough, the AG directed my attention to two provisions in AG 26 that 'establish conditions to protect the welfare of the detainee while he is in detention' and, on this basis, declined my request to visit him. Those two provisions required regular visits to a detainee by a state medical practitioner and secondly by a magistrate. I subsequently discovered from Josef that these had not occurred at all in Oshakati, and not with the required regularity in Windhoek.

Two days later, I nevertheless accompanied Nikodemus to the prison and was denied access. Nikodemus confirmed that Josef wanted to consult me during his brief meeting with him.

I then set about preparing an urgent application primarily directed at securing legal access for Josef. He had said enough to Nikodemus, however, for us to challenge the legality of his ongoing detention as well. This was something of a long shot. We decided to seek a provisional order calling upon the AG to show cause why Josef should not be released from custody. Given our experience in the Mariental case and the reluctance of the courts to order the release of detainees, I cautioned Nikodemus not to be optimistic about obtaining a release order. I thought we may at best secure legal access. This would establish an important precedent for future detainees under AG 26.

But we had not reckoned on the impact of a new appointment to our bench.

Harold Levy had practised for many years as an advocate in Cape Town. He had a reputation for being one of the more liberal members of that bar. Not long before we brought this application, his appointment as a judge in our court had been announced. He was to sit on this case together with Judge President Berker.

The AG opposed the application. AG 26 authorised him to issue a warrant for detention if he was satisfied that a person committed or attempted to commit an offence or in any way promoted or was promoting the commission of violence or intimidation directed at obstructing or threatening the peaceful and orderly constitutional development (of Namibia). In his affidavit, the AG said that he was satisfied that Josef was such a person. He supplied no reasons for his belief to that effect. He also opposed legal access to Josef. Jeremy Gauntlett skilfully argued the case for us. He cited recent English cases that supported the need for objective reasonable grounds for the AG's belief to exist (that Josef fell into the category defined in the proclamation). He argued that the AG's mere say-so (that he was so satisfied) was not sufficient and that an order should be granted calling upon the AG to show cause why Josef should not be released.

Both judges found resoundingly in Josef's favour. Harold Levy said that the right of access to a lawyer was a fundamental component of the right of access to the courts. Unless that right was specifically prohibited in a law, a detainee should not be deprived of the right to consult a lawyer. He ordered immediate legal access to Josef. He agreed with Jeremy's argument that, for the AG to be 'satisfied', he must establish the existence of objective reasonable grounds to justify the order of detention. In addition to ordering immediate legal access, he also issued an order for the AG to show cause, a few weeks later on 1 August, why Josef should not be released. Judge President Berker agreed with this order and added some further reasoning of his own in support of the principle that the AG would need to show objectively justifiable reasonable grounds for detention orders under AG 26.

This represented a significant legal victory. It not only set a new standard by granting legal access for AG 26 detainees, but – more importantly – required objectively established, reasonable grounds for detention orders under AG 26. The ruling was also hailed in South Africa, where increasing numbers of people were being detained without trial under the recently declared (first) state of emergency. It could and would be used to support detention challenges there.

Before the case returned to court on 1 August and after access was granted by the court, I visited Josef in prison. He made an affidavit, detailing his abusive treatment and the failure to ask him any further substantive questions after the end of May 1984 or charge him during this period of more than a year.

There had been another development of significance after the initial date of hearing and before 1 August 1985. An IG had been installed on 17 June 1985. The South African government had appointed a grouping of pliant parties to form this government. It comprised (and was dominated by) the ethnically based DTA, with some other smaller parties. Most of the administrative powers previously vesting in the AG were transferred to this new IG. There had been much slick South African government propaganda heralding this new order, said to be based upon the protection of human rights and which would lead Namibia to its independence, with or without the concurrence of the international community. The transfer of powers proclamation[32] from the AG to the IG embodied a bill of rights. The IG was precluded from passing laws that offended against that bill of rights.

It was now for the IG's cabinet to exercise the powers under AG 26, previously held by the AG. This was to be the first of several tests of its commitment to its own bill of rights contained in its establishing legislation. There was some speculation that the new cabinet may no longer oppose Josef's application when the matter would come back to court on 1 August. But that was not to be. Instead, the cabinet – through its first chairperson, the DTA's Dawid Bezuidenhout – supported the AG's original decision to detain Josef without advancing any reasons for this stance.

In the absence of establishing any objective reasonable grounds for the detention, the court on 26 August 1985 ordered Josef's release from detention: a first for me in my five years of practice. The cabinet appealed against that order. The court ordered Josef's release pending that appeal. The IG had dismally failed its first human rights test. It was the start of a pattern consistently repeated every time its own bill of rights was invoked against the arbitrary deprivation of rights, demonstrating its rubber-stamping role of the decisions of the South African security establishment to which it was beholden. Its professed commitment to human rights was exposed as utterly hollow.

---

32   Proclamation 101 of 1985.

It had heralded no change in human rights protection at all. Instead, it oversaw a steady decline in the enjoyment of human rights and a descent into lawlessness on the part of the State.

Armed with the order as soon as it could be typed and signed by the Registrar, Nikodemus and I proceeded to the Windhoek Central Prison. The political section of the prison had already received word of the court order. When we got there, an ecstatic Josef was inside its reception area, waiting for us, sporting his Stetson hat and ready to make a triumphant exit from the Windhoek Central Prison.

The IG's appeal was heard by the Appeal Court by Bloemfontein in August the following year. It lost the appeal because it had not itself, in as many words, stated that it was satisfied that Josef fell into the category, having merely relied upon the AG's prior satisfaction to that effect. The court was split, however, on the fundamental issue as to whether the AG (and later the IG) was to be satisfied on objectively reasonable grounds. The then South African Chief Justice Rabie, a staunch conservative, held that this was not the standard, declining to follow English precedent and finding that the mere say-so (as to being satisfied) would suffice for him. In other words, the court would not require that a reasonable basis would need to be established. One of his fellow ultra-conservative cohorts sided with him. Judge Trengove disagreed. He endorsed the approach adopted in Windhoek and said the standard required establishing an objectively reasonable basis. Another judge agreed with him. The fifth judge, who was ill at the time, declined to express a view on the issue because, he said, both factions agreed that the appeal should be dismissed. The underlying basis for the dismissal of the appeal was thus not conclusive. The Chief Justice subsequently saw to it that his approach was followed in a later case by ensuring that Judge Trengove never sat on another security-related appeal after that. From then on, he was more selective in composing his bench for political cases.

As a consequence of this case, AG 26 was never again, to my knowledge, invoked. Instead, the security establishment resorted to the less troublesome AG 9 for detentions without trial.

It was then time to turn my attention to AG 9 and find a way to gain access to lawyers under that noxious provision.

3

Access denied! Fighting for legal access to detainees

The spate of arrests in the Oniipa-Oneputa area – about 10 km south of Ondangwa in the Owambo area – during August and September 1985 was ominous. It had been preceded by a prolonged period of insurgency in the area. The rounding up of a large group of civilians in an area could mean that the security police may be building a case to take to court. A rare event.

John Akweenda, a former Mariental detainee who had been released in October 1984 after spending six and a half years in detention, had called me from Oniipa in mid-October 1985 and asked to see me. After a couple of days, he had made it to Windhoek and was seated across the desk from me in my office.

'My brothers Thomas and Martin, my brother-in-law Andreas Immanuel and a cousin Absolom Linus have been picked up by the security forces around the end of August and early September and have not been seen again. Please do something.'

John was concerned about their personal safety and Thomas's job. All except Thomas lived in the area. Thomas stayed in Tsumeb where held down a good position as a salesman with the local branch of a hardware outlet, CYMOT. Thomas had been arrested in Oniipa on one of his regular visits to his family home. The 200 km distance from Tsumeb meant he could travel to Oniipa on weekends from time to time.

I took down their details and promised to get back to him after making a customary enquiry to authorities. I feared there was little we could do about Thomas' employer except inform them of his position and keep them abreast of news as and when we had some and hope they would keep the position for him. He had worked for them for some ten years by then after all and they were, I tried to reassure John, known to be fair employers. They may be understanding.

My enquiry to the IG dated 17 October 1985 did not elicit any response, despite concerning the liberty of individuals. A further letter on 19 November demanded a response and threatened an application to compel one if it were not provided by 27 November. This at least resulted in an answer that the matter was being investigated, assuring me that a response would follow by 9 December.

Not surprisingly, the eventual reply on that date from the IG said that they were all being detained under section 5 bis of AG 9 and attached warrants of detention signed by the then chairperson of its cabinet. Under this provision, the cabinet could indefinitely extend the detention of those already detained for 30 days by security force members.

AG 9 detainees are expressly denied access to a lawyer during the initial period of detention for 30 days. But the extension of detention under AG 9, formerly by the AG and replaced by the cabinet as from June 1985, did not specifically prohibit legal access during the indefinite extended period of detention (after 30 days) under section 5 bis, even though the wording on the warrants sought to do that.

The *Katofa* case had established that AG 26 detainees were entitled to see lawyers, because that proclamation had not specifically precluded that right. That portion of the judgment had not been appealed against and had set a significant and meaningful precedent. The practical effect of the ruling meant that the authorities subsequently avoided AG 26 as detaining power and turned instead to AG 9, because it expressly precluded that right during the initial 30-day period of detention and was applied by the authorities to exclude access during the indefinitely extended period afterwards. This was confirmed to me by Brigadier Thomasse, then head of the security police under whose control the detainees had been held.

I felt that the time was now ripe to push for similar rights for AG 9 detainees whose detention had been extended by the cabinet under AG 9. It would also be yet another important test of the cabinet's commitment to upholding basic human rights, as promised in its empowering proclamation by the inclusion of a bill of rights and repeatedly emphasised in its self-promoting public statements because of the diminishing popularity of heavy-handed security force action in the eyes of a burgeoning politically conscious youth.

When I reported back to John about the response from the cabinet, I suggested that he return to Windhoek to discuss a challenge to secure legal access. My experience in the lengthy trial of Frans Angula and others had shown how crucial early access could be. Our clients had been charged with committing a number of acts of terrorism under the Terrorism Act in 1985. They had been assaulted and tortured by security policemen during the early phases of their detention. Some had made confessions or admissions, and had pointed out incriminating evidence to policemen. But they were only formally charged more than a year after they had been apprehended and interrogated. This was the first time they could see a lawyer or a private doctor. At that stage, all external signs of assaults had disappeared. It was virtually impossible to challenge the voluntariness of their confessions and admissions successfully. With early access, there were very real prospects of evidence of the assaults and torture that were vigorously denied.

In an earlier trial handled by Hosea involving two PLAN fighters, Sam Mundjindji and Veiko Nghitewa, under the Terrorism Act, they had likewise been assaulted and tortured. This was raised in cross-examination by an experienced counsel, David Soggot, who appeared for them. They, too, had been assaulted long before access to them was granted after they had finally been charged. The security police men were indignant in their denials of having beaten them. Without corroborating medical evidence, the assaults could not be established. In his judgment in that case, Judge Mouton disparagingly referred to this line of cross-examination, stating that it merely served to 'kick up dust' in that nothing had come of those allegations.

My tactic would be to challenge the legality of the detentions again in this case and press strongly for access. I figured that the chances were good that we could at least succeed with access and establish an important precedent for future detainees, helping us to prove assaults, mount stronger challenges to confessions and reduce the prospect of future abuse of detainees as the chances of exposing it increased. John was excited about our bringing an application to secure access and possibly securing the release of his relatives. I prepared draft papers, settled by the formidable team of senior and junior counsel assembled for this test case – Ian Farlam, assisted by Jeremy Gauntlett. After their combined effort, the challenge to the lawfulness of the detentions was excellently expanded and so convincingly set out that we stood a real chance of succeeding outright with a release order, instead of my earlier primary objective of achieving access.

The application including that part directed at legal access was strenuously opposed by the cabinet of the IG.

In his opposing affidavit of 27 January 1986, the then chairperson of the cabinet, Moses Katjioungua, confirmed that the cabinet had, on 26 September 1985, ordered the further indefinite detention of our clients. On 24 January 1986, Andreas Immanuel's release was ordered, but he said the continued indefinite detention of the remaining three was necessary for the maintenance of law and order, and in the public interest. He said that the cabinet was satisfied that Thomas was a member of a cell actively involved in acts of terrorism and sabotage. Katjioungua also confirmed that the cabinet had approved the conditions of detention, which included denying legal access.

A two-judge bench would consider the case on 13 February 1986. It comprised Johan Strydom and a new judge about to be appointed, Herbert Hendler. Not much was known about the latter. We did not know what to expect. What we did know, however, was that the approach of the two-judge court in the *Katofa* case would greatly assist us in seeking access as well as challenging the detentions themselves.

Our counsel delivered an expertly constructed argument persuasively. The detentions were attacked on a dual basis. Firstly, Ian Farlam contended that detention without trial conflicted with the bill of rights incorporated in the IG's empowering proclamation and that the detentions should be set aside for this reason alone. In the second place, he argued that detainees under AG 9 were entitled to be heard regarding why they should be further detained before the cabinet could make a decision about their further detention under section 5 bis. Turning to access, he cogently contended that detainees under section 5 bis were entitled to access to lawyers for the reasons articulated in the *Katofa* case. The judges listened attentively and asked him few questions.

In contrast, the court grilled our opponent, Jan Hugo from Pretoria, especially about why his clients had refused access to a lawyer. That approach clearly did not sit well with the court. At the end of the oral argument, they announced that a ruling would be made later on the same day, something rarely done. This was promising; I waited impatiently for the designated time in the afternoon.

For the first time, I felt we were on the front foot. There was a definite buzz of expectation as we returned to court for the ruling in the early afternoon. John was accompanied by some relatives and friends, representatives of the CCN and a few supportive journalists, all buoyed by the sympathetic hearing we had received. Our upbeat chatter fell silent as the judges entered. Judge Hendler announced that he had prepared a written judgment and, as was the custom, would only read out the order at the end. He announced that the release of the three remaining detainees was ordered by the court and declared that their detentions were illegal. He also ordered the IG to pay the legal costs.

Judge Strydom stated that he concurred in the ruling and the court adjourned. As quickly as that. I had the urge to jump up like a football player and punch the air, but I managed to keep my elation in check. Just as well: our state of euphoria was dampened when the security police in court informed me that Martin and Absolom Linus were then to be charged under the Terrorism Act and would, from then onwards, be held in detention under that law. Thomas was freed and was thrilled to return to his wife and young family in Tsumeb – and, thankfully, also to his job there. I represented Martin and Absolom in their lengthy and sensational trial that got underway later that year, together with Andreas Heita. Torture came under the spotlight as never before. Despite what Katjioungua had extravagantly stated, Thomas was never subsequently charged.

Even though Martin and Absolom had been charged, it was a huge victory, as the well-reasoned judgment soon revealed. Judge Hendler went out of his way to find that detainees under section 5 bis were entitled to consult lawyers during their extended detention. This, I knew, would be a game-changer. Although a trial under the Terrorism Act would always remain an unfair exercise, an element of its inherent, fundamental unfairness was now ameliorated. From now on, it would be more difficult for the security police to adduce confessions extracted after torture. This brought with it the prospect of less abuse of long-term detainees for fear of proof of being found out. And it forced the hand of the security police to charge Andreas Heita, then being detained under section 5 bis.

4

'As long as I don't kill him':
Exposing torture

A system of torture was central to political trials (and, for that matter, detention without trial) in Namibia in the 1980s. Not only were the defendants subjected to torture to extract confessions and admissions, but witnesses were also detained and tortured. This was because they were frequently civilian collaborators who would be tortured to incriminate insurgents and other civilian collaborators, who would then be charged under the Terrorism Act. Once information was coercively obtained from witness detainees, they would be threatened with prosecution or further incarceration unless they testified along the lines of what had been extracted from them by third-degree methods. Almost all defendants ended up making confessions and admissions after undergoing gruelling torture.

The odds were stacked against establishing torture, however. The biggest hurdle was having no access to detainees until they were formally charged, usually a year or more after they were apprehended when torture had usually taken place. Most, if not all, physical evidence of torture would have disappeared by then.

That was why it was so crucial to secure access to detainees.

The *Akweenda* judgment on 13 February 1986 had established a very useful precedent with far-reaching implications. Long-term detainees under section 5 bis of AG 9 would either have to be charged or released because they had not had a hearing (before the decision to issue a further detention order). Crucially, at the very least they would be entitled to legal access after their initial 30-day period of detention. AG 9 was the preferred power invoked for long-term detentions, given the wide powers of arrest and minimal safeguards during detention. Successive AGs had simply rubber-stamped orders for further detention under section 5 bis, instead of properly considering them. The *Akweenda* (and *Katofa)* cases had also shown that the new cabinet of the IG continued that tradition of lavishing approvals for lengthy detentions without trial without proper scrutiny – or any real scrutiny at all. This was yet another emphatic demonstration of its empty commitment to human rights protection.

Within days of the *Akweenda* ruling, two captured PLAN fighters were charged under the Terrorism Act in northern Namibia. This was because the security police had been forced by the *Akweenda* ruling to charge them. Importantly, this meant that we had access to them. I was instructed to defend them. I wasted no time in getting to them, as they had probably been tortured. It was critical to see them without delay. The day after being instructed to defend them, I called the security police in Oshakati to arrange a consultation with them on the very next working day – Monday 10 March 1986.

This was a first. Save for the AG's specific approval to consult Axel Johannes in detention in 1980, I had never been permitted to see any detainee while he or she was in custody at the hands of the security police, despite numerous requests. I arranged to see Andreas (Pwakela) Heita and Tangeni Paulus in the security police's offices at Oshakati.

As I entered those offices, the atmosphere of deep resentment of the *Akweenda* ruling was almost tangible. Andreas and Tangeni were present. I knew that my openly hostile reception and the ensuing aggressive exchanges with me would assist in building some trust in this first meeting, given the fact that they had not met me or heard of me beforehand. The security police insisted on being present in the consultation. I tried to resist that. They antagonistically asserted that Andreas and Tangeni were captured 'terrorists' and under no circumstances would they permit me to consult them without them being present and able to observe our every move, including me in their concern.

After a heated altercation, they eventually made a small concession. They would remain present but out of hearing range, so they said. Recording my objection, I decided to participate in this arrangement as I had travelled some distance to see my clients and decided to defer the final determination of this dispute, if it persisted, to a later date in Windhoek with the overall head of the security police – or, failing success with him, in court. But that was the nature of practising then – constantly having to press and know when to defer a dispute and adapt to what was possible. I could see that this was the best I could achieve that morning.

It was of course not possible to have any kind of meaningful consultation like that. I used the opportunity to introduce myself formally and explain that I had been engaged by the CCN to defend them. I would also see if I could glean whether they had been assaulted and then have a follow-up consultation very soon afterwards in better circumstances. Tangeni was in obvious pain and discomfort. His leg was plastered and his partially plastered arm was in a sling. His head was also heavily bandaged. He had been seriously injured in the skirmish leading to his capture. He had undergone major surgery at 1 Military Hospital near Pretoria and had been returned to hospital in Oshakati. He had been brought to the consultation from hospital, where he was being held under guard. He plainly needed to get back to his hospital bed without delay.

I asked a few questions about their personal circumstances and how to get hold of their families. In between taking down details, while fairly vocally seeking clarification about the spelling of a name that Andreas could see I had already written down correctly and without looking up, I very quietly whispered an enquiry to Andreas under my breath, asking if he had been assaulted. He gave a very quick nod before painstakingly repeating the spelling of the name, which he had seen had already been correctly transcribed. Even though his English at that stage could at best be described as very broken, it was clear from this and the expression in his eyes that he had instantly registered what I was after and had delighted in our private conspiracy. This exchange had gone unnoticed by our minders. Thus began a close relationship of trust. When I said I would return to see him soon to consult further, his face lit up.

I asked the local security police commander which police station he was being held at so that I could return in a week or two to see him. At first, the commander refused that information. I pointed out that Andreas had now been charged, was entitled to consult me, and that I would want to make a timeous arrangement to see him briefly again about practical issues in a week or two when returning to the north. He begrudgingly answered that he had been transferred to the Ondangwa Police Station. His reluctance to accept that Andreas could, as of right now, consult me was evident. It was new territory for him too.

This encounter had neatly coincided with my Sunday meeting with the four applicants in the 91 Koevoet detainee application. It was on the following morning.

Because of developments in that case, I returned to the north eight days later for my bizarre meeting with Brigadier Dreyer of Koevoet, in which we secured the release of former PLAN fighters from the Oniimwandi base. When Hosea and I dropped one of them off near Ongwediva afterwards, it was mid-afternoon. Our business in the north that day was not yet completed. There was still time for me to make a brief turn at the Ondangwa Police Station, which I had planned to do if time permitted. Hosea then dropped me off at the Ondangwa Police Station and returned to Ongwediva to collect his sister Leli who would drop us at Ondangwa Airport in her car, which she had lent us for the day.

I asked for the station commander at the counter in the charge office at the Ondangwa Police Station. A uniformed lieutenant appeared from an adjacent office. Addressing him in Afrikaans, I introduced myself as the attorney representing Andreas Heita. I apologised for not making a prior appointment. I explained that I had come from a lengthy meeting with Brig. Dreyer. It had finished earlier than expected and I had some time before I would return by plane to Windhoek from the nearby airport. This had afforded the chance to deal with a small practical matter with Andreas. It would be greatly beneficial to do so and save me from travelling all that way back for that single purpose when it could be quickly disposed of with his cooperation. It would, I said, take no longer than half an hour. I was able to say all this without being interrupted. Indeed, the lieutenant listened without evident impatience or hostility. But I could sense that I had not yet persuaded him. I switched tack and invited him to call the officer in charge of the security branch at Oshakati, who would confirm that I was acting for Andreas. He would also confirm that I could see him as charges had been preferred against him, which meant that he now had access to a lawyer. I detected some relief in his facial expression at my suggestion: he need not make the decision, but could defer it to somebody else.

He called the Oshakati head of the security police from the charge office in my presence. The phone was on a large desk a short distance from the counter. I could hear him provide an accurate summary of what I had said to him. A short silence then followed and the conversation was concluded with a brief acknowledgement in the affirmative. He turned to me and said there would be no problem. He called across to one of the uniformed policemen on duty in the charge office to escort me to Andreas's cell. I thanked him, unused to common courtesy and not the overt antagonism I had experienced at the hands of the security branch. He was a member of the uniformed branch, a different species.

The cell in which Andreas was held was some distance from the charge office, across a courtyard area, towards the back of the building. It was dark and dank. There was no table or chair inside the cell. I asked the policeman if we could use one of the empty offices off the courtyard as I needed to make a few notes. He took us to one of those offices. He hovered in the doorway. I politely asked for some privacy. He said that his instruction was to observe us and remain present throughout. Yes, I responded, no objection at all, but outside of hearing range, please. I motioned to the large window in the opposite wall and suggested that he lock us in and go around to the window and observe us from there. I would later indicate to him when we were done. In that way, he could watch us without being able to hear us – which, I added, was inherent to attorney–client privilege but would address his reasonable instruction to keep us under constant observation. He was fortunately persuaded.

As the key was noisily turned from the outside to lock us in, I whispered urgently to Andreas to remove his shirt immediately. He responded at once. As he did so, I grabbed my camera from my briefcase with equal speed. He turned around to reveal massive and unsightly scarring across his upper back and torso. It was a terrible and shocking sight. Five or six distinct tramline scars prominently covered large tracts of his back. They each had dark bruising in long, straight lines of some 30 cm or so, with a raw pink colour of freshly healed but swollen skin protruding between them in the form of gigantic blistering. He also had a scar on his head and some much smaller scars on his chest. I had little time to focus and snapped four or five photographs in double-quick time. In a flash, I was able to shove the camera back into my briefcase. Andreas managed to slip his shirt back on swiftly. By the time the policeman appeared at the window, he would have seen Andreas straightening his shirt and me rummaging in my briefcase as I hastily removed the film, only to emerge with my pad and pen in a deliberate manner while in earnest conversation with Andreas.

I jotted down a few details of the assaults. He had been repeatedly beaten with a piece of hosepipe, mostly on his back, by Capt. Ballach, who was attached to Koevoet. These assaults occurred over some days during interrogation immediately after his capture. The beatings were sustained over long periods and had ruptured his skin. He had bled from the wounds. Electric shocks had also been applied to his genitals. He had received a blow to his head, which had knocked him to the floor. There was a small bald spot on his head where an open wound had healed, corroborating this aspect. He had been blindfolded throughout. There was no let-up in the savage attack until he had pointed out explosives, made admissions and given sufficient details to satisfy his tormenters. He had later signed a statement. He was eventually treated for the ruptured skin and injuries to his back in hospital. He could not recall who treated him at hospital and the exact date. But I had enough to go on for the time being.

It turned out that there was no record of his treatment at the Oshakati State Hospital or at the military facility where he had received medical attention from army doctors. This was not surprising, given our experience at how scrupulous the security police (and Koevoet) were about covering their tracks.

After updating him briefly on the delays in obtaining details of his charges and a trial date, I called out to our observing policeman to come around and open up as I knew that Hosea and Leli would be waiting outside for me by then. Before he could unlock the door, I swiftly tucked the removed film into my underwear and put another roll of film into the camera, in case the policeman suspected something and decided to search my bag and person. But he took Andreas to his cell without further ado and acknowledged my thanks for enabling us to consult in the office.

Hosea could hardly contain his excitement when I told him of my photographs.

'This is going to be a major breakthrough. I know it.'

And so it turned out to be.

The next day, I called the officer commanding the security police in Oshakati about Andreas's injuries to insist that he be taken to a doctor. I was put through to the investigating officer in the case, Warrant Officer Van der Hoven; I expressed my concern about Andreas's injuries and insisted that he receive medical attention.

The full indictment took some time. Andreas and Paulus were charged with committing acts of terror under the Terrorism Act along with five civilian collaborators, including Martin Akweenda and Absolom Linus.

Months later, at the outset of the trial on 25 August 1986, we gave notice of an objection to the charges under the Terrorism Act on the grounds that it offended against the IG's bill of rights. The case was postponed to 10 September 1987 for argument on the objection.

The IG had been installed in 1985 by way of a proclamation that prohibited the National Assembly, established under the proclamation, from 'making any law abolishing, diminishing or derogating from any fundamental right' listed in the bill.

On the day of the argument, the prosecution produced a new proclamation[33] issued by the state president a few days before. Hot off the press, it amended the IG's empowering proclamation by inserting a new provision that precluded the courts from enquiring into the validity of any Act of the South African parliament. The procla-

---

33   Proclamation 157 of 1986.

mation was dated 5 September 1986. We had been unaware of it because gazettes from Pretoria usually only became available some days after their publication date. It had been hastily enacted to thwart our challenge.

Ian Farlam and Jeremy Gauntlett were engaged to argue the constitutional objection. They had argued a similar point for us in the *Angula* terrorism trial, although without success. We had drawn the liberal Harold Levy as the presiding judge in the *Heita* trial, however. We decided to argue that the earlier decision should not be followed. Much was at stake, and had caused the South African government to amend the IG's empowering proclamation. Ian argued successfully that the recent amending proclamation should not apply to the pending objection unless this was specifically stated in the amendment.

Judge Levy found that our objection was not affected by it. He also found that the Terrorism Act, with its onus on accused persons to prove their innocence, offended against the fair trial provisions in the bill of rights and upheld the objection. It meant that the defendants could not be charged under the Terrorism Act for anything done after 17 June 1985 (when the IG was installed and its proclamation took effect). Judge Levy said it was a question of policy and not of law for the authorities to decide whether to prosecute under the offending law for conduct prior to 17 June 1985. The prosecuting authorities decided to do so and confined the charges under the Terrorism Act to acts committed before the IG took office on 17 June 1985. This only eliminated a few counts, as most of our clients had been apprehended in late August 1985. The majority of the charges related to events before that date. The charge sheet was also amended to introduce charges under the Sabotage Act and the common law offence of malicious damage to property.

This liberal ruling had effectively been overturned in the *Katofa* appeal, however, with the conservative South African Chief Justice finding that the IG's proclamation precluded courts from pronouncing upon the validity of legislation in existence when the IG had been given its powers. This was obviously the cynical intention of the apartheid state and its obliging partners in the IG. They had both repeatedly argued for that position. It meant that the IG's bill of rights had almost no real value at all as it would only apply to passing future legislation and not to invoking a powerful battery of oppressive laws previously enacted by the apartheid state. The IG had happily inherited a wide range of draconian powers; it had little need itself to pass further nasty laws and less inclination to ameliorate the effect of them. Instead, it repeatedly invoked them.

Certain facts were admitted when the trial started, such as a meat factory being sabotaged by a bomb, several telephone poles and a water installation being blown up, and a few other occurrences that our clients could not contest. There were witnesses who put some of our clients on the scene when these acts of sabotage had occurred and who had seen them there in incriminating circumstances – being armed or in possession of explosives. But the case against two of our clients, Gideon Tangeni and Kakede, depended largely on the confessions and admissions extracted from them during their detention.

Most witnesses were civilian collaborators who had been detained for lengthy periods and tortured during detention, in most instances. They had been told that, unless they gave satisfactory evidence which accorded with the statements extracted from them by coercion during detention, they would be also prosecuted or simply not released from their indefinite detention.

During cross-examination, several of these witnesses confirmed that they had been assaulted by their interrogators during detention. Some had even seen Andreas or other defendants being assaulted, or seen evidence that they had been beaten. The purpose behind this line of cross-examination was to establish that there was systematic torturing of detainees by the security police and other security force elements such as Koevoet – with a view to our planned challenge to the admissibility of all our clients' admissions and confessions made during detention.

The civilian state witnesses incriminated our clients sparingly, much to the evident frustration of the prosecution. This meant that they would need to resort to the admissions and confessions in an attempt to prove several of the counts against our clients – especially against Gideon Tangeni and Kakede.

Despite the evidence of torture that emerged during cross-examination of detainee state witnesses, the prosecution said they still wanted to adduce the defendants' confessions and admissions. We then gave notice that all would be contested on the basis that they were not voluntary and had all been tortured to varying degrees.

I then engaged local senior counsel Bryan O'Linn to lead Theo Frank in what is known as a trial-within-a-trial, the separate phase of the trial to determine the admissibility of those statements. Bryan was an indefatigable cross-examiner and was especially effective with policemen. He had a way of wearing them down with his dogged persistence until he had obtained the desired concessions. He also had an uncanny knack for catching them off guard, and then pouncing upon an inconsistency and driving home his advantage to devastating effect. His cross-examination in this case would, I am sure, go down as the finest in his distinguished career, characterised by integrity and an overall commitment to championing human rights during his many years as leader of the bar.

In our first consultation with Bryan, Theo and I showed him the photographs I had taken of Andreas at the Ondangwa police station. He, too, was horrified by what he saw. We had already drawn the photographs to the attention of the Attorney-General. Bryan was rightly also astounded that the prosecution nevertheless wanted to adduce the confessions.

We also explained to Bryan the importance of the confessions to the prosecution's case against two of our clients as state witnesses had hardly connected them to any of the manifold charges against them. This was the last throw of the dice for the prosecution against them, as they had both made statements. The confessions would also to bolster the case against Andreas and others, as the state witnesses who had collaborated with them had not spilled all the beans on them despite being cajoled by the prosecution with leading questions. The prosecution team was led by a very seasoned political trial prosecutor, Mr A. Liebenberg, especially brought in from South Africa for the case.

Four police witnesses were called in the trial-within-a-trial.

Warrant Officer Nicky Nampala of the security police was present during much of the interrogations. He was the first to be cross-examined. He had captured Andreas, who had sustained a gunshot wound to his arm in the skirmish that had led to his capture. Nampala had taken him to a military sickbay, where the wound had been treated and bandaged. An intravenous drip had been inserted by the treating doctor into his other arm. Andreas had been released by the medical personnel so that he could be taken to the security police offices in Oshakati for interrogation.

In the meantime, Capt. Anton Bekker, the after-hours duty officer of security branch at Oshakati, had sent for Capt. Ballach of Koevoet after being informed by Nampala of Andreas's apprehension. By the time Nampala had arrived with Andreas at the security police offices at Oshakati, Ballach had awaited them. As Andreas had alighted from the back of the pickup truck, sporting his drip, Ballach had advanced upon him and yanked out the drip's needle from Andreas's arm before taking him to an office where he had proceeded to interrogate him. When it was put to Nampala that this was brutal and shocking, his answer was, 'Ja, dit was tot 'n mate (Yes, it was to an extent).'

It was not a promising start for the prosecution.

Ballach's reputation for torturing detainees preceded him. I had built a dossier of his assaults on serving political prisoners and former detainees, who would be called to give evidence to show a system of torture. Many had fingered Ballach. But their evidence would not be necessary after Bryan's cross-examination of Nampala, Bekker and Ballach himself.

Ballach's interrogation of Andreas had lasted for three days. Nampala said the most severe assaults were perpetrated on the first day. Nampala said that Ballach had flogged the wounded Andreas with a hosepipe on his back, arms and torso for lengthy spells.

During Bryan's cross-examination of Nampala, Bryan paused and asked Andreas to stand up and remove his shirt to show Nampala the scars across his back and on his chest. When Andreas did so, he was facing the judge. As his shirt came off, there were spontaneous gasps from the packed gallery. There was a sign of irritation on the face of Judge Levy at this courtroom disturbance. Realising this, Bryan immediately asked Andreas to turn around so that the judge could also see his back. Judge Levy's mood changed to justifiable outrage at the sight of the multiple scars that disfigured Andreas's back. There were still large patches of bright, shocking-pink skin between scars of a darker colour, graphically depicting the torture experienced more than a year before. At Bryan's invitation, Andreas also pointed to the scars on his head, ear and chest.

Nampala confirmed that Andreas had had none of these scars upon arrest. Nor had they occurred during his capture. They were, he confirmed, the results of sustained beatings after his capture. It was, he elaborated, normal practice to beat captured Swapo guerrillas and their suspected collaborators. He conceded that the usual rules governing interrogation simply did not apply to interrogating insurgents, as long as an insurgent's life was protected.

An incredulous Bryan exclaimed 'Ekskuus? (I beg your pardon?)'

Nampala repeated: 'Solank ek net sy lewe beskerm het (As long as I just protected his life).'

'Solank jy wat? (As long as you what?)'

'Sy lewe, ek het hom mos nie doodgemaak nie (His life, I didn't kill him after all).'

'Jy meen alles duskant doodmaak is, so geslaan as wat hy was, dié is "all right"? Net, net darem nie doodmaak nie? (You mean everything short of killing him, like beating him as he was, is all right? Just, just not actually killing him?)'

'Jy slaan dat hy bars maar tot hy uitwys wat hy uitgewys het (You beat him to breaking point but until he points out what he pointed out).'

'Vir die uitwys is dit geregverdig, jy slaan soos jy wil? (For the pointing out, it is thus justified for you to beat as you please?)'

'Maar daarna is hy nie meer aangerand nie (But after that he was not further assaulted).'

'Ja, maar jou houding is, en dit is die houding van jou hele veiligheidstak daar, dat solank julle wil inligting hê, is dit nou maar reg om die manne te slaan en te kere te gaan om die inliting te kry, reg? (Yes, but your approach is, and is it also that of your whole security branch, that as long as you want information, it is justified to beat men and go beserk to obtain the information, right?)'

The answer was in the affirmative.

This chilling testimony accorded with what numerous clients had consistently told us over the years, but had been so difficult to establish because we did not have access to them soon after their assaults. If they claimed they were beaten, a number of police officers would dutifully troop into the witness box to piously deny assaults of any kind. And they had been believed by judges in the past when doing so.[34]

---

34 Judge Mouton, in his judgment in trial of insurgents in *S v Mundjindji and Nghitewa*, had gone further and referred to cross-examination about police torture as having merely served to 'kick up dust'.

Access and the photographs of Andreas had changed that.

Nampala's admission about this approach was clearly a game-changer. But candid as he was about Ballach's beating of Andreas, he denied that electric shock treatment had been used on him. This type of torture invariably left small burn marks visible only for a short while afterwards. It could safely be denied without the fear of physical evidence to the contrary. It would, again, be a single detainee's word against several police officers' denials.

Nampala also admitted that Ballach had also badly assaulted two of the other defendants. He had thrown Gabriel Mathews to the floor wrestler-style, and struck him while he was down – and yet again when he got back to his feet, so that he had been struck down again. In the case of Johnny Nangolo, Ballach had thrown him to the ground and struck him down again at least three times.

Nampala had also testified that the rudimentary corrugated iron cells where detainees were held by the military were called the 'hokke' and acknowledged that this term, meaning a cage or enclosure, was commonly used to describe enclosures for animals. This was the term, he said, that was used by the military to refer to those facilities.

Except for *Die Republikein* and the state-controlled broadcaster, the local media and liberal South African newspapers prominently featured the story of Nampala's evidence of routine torture of detainees on their front pages, stressing how unprecedented it was.[35]

The investigating officer, Warrant Officer Hermanus van der Hoven of the Oshakati branch of the security police, followed Nampala on the witness stand. We soon knew that he was not being truthful. At the outset, he denied that I had called him in late March to express my concern about Andreas's injuries and request that Andreas receive medical attention. He was referred to the first medical record

---

35   The *Windhoek Advertiser*, 5 March 1987; *The Namibian*, 6 March 1987 and 13 March 1987; *The Cape Times*, 9 March 1987; *The Sunday Star*, 1 March 1987; *The Weekly Mail*, 27 February – 5 March 1987 and 6–12 March 1987.

of treatment given to Andreas, dated 25 March 1986. It was the first time he had obtained proof from military medical personnel that Andreas had been treated, shortly after my call. The fact that he denied my call, yet had taken Andreas for treatment soon after my visit to Ondangwa and obtained proof of that medical visit, meant that we had little confidence in his credibility.

He said that he had seen Capt. Ballach of the police's notorious Koevoet unit assault three of the defendants during interrogation. Under Bryan's cross-examination, he said Andreas had been repeatedly whipped by Ballach with a segment of hosepipe. Van der Hoven spoke of his Christian values and said he did not approve of violent methods used on detainees, but accepted that they were an 'essential' part of interrogation as this had led to the discovery of explosives. The end, he said, justified the means. After the initial beatings, Andreas was taken under a large escort to a place to point out explosives. En route, on the back of a Casspir, Van der Hoven had seen an unidentified member of Koevoet strike Andreas over the head with a large stick. He had approached Ballach to call the Koevoet member to order. Van der Hoven confirmed that Andreas had been detained at the time at a Koevoet base, and that Koevoet did not keep a cell register or an occurrence book at its main base where detainees were held. His evidence was also that those detained by the military were usually held in solitary confinement and that no record was kept of medical treatment received by such detainees.

At one point, Bryan enquired whether the piece of hosepipe formed part of Ballach's torture apparatus. Bryan scoffed at the instant denial, and retorted to the delight of the full court room: 'What was its use then, to water a garden in his office or what? (. . . om 'n tuin in die kantoor nat te lei of wat?)'

More was to follow.

Captain Bekker was called to testify about an oral confession allegedly made to him by Gideon Tangeni. There was almost no other evidence of Gideon's involvement. We had little to go on when preparing for Bekker's cross-examination. No other clients had been assaulted in detention by him – except for Gideon being roughed up and then assaulted on that occasion. Bekker simply did not feature in any accounts of torture upon the serving political prisoners and former detainees. We soon found out why.

It turned out that Bekker had previously been stationed in the Eastern Cape of South Africa. After being posted to Oshakati, he had been more involved in the intelligence side of security police work, as opposed to investigation for prosecutions. He was a poor witness, already ill at ease and shifty in his evidence-in-chief, long before his cross-examination even started. Bryan quickly disposed of his version. Within minutes, he stumbled and stuttered and was grasping for answers. He soon made concessions about failing to provide the customary warnings to Gideon before receiving his oral 'confession'.

He confirmed that he had seen Ballach beat Andreas and conceded that he deliberately concealed this from his commanding officer out of fear that it would be stopped.

Bekker also conceded that he had done nothing to stop Ballach's brutal beatings because he felt that the use of violence had been justified. He said he had not seen any injuries at the time. This severely dented his credibility. Bryan asked Andreas to remove his shirt again and Bekker was obliged to concede that the very visible wounds were marks of assaults. This led to Judge Levy intervening:

'Ek meen dit is 'n baie ernstige slanery daardie, dit is 'n wrede slanery wat gedoen is. Hy is pap geslaan. Kyk na die rug? (I think it was a very serious beating, that; it is a gruesome beating perpetrated. He was beaten to a pulp. Look at his back?)'
   'Ek sien so, U Edele (I see so, my Lord).'
   'Sal jy saamstem hy is pap geslaan? (Would you agree that he was beaten to a pulp?)'

'Wel, die merke sit daar. Dit lyk lelik. (Well, the marks are there. It looks ugly).'

His account of a confession by Gideon was entirely discredited in Bryan's short and devastating cross-examination.

The fourth and final police witness was Ballach himself. A man of no more than medium height, of wiry and muscular build, he admitted in his evidence-in-chief that he had assaulted Andreas by striking him on his back with a length of hosepipe about a metre long.

But, he said, the subsequent confessions made before a magistrate had been voluntary and had not been tainted by his prior assaults.

Soon into his cross-examination, he conceded that he didn't warn Andreas, as is required, that he need not answer questions. Bryan put it to Ballach that he had pulled the drip out of Andreas's arm to demonstrate his brutality upfront and to instil the fear of God into him. This he denied. He was soon reeling against the rope like a swaying boxer, however, after fielding a few quick body blows powerfully administered by Bryan. First, he said that he had merely struck Andreas lightly a few times on his back. Bryan again asked Andreas to remove his shirt. He conceded that the scarring was the consequence of his assaults. Bryan put to him that it amounted to an extraordinarily serious assault.

His response: 'U Edele, ek het die man, kom ons praat nou soos ons altyd sê, 'n goeie pak gegee. (My Lord, I gave the man, as we would say, a good hiding).'

Judge Levy intervened: 'Die vraag was, sal u erken dat die letsels buitengewoon erg is? Kan u daarop antwoord? (The question was if you would admit that the scars are extraordinarily severe? Please answer the question?)'

'Die letsels blyk so te wees, U Edele (The scars seem so, my Lord).'

Judge Levy then asked if he would admit that the assaults upon

116

Andreas were very serious and the response was only on the first evening.

After going through the assaults on Andreas in more detail, Bryan put to him that Andreas had been beaten in a brutal and barbaric manner. He denied that. The follow-up proposition was that the assaults had not been beyond limits for him. That, he agreed with.

Ballach denied some of his assaults as had been testified by Van der Hoven and Nampala, and could give no explanation why they would give false evidence to that effect.

The assaults, he said, delivered results, as Andreas had later pointed out plastic explosives at a location. He had 'flogged (Andreas) because he told lies', but after being assaulted, Andreas, he maintained, was then completely willing to tell the truth.

Capt. Ballach eventually conceded that Andreas had been severely beaten and that these vicious assaults had been perpetrated with a view to secure a confession.

At Koevoet, he said the objective was to 'hunt down and eliminate' Swapo guerrillas. He confirmed that Andreas had been blindfolded during the assaults. He also said that Koevoet kept no records of their detainees and he kept no record of his interrogation. The military medical officers likewise kept no record of the treatment of detainees. Bryan put it to him that the reason for all this was to cover up ('verdoesel') evidence. When Ballach denied this, he could not give any other reason for the absence of records. Tellingly, he also confirmed that Koevoet did not follow inquest legislation in respect of the deaths of guerrillas or suspected guerrillas; the deceased were buried in unmarked graves.

It was put to him that those captured by Koevoet had no rights. He denied this. But he acknowledged that he had not warned Andreas before his questioning that his answers could be used in evidence against him. When asked why he had pulled out Andreas' drip, he said that Andreas looked in reasonable shape. Judge Levy intervened

117

to ask whether he was not concerned that his wound could go septic. He said not. It was all too clear from his response that this had not remotely occurred to him and was of no concern to him. Ballach, too, denied that electric shocks were administered to Andreas during his interrogation and that he had passed out during shock treatment.

Bryan also put to Ballach that he was specially brought in to interrogate Andreas as a third-degree specialist. This he denied. He later amplified his answer by pointing out that the assaults on Andreas were not 'outside limits' but conceded that if others were to have assaulted Andreas 'problems could have arisen'.

When Ballach said he did not know how the scar on Andreas's head had been caused, he agreed with Bryan's proposition that he was unconcerned about whether and how injured his subject became, as long as the assaults brought results. He evaded questions about, and denied assaulting, Thomas Akweenda, who had been called as a state witness. Thomas had made mention of such an assault during his cross-examination. He also denied assaulting three of the defendants in the earlier *Angula* terrorism trial who were ready to testify to those assaults.

When Ballach's cross-examination came to an end, the prosecution formally withdrew their attempt to adduce the confessions and admissions. The prosecution closed its case in an air of ignominy. We could not and did not call any of the defendants to testify in their defence, as far less was established against them than expected.

After argument, the court adjourned for a few weeks to prepare its verdict. As there were so many charges and and so much testimony spanning some months, Judge Levy's judgment was lengthy: it ran into 125 pages. Its delivery was at a pedestrian pace. At the end of every sentence, Levy would pause for it to be translated into Oshiwambo for the defendants (and their relatives and supporters in the packed court room). The laborious delivery meant that he was not able to complete the task by the end of the day. We gathered again the next morning for him to continue. Because the attempt to adduce the confessions and admissions had been abandoned, it was strictly speaking not necessary to deal with the evidence of torture. But Judge Levy went out of his way to castigate the security police at length. He first referred to our cross-examination of detained State witnesses who had testified that they had been beaten. He accepted that this was in a bid to show a concerted method on the part of the police in an investigation process that systematically included assaults in order to obtain confessions or admissions. He found that Andreas had been 'beaten mercilessly on the three days following his arrest. His back is at present a mass of raised discoloured scars. His back must have been beaten into a pulp.'

Judge Levy also referred to the injury to Andreas's head 'which had left a bald patch with a scar' and his injury to his ear. Levy also disparagingly referred to Ballach plucking the drip from Andreas' arm.

Judge Levy roundly rejected the justification of police officers that the end justified the means, adding:

> An assault is a crime and no exceptions can be permitted. Any exception could undermine the very existence of law and order and make a farce of all those concerned with the enforcement of the law. What it amounts to, is that the police are doing exactly what they are there to prevent.

He held that Ballach should be prosecuted for the assaults that he admitted.

Andreas was convicted on multiple counts of terrorism. Paulus and Martin Akweenda were also found guilty of contravening the Terrorism Act. Three of the other defendants were convicted under legislation relating to possession of explosives. And then, towards the end of his lengthy verdict, the crowning moment came.

Judge Levy turned to Gideon Tangeni and Kakede. He found that the evidence against both was inadequate and that the case against them had not been proven beyond reasonable doubt. Tangeni and Kakede were acquitted on all charges. The gallery erupted and the court hastily adjourned to a future date for sentencing. Amidst ululating and uncontained jubilation, Kakede flew from the dock to embrace me and then his aunt, who had managed to press through the throngs of well-wishers. She had devotedly attended his trial throughout. Tears were streaming down her face.

There were seldom acquittals in political trials. The fact that both defendants and witnesses had been detained without trial for lengthy periods to extract statements favourable to the prosecution usually meant a positive outcome for the prosecution in these show trials. Despite six of the eight defendants being found guilty, it felt like a major victory – which it was.

The victory was, of course, not confined to that success.

For the first time, we had been able to expose systematic torturing of detainees with a view to extracting confessions and admissions from them. Political trials were finally shown up for what they were – shams tainted by a routine resort to torture of detainees, defendants and witnesses alike. The credibility of political trials in Namibia was finally and forever undermined. In the years that followed before independence, very few people were again brought to trial for political offences. This was the real victory.

When it came to sentencing, we called a political scientist to give expert evidence about what had given rise to the liberation struggle and the resort to armed resistance to South African rule. The conduct of the defendants was placed within this context. Judge Levy listened attentively to Professor Gerhard Tötemeyer's evidence. Although it was not as cogent and structured as the evidence that Professor André du Pisani had given in the earlier *Angula* terrorism trial, he made the salient points with credibility.

Andreas received a hefty sentence of 18 years imprisonment on 22 May 1987, however. The other defendants' sentences ranged from an effective eighteen months' imprisonment for the young Sagaria Barakius Namwandi (who was only sixteen years old when he was arrested and detained, but eighteen years old when sentenced) to twelve years. We unsuccessfully appealed against the sentences. Andreas and his co-defendants did not serve their terms. Except for Sagaria, who was released after serving his sentence in full (political prisoners did not receive early releases on parole), all the others were released as part of the UN peace plan in July 1989.

5

In the court of the Koevoet king

The summer months at the end of 1985 and in early 1986 saw an upsurge of security force atrocities in Owambo on a scale not previously encountered. This necessitated several trips to northern Namibia over that period.

During one of these visits, I received an urgent message from Skinny Hilundwa to drop by at his office at Ongwediva before heading back to Windhoek. It was a hot February afternoon. My consultations had taken longer than expected. I was in a hurry to head south in order to make it to the military checkpoint at Oshivelo before sunset and the onset of the curfew.

Skinny was a seasoned activist who had been detained without trial under security legislation for a long period before I started to practise. I only came to know him well around 1984 when he ran the Owambo office of a literacy programme funded from abroad, based at the ELCIN complex at Ongwediva. Ever friendly, with an easy air, he was understated and humble, yet had acute powers of observation and his finger on the pulse of developments in the northern regions. An opportunity to hear his analysis of the latest developments was always a welcome and stimulating prospect. He realised my need to rush and came to the point at once and handed me a letter.

'It's from some former PLAN fighters who have been captured and are being sort of detained. This is a tricky one, very tricky. Please have a look and see what you can do.'

I promised to do so and get back to him. There were three signatories to the letter. It said that they were former PLAN fighters and were being held against their will at the Oniimwandi base camp by the Koevoet Counter Insurgency Unit of the Police. They feared for their lives and asked me to secure their release and to do the same for some 130 others in a similar position. A list of 136 names was included in the envelope.

The day after my return to Windhoek, on 19 February 1986, I sent a letter to the cabinet of the IG, attaching a list of the 136 names, enquiring as to the legal basis for their detention as well as the dates of their seizure and copies of warrants or orders authorising their detention. The then rotating chairman of the cabinet, Moses Katjiuongua, wrote back to say that, '. . . after an investigation, it appears that no such persons are being detained.'

The blanket denial was baffling. I had encountered cases of individuals who had been picked up by the security forces whose detentions had been denied. On rare occasions, there was a subsequent acknowledgement of a detention initially denied, coupled with an explanation that a different name had been supplied by the detainee in question to the one contained in my enquiry. But on most occasions, these disappearances were unresolved and the people were not heard of again. Their fates sadly still remain unresolved. One exception was Johannes Kakuva, who had been picked up by the security police near Opuwo in the area known as Kaokoveld in the far northwest of Namibia in August 1980. His detention was denied in a protracted exchange of correspondence that I had directed to the authorities. When I had left for my studies in the US, we had decided to investigate the circumstances of his disappearance further. During my absence, my colleague and friend who had joined the firm a year after me, Hartmut Ruppel, had diligently built a case from affidavits he had secured from a number of people detained with Kakuva, and who had seen him beaten badly and had also heard him scream during his detention. Hartmut successfully launched an application on behalf of his family for the presumption of his death. The case was referred for oral evidence. The ensuing evidence was overwhelming. Judge Mouton had no difficulty in making a ruling to that effect – declaring a presumption of his death in detention at the hands of the security police.[36]

In the other cases of disappearances I had dealt with, we lacked sufficient evidence for which security force elements were involved and where the detainees had been taken. These incidents had invariably occurred under the cloak of darkness in isolated rural areas without electrification. These people had simply disappeared in the night, never to be seen or heard of again. Recent revelations of Koevoet's operations in books about the notorious Eugene de Kock, who had been a company commander with Koevoet from its inception in the early 1980s for a few years, would suggest that some – if not most – who disappeared in this way may have died at the hands of Koevoet after torture and interrogation about the movements of insurgents.[37]

I read the cabinet's response to my enquiry over the phone to Skinny. 'Can you come this weekend?' was his reply. 'It must be over the weekend and not during the week.'

On the following Sunday (9 March), we met at our cryptically pre-arranged venue, behind a small shop nearby Ongwediva. We separately drove from there to a small business complex closer to Oshakati.

---

36   *Kakuva en 'n ander v Minister van Polisie* 1983 (2) SA 787 (SWA) and 1983 (4) SA 787 (SWA). Despite the court finding and evidence of assaults, no one was ever prosecuted for his death or those assaults.

37   Pauw, J. 2017. *Into the Heart of Darkness: Confessions of Apartheid's Assassins.* Jonathan Ball Publishers: Cape Town, pp. 37–42; Jansen, A. 2015. *Eugene de Kock: Assassin for the State.* Tafelberg: Cape Town, pp. 88–125 and 126–127.

Four men were waiting for us inside a back office on the premises. This venue had been made available by the owner, a trusted Swapo member and a friend of Skinny's.

I was introduced to Immanual Hashiko, Vincent Haushona, Onesmus Shikongo and Aktofel Shiluwa. All had been PLAN fighters. They had left their homes in different parts of Owambo in the mid- to late 1970s to go into exile and join Swapo. Each had undergone military training and returned as PLAN combatants, operating inside northern Namibia, on varying missions and sometimes for lengthy periods. They had, on different dates and at locations, been captured by Koevoet. They had then been incarcerated at the detention facility within Koevoet's Oniimwandi base camp. In Immanuel Hashiko's case, he had first been hospitalised for some time under guard at the Oshakati State Hospital and also at the Ondangwa Military Hospital at the Airforce Airbase. This was because of injuries he had sustained in the sortie leading to his capture.

I put the obvious question to each of them.

'But, if you are being detained, what are you doing sitting here in civilian clothes at this business complex about 1 km from Oniimwandi on a Sunday afternoon and without any trace of an armed guard in the vicinity?'

Their responses were to identical effect.

After their capture, they were at first tortured and interrogated and locked up in cells in the Oniimwandi base camp. At a later stage they were confined to barracks in that camp. After a few years, they were allowed out for over weekends, primarily from Saturday afternoon until 7 am on Mondays. It was made clear to them that they could never leave the Oshakati area on these free weekends. If they dared to do so, they would be summarily executed upon recapture. Given the ruthless methods used by their captors, which included summary executions, they feared for their lives if they were to leave that immediate vicinity and leave the base. They did not dare do so.

Each referred to cases of two captives who had been summarily executed in the camp. They also all recalled the case of another inmate who was taken away at night by their Koevoet captors and was never seen again, also suspected of being summarily executed. A fourth had died in suspicious circumstances – and had been found hanging one morning in the camp. The fear felt by each throughout my consultations was palpable. Their captors had not at any stage informed them how long their strange state of semi-detention would endure. But they wanted to put it to an end and to leave that Koevoet camp permanently.

I proposed to take down written affidavits from them there and then, as they would have to report for duty at the camp early the next morning and would only be out again on the following Saturday. But this would have meant going to the Oshakati Police Station to have the affidavits commissioned. Police officers would be the only commissioners of oaths available in Oshakati on that Sunday afternoon. This they each empathically resisted. They feared for their lives if they were to swear to an affidavit before a police officer because Koevoet formed part of the police and they would be found out. They provided me with a revised list of 91 names, including their own. All those on the list were also captured PLAN fighters in a similar position. They also supplied the names of three Koevoet captains (Ballach, Potgieter and Botha) who performed duties at the Oniimawandi detention camp. They each struck me as credible. I believed them.

I also knew of Captain Ballach, a member of the security police assigned to Koevoet. He had formed part of an investigation that had led to a lengthy trial involving three insurgents and four civilian collaborators. They were charged and later convicted under the Terrorism Act. I had been their instructing attorney during the trial.

Some of these defendants had complained that Captain Ballach had viciously assaulted them during their detention while they were being interrogated. We had not been able to obtain any corroborating medical evidence to prove this, because we had only gained access to our clients after they had eventually been charged – more than a year after the assaults had taken place. Most no longer had any scars or visible evidence of the assaults to support their version. It would be their word against that of a senior police officer. Several other police officers would also be produced to parrot the police version piously that they do not assault detainees and would not dream of doing so. Our clients, in that case, were not able to dispute the truth of the main features of the evidence given by Ballach. It was not in their interests to testify in their defence and be subjected to cross-examination because state witnesses, drawn from the community who had also been detained, gave evidence that was far less incriminating than we anticipated. The state witnesses were largely collaborators and were sparing in their details of events. Unknown to me at the time, Ballach's torture exploits would be graphically exposed shortly afterwards in the *Heita* trial.

In the absence of affidavits from any of the four persons I had consulted that Sunday, I got each of them to sign a power of attorney to authorise me to take whatever steps I could in order to secure their release from this strange netherworld of quasi-detention.

It would mean that I would need to make an affidavit setting out what they had said to me concerning their circumstances and attach their powers of attorney. I discussed this approach with my colleagues in my firm upon my return to Windhoek. The senior partner of my firm, John Kirkpatrick, was dead against this course.

'You are becoming far too involved. It is as if you are now becoming an applicant and no longer have any professional detachment. I'm against this in principle. You should not proceed with this application.'

The underlying reason for this sharp and unexpected rebuke then emerged. Resuming his tirade, he elaborated: 'Dirk Mudge [a cabinet member of the Interim Government and its unofficial leader] yesterday at a mining function especially collared me to complain about the way in which you address the cabinet in your correspondence. He found it offensive and disrespectful and felt he should draw it to my attention as they did not expect this tone and attitude from a leading law firm.' (John was prominent in business and mining circles and had become the chairman of the board of the major uranium mining company, Rössing Uranium Limited.)

There was clearly to be a showdown if I persisted with this application.

I was taken aback on both scores. I decided to deal with them separately. I said that I differed with him on the approach to the application and very briefly explained why. But before completing my short reasons, I proposed that we ask Arthur Chaskalson for his view.

'If he says that I should not proceed, then I'll back off. But would you accept that I can go ahead if he gives it the green light?'

To my relief, John had calmed down after airing his grievance and agreed to this proposal, as he held Arthur in very high regard.

As to the complaint about my correspondence, I responded that I thought I knew which letter had offended. I offered to collect it forthwith from my office, adjacent to his, and show it to him. He could not decline that offer. Within an instant I returned and placed a letter of demand before him. It required the cabinet to respond to an enquiry made concerning a cabinet ban on marches and meetings for a certain date. There had been no response to my initial enquiry. My follow-up letter was, upon reflection, somewhat assertive – probably due to the date of the proposed banned march rapidly approaching. It insisted that, if no response were to be given within a specified period, an inference would be drawn that there were no reasons or any reasonable basis for the ban. I told John that the wording of this letter had been settled by experienced counsel in the person of Jeremy Gauntlett. He likewise respected Jeremy's ability and judgement, accepted my explanation, and graciously said that he felt Mudge had hopelessly overreacted to it.

A confrontation had been averted, one that would have resulted in my departure from the firm. I was not yet ready for that. I also did not want to leave the firm on acrimonious terms. It had been largely supportive of the work I was doing, even though there had been some tension from time to time. But the overall atmosphere was friendly and collegial.

I had heard that Oniimwandi was a Koevoet base, but had no confirmation of this. On 13 March, I called the security branch at the Oshakati Police Station and asked to speak to the Commander of the Oniimwandi Detention Centre. I was directed to the special unit 'K', which had become the new and preferred way of referring to Koevoet on the part of the police. I was put through to a Capt. Botha. He said he was commanding officer of that base. He denied that any people were being detained at his base. I started to read out the 91 names in my possession. He interrupted and said that it would be pointless for me to read through each of the names. There were no detainees in his camp. Period. If I wanted to make an official enquiry, I should direct it to the security branch in Oshakati.

I tried to get hold of Arthur. His office said he would be unavailable and in court in the Delmas treason trial for the next few days. That bitterly disputed case had reached a pivotal point. Arthur had been briefed to come into the case to lead his old friend George Bizos to argue an important aspect.

I reached him at his home that night. He was totally immersed in a tense argument in that case and sounded strained and worn out. He could not consult me for the next few days about another case. I impressed upon him that it was an urgent matter that had placed my position in the firm in jeopardy. He was at once very concerned and said that I could come and stay overnight either on the next day or the day after that but that he would only be able to chat with me at home over dinner, given the heavy demands of the argument in the Delmas trial.

As it turned out, I did not need to travel to Johannesburg the next day to see him. Another eminent senior counsel, Ian Farlam, was, by chance, briefed in Windhoek the next day in a case by another lawyer, and had agreed to meet me after court. John Kirkpatrick agreed to abide by his view on the matter.

Ian listened carefully as I set out the facts.

'But of course you should bring the application. You would merely be a witness and not an applicant. Your four clients would be the applicants,' Ian calmly said.

I explained that I would approach the three bishops again as applicants to apply for the release of the others named on the list. He sanctioned that approach and undertook to phone John Kirkpatrick if I wanted him to do so. Early the next morning, John said this would not be necessary. He no longer objected to the application going ahead. The bishops were on board. The application was served later that day and set down for the following Tuesday.

On the intervening Sunday morning, Chris Brandt, the Deputy Government Attorney, called me for an urgent meeting at his office that morning to discuss the case. In those days before cellphones, I was unable to get hold of Hosea or Hartmut to accompany me and went on my own. There were three Koevoet captains in his office. I was introduced to Capts Ballach, Botha and Potgieter. Brandt took me aside and said that all of the persons listed in the application were, in fact, paid employees of Koevoet and not detainees in any sense at all. That, of course, conflicted with my instructions. I pointed that out to him. He then called across to one of the captains, who produced a wage register. It listed virtually everyone included in our application. The worn and dog-eared register seemed completely authentic and indicated monthly payments made over a period of a few years in favour of those listed in our application. He assured me that they were all on the police payroll and that there could be no question of them being detained in those circumstances.

Brandt pointedly turned to me. 'I am showing this to you now so that you can see for yourself and satisfy yourself. You must drop the case at once.' He was not known for a tactful a bedside manner in his dealings with his opponents.

'Not so fast', I responded. 'I would need to check this out with my clients first. I can't and won't withdraw the case without first canvassing this with them.'

I added that it was my duty to do so.

I waited outside his office as he conferred briefly with his clients. He then emerged, asking me to confirm my position, which I did. He paused as if for effect and to summon a deliberately stern tone: 'Well, in that case my clients can no longer guarantee your safety in the north.'

I was instantly outraged by this threat. 'I give you 30 seconds to withdraw that threat or we'll go right now to the home of the Judge President so that I can explain to him why I cannot continue to represent clients in his court if the Government Attorney and his clients make threats of this nature against me in the conduct of my practice.'

'It's not a threat. Nor is it intended to be. I am just stating a fact. My clients tell me that many people would be extremely unhappy with you if their source of income were to be taken away from them and they think this could adversely affect your safety.'

'Oh, please. It clearly remains a threat. Either you unequivocally withdraw it at once or I am leaving now for the Judge President. And I'm formally inviting you to be present when I approach him on the issue.'

'Well, if it came across like a threat, I'm prepared to withdraw it.'

I said that I would accept his withdrawal of what was said.

I reiterated that the application would not be withdrawn by my clients unless I was given unqualified access to those on the list to take instructions from them. This was refused point-blank by Brandt after again briefly conferring. My patience was wearing thin.

'Very well. I shall then tell the court on Tuesday that, despite your assertion, supported by the register, access has been refused for me to consult my clients on the issue. I shall then formally ask the court to require that every single one of them be brought to court and for each to be questioned in court as to whether they are being held against their will or not, seeing that your clients are refusing access to them. You will then see what the court's attitude will be. It serves no purpose in talking any further to you on the issue. I'll see you in court on Tuesday.'

I turned to leave. 'Wait,' was the response. 'Let me confer one last time, before you go'.

Again, I waited in the passage – for much longer this time. I assumed that calls were being made to those more senior. Eventually he emerged and told me that I could consult with those within the base the next day or on Tuesday. I accepted Tuesday and we agreed to postpone the case for a few days to enable me to do so.

I asked Hosea to accompany me to the north for this consultation. We chartered a small plane, a single-engine Cessna 210. The flight was smooth until we reached the Etosha Pan. The pilot gave us the customary warning that we would drop from an altitude of about 10 000 feet to fly the last 100 km or so at what was termed treetop height. It was actually about 100 feet above the ground. This was the standard practice during the 1980s to avoid radar detection because of insurgency. (Swapo guerrillas had rocket-propelled grenades [RPGs] and other sophisticated weaponry and had shot down some SADF helicopters.) It was the rainy season. There were clouds around and the weather was unsettled. The last 30 minutes or so, which seemed interminable. Our stomachs seemed to move up and down with every bump that shook the small aircraft. Somehow I managed to retain my breakfast, as did Hosea. But it was a near thing.

We were received at the Oniimwandi base by Brig. Dreyer, the head of Koevoet. (He was later promoted to the rank of major-general.) It was a first time for both of us. We had not expected to meet him. He was dressed in camouflage fatigues, his eyes concealed behind opaquely tinted glasses, his face tanned, yet slightly ruddy. His movements suggested agility and a level of fitness, confirmed by a physically trim frame. He addressed me from the outset and throughout on my first name and took no notice at all of Hosea, whom I introduced to him. He said he first wanted to brief me fully personally, again completely ignoring Hosea. I politely explained that our purpose there was to meet those on the list and that it would not be necessary to confer at any length with him. I disliked the forced familiarity and informality he displayed towards me, almost congeniality, a common tactic used by security policemen. I also pointed out that he was represented in the court proceedings and it would not be appropriate to hold discussions with him without someone from the Government Attorney's office in attendance. He would have none of that. He had spoken to the Government Attorney and said he would meet us to give us the necessary background. He invited us to a spacious office. Tea and coffee were served, with rusks and biscuits.

What then ensued will always stand out as one of the most bizarre experiences of my career. He addressed me throughout in Afrikaans. Despite Hosea's presence throughout, everything remained directed at me, as if Hosea was simply not there.

Dreyer gave a detailed account of the history of Koevoet, which he had founded.

'You know, the SADF was faring very poorly here in the late 70s. You can actually say they were losing the war. They simply did not understand how to deal with guerrilla warfare and could not adapt to it. They had no clue and their methods, training, structure and tactics were completely unsuited to it. With their conventional approach, they were having setbacks – one after another – and had nothing to show for themselves. More importantly, they were simply getting nowhere against Swapo. So, in 1978 John Vorster [the then prime minister of South Africa] called me in and asked me to establish this counterinsurgency unit. I had gained some very useful experience in counterinsurgency work in Rhodesia. The success rate there was very good, particularly because of the quality of intelligence. He asked me to set up Koevoet and turn the tide in the fight against Swapo. And that's what I did in January 1979. And I can tell you, I've not looked back since. Our methods are of course unconventional. We ferret out information and effectively act upon it. But we get results. And that's what counts. We have turned things around.'

As we sipped our tea and coffee, he proceeded to provide details of some of those military successes. He took out a scrapbook, filled with graphic photographs depicting the death and destruction of Swapo insurgents at the hands of Koevoet members. He described with evident pride some specific incidents where insurgents had been killed or captured, often with arms and explosives in their possession or at scenes of arms caches that had been pointed out by Swapo insurgents after their capture. He also provided some statistics of Koevoet's kill rate and ratio.

'We are extremely tough and have an excellent success rate against Swapo. Although our kill rate is high, this doesn't mean that we kill all the insurgents we encounter. We in fact capture many. And, let me tell you, many of those we are actually able to deploy later. Some are in fact very useful to us. There were some [in the security establishment] who didn't like the idea. But I can tell you that Owambos can be useful, very useful in this fight.'

It seemed lost on Dreyer that Hosea, an Oshiwambo-speaking person, was present. Gauging from his manner, he probably thought it was complementary and not racist, having put a distance between himself and other more right-wing security force colleagues who balked at the prospect of black members in their forces. I darted a look in Hosea's direction. He lifted his eyebrows ever so slightly in acknowledgment of what we needed to get through and I picked up just the faintest suggestion of humour in his eyes.

I interrupted Brig. Dreyer in full flight at this point: 'But you did not take them prisoner out of any humanitarian motivation. It was surely and probably purely for the purpose of obtaining information from them.'

He was constrained to agree. But he hastily added with the same degree of strident conviction that had characterised his entire presentation: 'Ja sure, intelligence is vital in any war. But let me tell you again, these people can be extremely useful. We have turned many into very valuable fighters and trackers in my unit. They are tough and skilful and get me results. I would not have it any other way'.

We were then taken to inspect a large quantity of arms and munition which, he said, Koevoet had captured from insurgents. It was mostly of Soviet origin, as he hastened to demonstrate.

When I next managed to get a word in, I asked when we would be able to see our clients.

'Ag ja, man, I'm coming to that. I was explaining that many of those we capture later join us as fighters. We carefully select them and they do excellent work for us. But there are others who are not suitable to fight for us. They are then used in other ways. They help in the camp and outside, and do a range of tasks. We pay them to do that. They are free to go out of the base at night. Some stay with their families in the nearby settlement, while others sleep in their barracks in the base. They are free to come and go as they please after hours. But you see, and I'm sure you would understand this, they can't go back to their people [presumably meaning PLAN]. They'd be persecuted, you know. So they prefer to stay with us and are employed in different capacities within our unit. Paid nicely for that too, mind you, and also very well fed. And here they can wipe their arses with toilet paper, not the mealie leaves they have to use at home. But you can hear that from them yourself.'

(He continued to ignore the presence of Hosea, who, at his first chance, muttered indignantly in my ear that mealies were not grown in Owambo and that mahango, a form of millet, was the staple, adding 'Shows how little he really knows.')

It had taken far more than an hour to get to this point. I thanked him for the tea and for taking the time to provide such detailed background. I was anxious to get on with our consultations with those within the base, not knowing what to expect and how long it would take to complete. We were, after all, scheduled to fly back to Windhoek late that afternoon.

As he finished and we were already getting up to move, he mentioned for the first time, almost in passing, that several of the people on our list were out on patrol or on other tasks and not on the base at the time. This annoyed me as he would have known about our visit since Sunday. But, he said, we could meet with all of those currently in the base who were on our list. I suspected this was a deliberate ploy, as was soon confirmed. I reminded him of the agreement reached with Deputy Government Attorney Brandt – to be able to meet and consult with everyone on the list. I reserved our position concerning those not on the base and said that we would go ahead to meet with those available in the meantime.

He barked a brief instruction to an underling. Dreyer then took us to an open area on the base. Within minutes, about 45 men appeared and were standing there, as if on parade. I soon realised it was no coincidence that our four applicants were not in the group, and had been sent away from the base for the day. This, too, would have been deliberate, as I had had no prior personal contact with any of the others. My clients were courageous in coming forward. They would be less susceptible to being influenced against us, and would instead influence their fellow inmates. The absence was disconcerting.

We were introduced as the lawyers who had applied for their release and that we would address them concerning our purpose. Dreyer then returned to his office. A few of his subordinates hovered around on the fringes to observe us. I asked them to move out of hearing range and also asked that we could sit down in an area where we could speak to the group. The open area was an assembly point on the base. On one side, there were corrugated iron cells. A few Casspirs with mounted machine guns stood on another side and a block of barracks was also evident. The setting had a military feel, yet not as ordered. Some of the Koevoet members around the base looked dishevelled in their shorts and T-shirts. There was an ominous and seedy feel to the place.

In a shaded part of the open area, Hosea and I explained the application to them. We referred to the payroll and said if they were employees who wanted to stay in the employ of Koevoet, then they should stay. But if they considered themselves to be there against their will and wanted to be released and sever their ties with the unit, then they could also do so and should say so. The atmosphere was tense. The fear on the part of those present was tangible. It was clear to us from our very wary reception that they had been spoken to before we had arrived there, as was confirmed to us by one of their number afterwards. None of them wanted to engage in any discussion initially, their uneasiness all too apparent. There were not even any questions at first.

After a while, one of them who had fortunately known Hosea from their high-school days, Karl Ndoroma, spoke up. He asked questions about the application and whether we could guarantee that he could leave the base permanently without any consequences. We did our best to address his fears. He said he was interested in being released. One or two others asked if we could negotiate an improvement in the conditions under which they stayed in the camp and wanted to discuss their grievances about those in command and conditions in the camp. We explained that our purpose was to secure the release of people who considered that they were not free to go.

After some more discussion and some internal caucusing, where we could see Karl explaining matters to others, about fifteen said that they wanted to be released and leave the camp. I then conveyed this to Brig. Dreyer, who was unable to conceal his surprise at this development. After consulting his subordinates, he said that they would need to wait until the next day so that the necessary paperwork could be finalised for them to process a final payment due to them to date. They were plainly unprepared for this outcome.

I conveyed this to Karl. He conferred with the others. They were adamant that they would not leave under any circumstances unless they could walk out of the base with us. I explained that they may need to forego any payment for that month. They were all happy to do so. It was not at all an issue to them and had not been raised at all in their deliberations.

This was initially not acceptable to Dreyer. After some negotiation with him, he was eventually constrained to agree to this proposal after I said that they would formally waive their payments for that month in writing and that there could be no valid reason at all for them to wait to receive a payment if they did not want it. It became increasingly apparent that he had not expected that any of the men would want to leave.

It took only a few moments for them all to sign that they had no claim for pay and collect the meagre possessions accumulated in the past year or two, stuffed hastily into a mere gym bag. The fifteen former PLAN fighters walked slowly with us as we made our way out of the base that afternoon towards our borrowed car. Each clutched no more than that single gym bag as we walked abreast on the dusty, white, open calcrete (clay) area towards the camp entrance. It felt like a scene from some corny and dated western, all of us gazing ahead, strutting abreast in silence with a feigned and uneasy confidence and not so much as casting the slightest glance behind or even sideways. The almost staged manner of this exit served to underscore the surreal feel to the base and the earlier meeting with Dreyer. Strains of King Crimson's song 'In the Court of Crimson King' and the disturbing image of the famed record cover ran through my mind, with visions of Marlon Brando's character in *Apocalypse Now* closely resembling Dreyer. Not a word was spoken until we had reached the car, parked in the shade of a tree a short distance from the camp entrance. The relief felt all round gave way to everyone suddenly speaking all at once. Our contact details were sought and given. They all said that they would go to their family homes, and spend time there before planning anything.

We gave Karl a lift to his family home near Ongwediva as it was on our way to Ondangwa. He then confirmed that they had been intensively briefed about our visit. It had been made clear to them that none should indicate that they were there against their will. If they did, they would forego their pay and privileges, and other unspecified bleak consequences could be visited upon them. He embraced Hosea and then me as we parted. I promised to look him up on my next trip to the north.

The application did not proceed any further although I did reserve the position of those whom we had not consulted. Some of those who were not on the base when we were there, including our applicants, very soon afterwards abandoned Koevoet when they saw that nothing had happened to those who had accompanied us out of the base. That number grew over the following months.

Karl became a loyal and good friend. He helped me to establish the Legal Assistance Centre some two years later and was a founding employee at its satellite advice office – the Human Rights Centre at Ongwediva in northern Namibia, which opened on 9 July 1988. I learnt from him that life in the Oniimwandi camp had been lonely and difficult. He had been captured in 1983 and spent almost three years there. He had operated as a PLAN fighter in Owambo over the course of a few years on several missions, until one day a heavy machine gun mounted on a Casspir had been trained on him in a temporary position he occupied. This had occurred after he had been subjected to mortar fire. Interrogation and two months' confinement in the rudimentary corrugated iron cells within the Oniimwandi base camp later made way for staying in one of the barracks inside the camp, each of which slept six former PLAN fighters. He found that he could not talk much to the others. Many of the former fighters had become Koevoet informers; he could trust no one. Inmates were told by Koevoet members that they were all legally 'dead'. They had no identity documents and would get none. No one would know or care if they disappeared and they could go nowhere without identity documents. There would be no consequences at all if they disappeared, or worse. This threat was backed up by the very real fact that some did disappear, never to be seen again, and were feared dead as I had been told by the four applicants. Karl confirmed this trenchantly.

After some time, he was allowed out on weekends like the others, but restricted to the vicinity of Oshakati. If he ventured further, he was told that they would come after him and eliminate him. But most of the former PLAN fighters, like Karl, were required to sleep in the barracks in the camp during the week. They performed various tasks inside the camp or were drivers (collecting supplies). Some former PLAN fighters even got married or cohabitated with their partners in the sprawling informal settlement that had sprung up nearby the camp. Some soon had children there too, and spent their weekends there. Some were later even permitted to stay there full time and only reported to the camp on weekdays for their duties.

Before going into exile, Karl had undergone some training in welding and was adept at repairing vehicles. These became his tasks. He was involved in constructing a large store facility for the camp, and fixed vehicles. It also helped that he could speak and understand Afrikaans. He kept to himself and got on with his tasks under the command of a captain responsible for maintenance issues. The camp inmates received monthly allowances and, he said, were well fed.

According to Karl, some former fighters were selected and invited to join Koevoet as fighters or trackers. Their pay was excellent. They earned more than teachers. There was talk of extra bonuses if they killed PLAN fighters or alleged fighters – a form of bounty money, chillingly referred to as 'kopgeld' (literally translated as 'head money'). There had been rumours circulating to this effect within the community for some time until it had been stated under oath by Koevoet members in court proceedings that they were paid 'kopgeld'. This practice no doubt led to them sporting T-shirts with an inscription emblazoned on them: 'Killing is our business, business is good.' Another Koevoet T-shirt I saw worn by an off-duty policeman at the Windhoek Police Station one evening boldly proclaimed 'Kill 'em all, let God sort 'em out'. These T-shirts spoke volumes of the mindset of Koevoet members and those in charge, who would have vetted them and inculcated that approach.

Karl said the former PLAN fighters within Koevoet ranks were ruthless and effective. They would disguise themselves as PLAN guerrillas to gather intelligence from civilians about the movements of actual PLAN fighters operating in those areas. Some were also used as interpreters in operations to interrogate civilians or captured fighters, often accompanied by a resort to excessive force. These new Koevoet members lived in the settlement next to the camp. They were a violent bunch and were frequently given to gratuitous violence in their off time, too, especially when fuelled by the excessive alcohol consumption to which they were prone.

Karl confirmed much of what Dreyer had said. Operating as a PLAN fighter in Owambo had become far tougher after Koevoet was established. The SADF was ineffective. At the time, he and other

PLAN fighters were able to evade them with relative ease and were more effective in their insurgency. But Koevoet used trackers and unconventional (and invariably unlawful and ruthless) methods to gather intelligence about PLAN fighters from civilians and captured fighters, and became even more effective after using increasing numbers of captured PLAN fighters.

Dreyer's presentation, tempered by Karl's experience and perspective, clarified so many incidents reported to us over the years – of brutal beatings of civilians by paramilitary operatives bent on obtaining information about the movements of PLAN fighters. At least some, if not most, disappearances of people who had never been seen again could also be explained. The details of their deaths and the whereabouts of their remains will sadly never be known to their next of kin, after they had either succumbed to excessive torture or simply been summarily executed after torture.

But what certainly crystallised were the systematic, covert paramilitary operations deliberately outside the framework of the law – and often against the law. These included the most serious crimes, such as extrajudicial killings being committed by agents of the state whose official mandate as police officers was to combat and prevent crime. Koevoet's mandate was repeatedly stated as being to 'eliminate' Swapo guerrillas.[38] One manifestation of this was the absence of any inquests held into the deaths of persons killed by Koevoet. The inquest legislation at the time[39] required that all deaths by unnatural causes should be the subject of inquests. In the *Heita* trial, Capt. Ballach confirmed that Koevoet did not consider the Inquest Act as applicable to the deaths it caused – a profoundly far-reaching step in Koevoet members' elevating themselves above the reach of the law and basically any form of accountability.

---

38   This was repeatedly stated in the media and confirmed by Ballach in the *Heita* trial.
39   The Inquest Act, 1959.

A book by a right-wing journalist embedded with Koevoet asserts that, in its ten-year existence, Koevoet killed or captured 3 225 alleged PLAN fighters. The term 'alleged' is, of course, not used in the work.[40] I use it because I would think that civilian collaborators or suspected collaborators who had been killed were included in that number. It has, after all, emerged in a book on the infamous Eugene de Kock that bounty money was handsomely paid to Koevoet members for killing Swapo fighters. Attributed to De Kock was a concern he had about 'an abscess of corruption' that had developed in Koevoet. According to De Kock, the corruption related to irregularities surrounding the amounts of bounty money paid to Koevoet operatives for every PLAN fighter killed.[41] I suspect that some of the bounty money claimed may also have been in respect of captured fighters who were then executed, or civilian collaborators who died from injuries sustained during questioning and torture or who were summarily executed when they were no longer of use. De Kock commanded one of Koevoet's company units from the inception of Koevoet in 1979 until he was transferred to Pretoria in 1983, later to head the notorious Vlakplaas covert assassination unit in 1985.[42] Koevoet companies were led by white security policemen from South Africa; the members comprised former Angolan FNLA fighters turned mercenaries, some locally recruited trackers and former PLAN fighters, and some security policemen.

The accounts of Koevoet featured in these works are told in glowing terms and, in the case of Stiff, as heroism – but without any regard for, or even reference to, Koevoet's extrajudicial killings, torture and lawlessness, or the brutality Koevoet inflicted upon the people of Owambo and the wanton destruction of their property

---

40   Stiff, P. 2004. *The Covert War: Koevoet Operations Namibia 1979–1989*. Galago Publishing: Johannesburg.
41   Jansen, A. 2015. *Eugene De Kock: Assassin for the State*. Tafelberg: Cape Town.
42   Jansen, A. 2015. *Eugene De Kock: Assassin for the State*. Tafelberg: Cape Town.

and crop fields and, crucially, the corrosive effect of this criminal conduct upon the rule of law. It was, after all, a police unit with a mandate to operate outside the law and commit crimes on a serious scale, in direct conflict with the law. Its crude and unlawful methods may have produced a kill ratio in which its protagonists took pride, and made them more effective against insurgents than their SADF counterparts. But despite claiming expertise in guerrilla warfare, they – like the US military command in Vietnam, which similarly boasted 'effective kill ratios' – failed to understand that insurgency would not be overcome in that way. I believe that Koevoet was, unwittingly, probably the most effective campaigner for Swapo in the independence elections in the areas in which it operated.

6

By order of the cabinet:
Murder covered up

The oppressive heat of a late November afternoon in 1985 was eventually beginning to abate sufficiently in a remote rural settlement in northern Oukwanyama, close to the Angolan border, for a few local residents to assemble to welcome home one of their number: Frans Uapota. He had come home to spend a few days' leave with his wife, Victoria Mweuhanga, and their children. Frans and Victoria had gathered that late afternoon with a few of their friends at the cuca shop close to their homestead in the vicinity of the rural village of Onengali. Their friends were almost all women from the neighbourhood whose men were away at work in the towns or city or mines several hundred kilometres to the south, or had left for war to join PLAN. They thirsted for the latest news from the city and relished the chance to catch up with Frans while sitting outside Gottlieb Haupito's cuca shop.

The sultry stillness of the late afternoon was rudely ruptured by the sudden appearance of a group of heavily armed SADF soldiers of the crack parabat fighting unit on a foot patrol as they entered the clearing around the small cluster of cuca shops. Being on foot, none of the usual warning signs, like the powerful roar of approaching armoured or mine-protected vehicles or, more rarely, the clatter of a hovering helicopter above with its mini dust storm, preceded their arrival.

Instead of the customary practice of asking for identity documents or asking about the movement of insurgents, one of the soldiers screamed an order in Afrikaans for everyone to lie, face down, on the ground. Frans and Victoria were seated next to each other and were soon flat on the ground. With weapons trained on them, the soldiers weighed into Frans with their heavy boots and rifle butts as he lay there. No reasons were given for the vicious attack. In fact, nothing at all was said to anyone after the order to lie on the ground. A couple of the soldiers then entered the cuca shop.

Frans was pulled to his feet by one of the soldiers and told to re-move his shirt, which was used to blindfold him. The other soldiers kept their rifles trained on those lying prone on the ground. Victoria glanced nervously sideways to see what was happening, but her vision was obscured by her position on the ground. She could hear the soldiers relentlessly beating Frans nearby, however. She could only snatch brief glimpses of what was happening out of the corner of her eye, but the sounds of the assault were unmistakeable, as were his groans of pain. Finally, Frans lay motionless. The soldiers then dragged him away by a rope tied around his neck. They also took away a neighbour, Nikolau Angelu, who had been inside the cuca shop when the troops had descended. They disappeared in the fad-ing light.

Nikolau was also on his annual leave from the Swavleis abattoir in Okahandja. He was inside the cuca shop with his two much young-er cousins when the soldiers entered. He understood Afrikaans. One of soldiers told his two young cousins that they could go immediately on account of their age but pronounced that Nikolau was clearly a 'terrorist' because he had a beard. The soldier ordered Nikolau to remove his shirt, also used to blindfold him. He was led away for about 30 paces and ordered to lie flat on his stomach. His hands and legs were tied together and the soldiers started to kick him in the face and ribs. The soldiers questioned him about his identity and employment cards, which they found on him. He was carried to a spot a bit further away. His legs were untied and he could sit. He overheard the soldiers talking to each other in Afrikaans. One of them plaintively posed the question 'Noudat ons die ander donner doodgemaak het, wat moet ons nou maak? (Now that we have killed the other bugger, what should we do now?)' Another answered that they could say that he had fallen onto a stone after being pushed. Yet another quickly chimed in to say that that explanation would not wash as there were no stones in the area. The next thing Nikolau heard was one of the soldiers speaking on the radio, reporting that they had killed a terrorist and captured another. The response was an instruction to stay in their position as night had fallen.

The frightened villagers back at the cuca shop had not dared to move for some time. The soldiers had not gone far from them. The sound of their voices carried to them. Darkness had by now also overcome the dusk. Gottlieb Haupito quietly suggested that all discreetly go to their nearby homes as that would be safer. If anyone were then to search for Frans and Nikolau, they would most probably be shot at. It would, he said, be best to defer further action to morning. They were terrified. Paralysed by fear and a sense of foreboding as well as by the curfew, Victoria and her friends cautiously departed home.

At first light, Victoria returned to the scene, accompanied by some supporting neighbours, to search for Frans in the direction where he was dragged. The site of the assaults nearby the cuca shop was clearly visible, as was a gruesome trail of blood along the ground, revealing the exact trajectory where the soldiers had dragged Frans for a distance of 96 metres. They soon realised that the soldiers were still in the vicinity. Victoria and her neighbours thought it prudent not to confront the soldiers or even make an enquiry. They decided instead to report the matter to their local headman, Haimba Uandja, who accompanied Victoria to the scene. As they approached, the soldiers ordered them not to come any closer.

The headman proceeded instead to report the incident at the nearest police station at Ohangwena. Several hours later, the police arrived at Victoria's homestead, bringing Frans' body for identification. His identity document and employment papers were on him when they brought his battered body to her. She saw multiple signs of assault and a raw scar around his neck that a chafing rope would leave. On the advice of her headman, Victoria laid a charge of murder against the soldiers and informed the police that she would be able to identify the white soldiers involved.

Nikolau had, in the meantime, been forced to spend the night in the bush with the soldiers. Early the next morning he was taken by military vehicle to the Etale military base not far from Engela. There, he was tortured during the interrogation that followed. He was taken back to the scene later that day where he encountered police who showed him the corpse and took him to Ondangwa to make a statement about what had happened.

The headman also decided to report the incident to Oswald Shivute, Secretary to the Owambo Administration based in Ondangwa, one of the ethnic-based administrations set up by the apartheid state for eleven different 'ethnic' groupings in Namibia as part of a grand apartheid-style scheme imposed upon Namibia. That administration was headed by Peter Kalangula. Although many of its members supported the status quo because of the benefits they received from it, several others were becoming increasingly uneasy and troubled by security force excesses and abuses. Oswald was an employee – as opposed to the compromised officials of Kalangula's party who held office in the Administration – and was given a free hand by Kalangula to take up community members' grievances against the security forces.

Top: On holiday with my mother and my sister at Knysna in 1963.

Above: Graduation at Harvard in 1983. Photographed with my mother on my left.

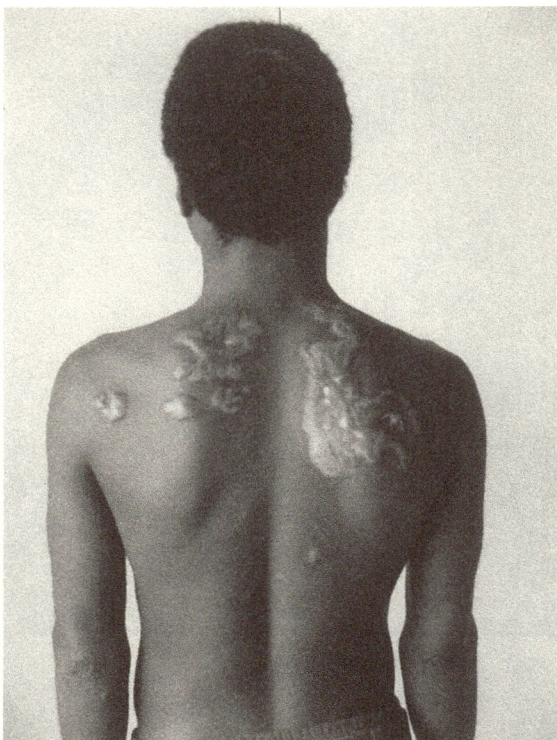

Right and below: Photographs discreetly taken of Andreas Pakwela Heita at the Ondangwa Police Station in March 1986. The photos were used in evidence at his trial later that year. They were taken nearly six months after he was subjected to torture.

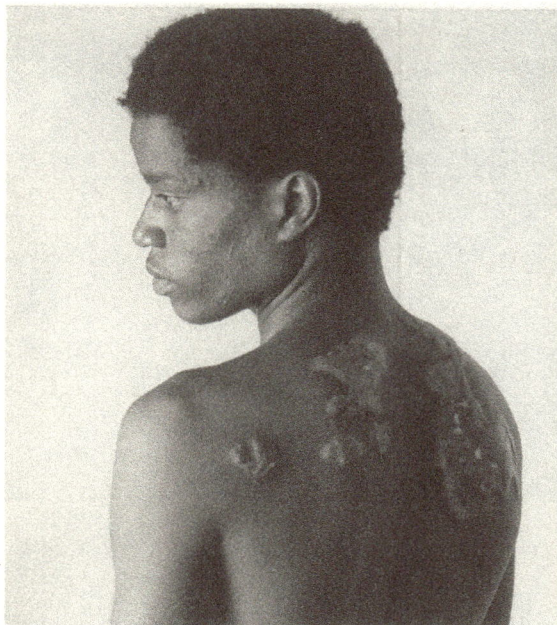

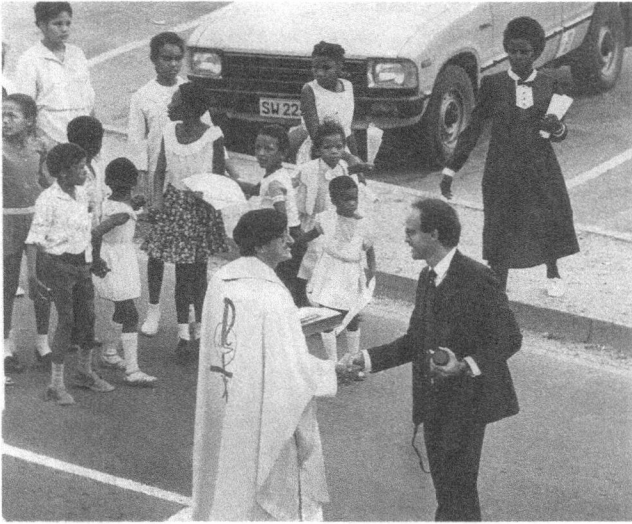

Top: The Cabinet of the IG banned a Corpus Christi procession organised by the Roman Catholic Church for Sunday 1 June 1986. We brought an urgent application on Saturday 31 May 1986 which set aside the ban under the Riotous Assemblies Act, 17 of 1956. I was on hand the following morning to greet Father B Wolf, the applicant, at the outset of the procession in which several thousand people walked from Katutura to Windhoek. (Photo: *The Namibian*)

Above: 1986 – Invited to attend a meeting hosted by President Kenneth Kaunda in Lusaka involving the frontline states, Swapo and the ANC. Pictured with Festus Naholo (to the right), then Swapo Secretary for Logistics and leading Women's League member, Pendukeni Iivula-Ithana.

the namibian

Bringing Africa South · No 43 · Friday July 4 1986 · 50c

SWAPO RALLIES LEGAL

Judge says that violence is not Swapo's sole objective

BY CHRIS SHIPANGA and GWEN LISTER

FOLLOWING A JUDGEMENT of the Full Bench of the Supreme Court with Justice Harold Levy presiding, Swapo may now legitimately hold public meetings, and all that is required is notification to a Magistrate 24 hours before the meeting is held.

In the matter between the State and Immanuel Gottlieb Nathaniel, Swapo Acting President; Mr Jerry Ekandjo, Swapo Secretary for Youth; and Mr Frans Kambangula, Swapo Secretary of Transport, who were all charged for contravening the Notification and Prohibition of Meetings Act of 1981 by holding an 'illegal' Swapo rally in Katutura on April 21 last year, the Supreme Court ruled that the charge sheet be quashed (declared invalid) on the grounds that it was not the sole objective of Swapo to violently overthrow the government.

Legal sources said that the

MARCHERS at a massive Anti-Apartheid rally in London on Saturday. Full story inside today.

---

the namibian

Bringing Africa South · No 63 · 50c · Friday November 21 1986

★ VICTORY ★

Another Supreme Court defeat for the interim government

STAFF REPORTER

THE DEPOSIT of R20 000 levied on this newspaper in terms of Section 6 of the Internal Security Act, was set aside by the Windhoek Supreme Court on Wednesday in an historic judgement which marked yet another courtroom defeat for the Cabinet of the interim government, who were also ordered to pay the costs of the application.

The then Cabinet Chairman, Mr Moses Katjuongua, in a sworn statement, said that the Editor of The Namibian, Ms Gwen Lister, had in the past written articles critical of Cabinet members, thus lowering the Cabinet in the esteem of the public. These articles adversely affected the political integrity and credibility of the Cabinet which had a cumulative effect of presenting a 'threat to the security of the state and maintenance of public order.' But Mr Justice Harold Levy dismissed these arguments, saying that "to maintain that Lister's personal criticism of members of respondent will bring respondent into contempt and that this criticism 'will only be to the benefit of Swapo' is not a sound logical conclusion and there is nothing on record to justify it".

The Internal Security Act, in terms of which the R20 000 deposit was levied on The Namibian, provides for a newspaper to be closed down if it is found that such a newspaper posed a threat to the security of the state or promoted the aims of communism and banned organisations.

Mr Justice Harold Levy, in a written judgement, upheld the freedom of the press and freedom of speech as guaranteed in the interim government's Bill of Rights, constructive criticism by newspapers, provided it was factually correct and fair, was fundamental to a healthy democratic society.

He said that public figures who felt aggrieved about unfair attacks

continued on page 2

SEEN leaving the Supreme Court on Wednesday after Judge Harold Levy set aside the R20 000 deposit imposed on The Namibian by the interim government Cabinet, is Editor Gwen Lister, with the newspaper's attorney, Mr Dave Smuts of the law firm Lorentz and Bone.

Top: This followed the legal victory in which the indictment of three Swapo leaders was quashed and had the effect of rendering Swapo meetings legal following the ruling.

Above: Emerging from court with Gwen Lister after succeeding with the challenge to the maximum deposit imposed on *The Namibian*.

Top: Inspecting the severely damaged Roman Catholic Church at Omuulukila in north-western Owambo in September 1987. The local community suspected it had been blown up by the SA security forces. However, the security forces denied these allegations. The church was left in ruins although the golden box cupboard housing the Holy Sacrament was unscathed.

Above: At the opening of the Human Rights Centre at Ongwediva on 9 July 1988, Hosea Angula in conversation with Frans Aupa Iindongo, a leading business personality who strongly supported the opening of the Centre. Behind are Swedish Ambassador to South Africa, Jan Ludwig, and myself.

Top: In March 1989, Anton Lubowski, Barnabas Tjizu and Gwen Lister appeared briefly in the Magistrate's Court on charges relating to union activities and a report concerning those activities. Michaela Clayton, with gown, represented them and the charges were soon dropped. (Photo: *The Namibian*)

Above: Corpses of Swapo insurgents at Ondeshifilwa left by the security forces on 3 April 1989. I needed to take photos as evidence of the brutality meted out to liberation fighters, and to use as evidence in the case that I was building against the security forces.

Above: A crudely put together pamphlet with images of Gwen Lister, John Lieben-berg and myself as a target and inviting the "Wit Wolwe", an apparent right wing vigilante group, to kill the three of us. It was disseminated at the Academy, the tertiary educational institution which now houses the Namibia University of Science and Technology (NUST), in 1988 and early 1989. The *Windhoek Observer* reported in September 1989 after Anton's assassination that they had received two anonymous calls before the assassination to say that I would not see April of the following year. Gwen received many such threats and John was much dis-liked by elements in the security forces because of his powerful images of human rights abuses.

Top: Accompanying one of the observer groups of the US Lawyers' Committee for Civil Rights under Law to northern Namibia during the implementation of Resolution 435 in 1989. Pictured are former Senator George McGovern (left) and Gay McDougall (right), director of the group's Southern Africa Project.

Above: August 2005 with (right and far right) Lorraine and Arthur Chaskalson, then Chief Justice of South Africa visiting Windhoek. (Photo: Tony Figueira)

A liaison committee comprising members of the Administration and the security forces had been set up in response to repeated concerns raised by the Administration about security force conduct and abuses. Oswald served on it. This committee was largely ineffective and did not provide any real accountability for atrocities. The security forces did not take it seriously and resented Oswald's complaints and enquiries. Oswald increasingly contacted Hosea and me on behalf of victims of abuse and also gave details of the more severe cases to Gwen Lister and Chris Shipanga of *The Namibian* after the newspaper was founded in August 1985.

Faced with the headman's report, a frantic Oswald called later that day (on 29 November 1985). Our tapped phones meant that only sparse details could be given. But Hosea and I at once understood from his use of metaphor that a serious atrocity had occurred and that someone wanted to see us urgently about it.

Within a day or so, Hosea and I were in Oswald's office in Ondangwa where we heard Victoria's account of the brutal murder of her husband. As a docket had been opened with the police, I asked them when the post mortem examination was to be performed, only to be informed that it had already taken place. I asked for a copy of the report. It was categorically refused. In response to my further questions about progress in the police investigation, I was tersely told that the matter was still being investigated. We were not optimistic about any prosecution going ahead because Frans had been labelled by the military as a suspected 'terrorist', even though this was totally unfounded. But we felt that the exposure of the circumstances surrounding his death could conceivably result in a prosecution, or at least an inquest. This meant frequent follow-ups with the authorities on Victoria's behalf. Victoria and Frans had five children. Four of them were still underage and a civil action for damages against the military would be prepared.

The police remained uncooperative. As I heard nothing further from them in Oshakati, I approached the Attorney-General in March

1986. In pre-independence Namibia that functionary was in charge of prosecutions. A few months went by as we awaited his decision. The incumbent at the time was Tielman Louw. He had a reputation for fairness and was approachable. The wait seemed worthwhile when I eventually received a letter in June from his office to the effect that four SADF members of the Parabat Battalion would stand trial for Frans' murder. They were C.J. Harmse, F.J. Herps, D.F. Esselen and J. Fernando. They would be arraigned and a murder charge would be put to them in the Ondangwa magistrate's court on 23 June 1986 as a preliminary step to the murder prosecution.

My subsequent enquiry as to how the accused had pleaded was met with an astonishing response. The senior public prosecutor for the northern division, based in Tsumeb, replied that the accused had not in fact pleaded at all. Instead, a certificate to stop the prosecution in terms of section 103 ter of the Defence Act was handed in at court. As a result of the certificate, the accused were not required to plead. They were excused and free to go; the criminal proceedings came to an end.

The certificate had been issued by the cabinet of the IG, which had assumed the statutory powers in Namibia of the (South African) minister of justice in Namibia accorded to that minister in Namibia after the IG had taken office in June 1985. The certificate read:

> Certificate in terms of section 103 ter of the Defence Act, 1957 (Act 44 of 1957):
> The State versus: (1) C.J. HARMSE
> (2) F.J. HERPS
> (3) D.F. ESSELEN
> (4) J. FERNANDO
>
> WHEREAS the State President of the Republic of South Africa is, according to an authorization issued under subsection (4) of section 103ter of the Defence Act, 1957, of the opinion –

(a) That the acts done by the above-mentioned persons, being all members of the South African Defence Force, which allegedly gave rise to the death of one FRANIS MAPOTE [*sic*] have been done in good faith by those persons for the purpose of or in connection with the prevention or suppression of terrorism in the operational area; and

(b) That it is not in the national interest that any criminal proceedings instituted or about to be instituted against them on account of those acts shall be continued

AND WHEREAS the Cabinet is in the circumstances called upon, in terms of the said subsection (4), merely on account of the fact that it is charged with the administration of the laws governing the functions of the courts of law to give effect to the opinion of the State President.

IT IS THEREFORE hereby, under the said subsection (4), ordered that any criminal proceedings instituted or about to be instituted against the said persons shall not be continued.

By order of the Cabinet

Signed
CHAIRPERSON OF THE CABINET
DATE: 1986-06-27

The Attorney-General stated that the trial could not proceed any further against the four accused.

This was profoundly shocking. Quite how the South African state president and the cabinet could consider that this brutal murder could conceivably amount to an act done in good faith in connection with the prevention or suppression of terrorism in an operational area simply strained belief.

This was, to my knowledge, the second time that this power had been invoked in the superior courts. Our appeal against the Mariental detainee ruling had not yet been heard. The full bench's narrow, executive-minded interpretation of the section loomed large as a potential barrier in any court challenge against the exercise of the draconian powers under that section. Despite that, the facts in this case were so egregious that a court would be hard-pressed not to interfere with this appalling abuse of power.

Hosea and I travelled to Victoria's remote village in northern Oukwanyama to explain this development to her and receive her instructions. Getting there was no mean feat. Our directions from Oswald turned out to be hopelessly inadequate. After turning off the main road near Oshikango in the right direction, we continually faced forks in the rudimentary tracks we followed. Obtaining directions from villagers in the area was arduous and time consuming. Obviously, a white and black person travelling together asking for the whereabouts of her headman would be treated with grave suspicion. Cooperation was not easy or expeditious. It took time on each occasion to explain our mission. When this was eventually understood, directions were forthcoming and we were on our way again, only until the next fork not much further along and the laborious exercise was repeated. When we reached Victoria and the headman, the latter found our account of our difficult journey hilarious. We explained to Victoria what had happened. She was aghast and could not comprehend how the authorities would no longer want to proceed with the murder prosecution.

'He was so brutally beaten to death,' she repeated to us again and again. She also kept saying that 'he had done nothing wrong', 'he was beaten for no reason' and 'he was beaten again and again and again'. (Speaking Oshikwanyama, she repeated the verb for 'beaten' many times for emphasis, as is often the case with speakers of that language.)

Her instructions were unequivocal. Those implicated in the killing should be brought to justice. We were to take whichever steps we could to ensure that. We prepared an application directed at setting aside that certificate by way of a judicial review. We prepared a draft and sent it to Jeremy Gauntlett to settle. After his refinement, the application was launched.

When it became known that the certificate had been issued by the IG, its cabinet was lambasted by *The Namibian* and most church leaders and community organisations in Namibia. The Bar Council under Bryan O'Linn's leadership condemned the certificate as a 'gross breach of the rule of law and the rape of justice in this country'. Foreign media and human rights organisations outside Namibia also roundly criticised the cabinet for issuing the certificate. Its establishing proclamation had, after all, included a bill of rights that was supposed to govern its future conduct. Some members of the cabinet had also spoken in general terms in support of human rights and the importance of protecting them in Namibia. In response to the mounting criticism of the certificate and the cabinet's human rights record, the IG issued a media statement, declaring that it had issued the certificate on the basis of legal advice it had received – which had been to the effect that it had no option but to issue the certificate once the South African state president had formed an opinion that the soldiers should receive immunity from prosecution under section 103 ter.

The sincerity behind the IG's media statement – or lack of it – was soon exposed when the cabinet gave notice that it would oppose Victoria's application to set aside that certificate, instead of simply abiding by the decision of the court, which would have been the principled course if it had reluctantly issued the certificate or even had no interest in it. Indeed, the IG vehemently opposed the application. It inexplicably found it appropriate to challenge Victoria's standing to apply to set aside the certificate that had stopped the prosecution of those charged with murdering her husband.

The application was also vigorously opposed by the South African state president and minister of defence. The former murder accused were also cited. But they did not participate in the proceedings. There was no need for that because of the strenuous opposition by the other respondents.

P.W. Botha, the South African state president, himself made an affidavit opposing the application. He said he had relied upon a report provided to him by the minister of defence and the considerations contained in it for his conclusion that it would not be in the national interest for the murder trial to continue. The minister's report had been prepared by Colonel de Klerk in the SADF's legal department. De Klerk said in his affidavit that his report had been prepared after a 'comprehensive investigation'.

It was evident from the affidavits, however, that this investigation had been based only on the statements of the murder accused them-selves and possibly other military personnel on the scene. It took neither Victoria nor Nikolau's evidence into account. Neither of them had been approached to provide information to the investigation. Both had been available to do so. Nor had any other civilian present at the cuca shop on that fateful evening ever been approached.

This did not surprise me. The military regarded local residents as hostile at best, or had no regard for them at all. It was almost as if they did not exist, except to be regulated or abused when in the way. They had no human face.

It was suggested in the report that Frans had been a suspected 'terrorist', although no facts of any nature were provided in support of this baseless assertion. Nor did the report explain why – even on this unfounded version – it was necessary for a squad of highly armed soldiers of a crack unit to inflict multiple and severe injuries on the unarmed, slightly built Frans in order to arrest him.

As to the requirement of being in the national interest to issue a certificate under section 103 ter, prominent in the considerations listed by De Klerk – and embraced by the state president – was 'to permit the accused under these circumstances to be prosecuted would have a demoralising influence upon them and on the SWATF which would have a detrimental effect upon the military conflict against Swapo'.

Another fatal flaw in the report was the failure even to refer to the post mortem report. When it eventually became available to us, we discovered that it described the multiple injuries upon Frans's body. These were not even disclosed to the state president in the report De Klerk had prepared. There was merely a reference to Frans dying from a 'massive subdural haematoma' which, De Klerk stated, could be reconciled with the version of the murder accused. The impact of these shocking omissions was not yet fully apparent to us as the post mortem report had still been withheld from us. What was already more than plain to us was that the report was misleading, partial and very selective.

To deal with De Klerk's affidavit, we needed access to the post mortem report and the actual report provided to the state president. Before the case was set down, we applied to court to obtain a copy of each of these reports. The government respondents persisted in their refusal to make these reports available to us and opposed our bid to see them. Shortly before this discovery application was due to be heard, only the post mortem report was provided to us; the court refused, on the grounds of state privilege, to order the disclosure of the report supplied to the state president.

The post mortem was most revealing. The massive subdural haematoma it listed as the cause of death covered the entirety of the brain, resulting from a head injury. In addition, there were several serious injuries listed in the report. They included nine broken ribs, a ruptured spleen, a fracture of the neck and various other lacerations and injuries, particularly around the neck, consistent with a rope having been tied around it.

Upon Jeremy's advice, we engaged two eminent medical experts to explain the post mortem findings in the context of the case. They were Prof. L.S. Smith, one of South Africa's foremost forensic pathologists, and Dr J.W. van der Spuy, a leading trauma expert. They prepared a joint affidavit which included:

> It is further apparent to us that a considerable amount of blunt force was applied to the chest cage of the deceased, giving rise to the pattern of serious injury to the upper abdomen and chest (including nine broken ribs and a ruptured spleen).
>
> In our view, the constricting force applied to the neck by the rope caused a massive venous congestion within the skull, and accentuated the bilateral venous bleed into the subdural space within the skull. The bilateral rib fractures would have compromised breathing and aggravated the effects of the head injury. The overall consequence was in our view to contribute to the severity of the massive subdural haematoma described.

The experts concluded:

> In our view, the cause of death of the deceased was a massive subdural haematoma covering the entirety of the brain, resulting from a head injury. It is further our view that the application of constricting force around the neck of the deceased (in the form of the rope . . .) together with the chest injuries probably contributed significantly to the cause of death . . .

The post mortem report clearly demonstrated the hopelessly misleading nature of De Klerk's report, which had formed the basis for stopping the prosecution. Despite De Klerk saying that information had been obtained from 'all available persons', he conceded in his opposing affidavit that state witnesses had not been approached.

This was offered as a rationalisation for not approaching Victoria and Nikolau. This fundamentally flawed approach was exposed as untenable in Hosea's replying affidavit, settled by Jeremy. It was explained that presenting the statements of Victoria and Nikolau and others would not offend against any ethical rule, especially in view of the purpose of the report – to terminate the criminal prosecution of the murder accused. The point was made – and later eloquently developed in argument at the hearing – that De Klerk chose not to obtain further evidence that would have enabled him to present a report to the president which was not so one-sided and misleading.

Jeremy suggested that Sydney Kentridge be brought in to lead him in the argument in view of the importance of the matter. We agreed and were delighted that Sydney agreed to return to Namibia to argue this case on 22 September 1988.

Sydney was at his imperious best in exposing the perversity of the certificate and destroying the arguments mounted in support of it. He convincingly argued that De Klerk's report did not constitute a report contemplated by section 103 ter, given its one-sided and misleading nature. He said that, in the absence of a proper report, a prerequisite for any decision by the state president, a valid decision could not be made as he would not have had the material facts before him. Sydney also argued that, even if the full facts had been placed before the state president, he could not have honestly formed the opinion that the four murder accused had acted in good faith for the purpose of preventing or suppressing terrorism in an operational area. No one, he added, could honestly believe that a group of highly armed soldiers from a crack unit would be acting in good faith when they battered the skull of an unarmed 45-year-old man of slight build, broke his neck, partially strangulated him with a rope, broke nine of his ribs, ruptured his spleen and left him with multiple bruises, abrasions and burns on his arms, thorax, abdomen and back. This was met with audible exclamations from the packed courtroom. Sydney also argued that the effect of a prosecution upon the morale of the murder accused and SWATF could not amount to a proper consideration of national interest. This was so sectarian that it failed to reflect a balancing of other wider and compelling interests.

Much of the argument advanced on behalf of the cabinet of the IG as well as the South African government respondents, and centred on an attack upon Victoria's standing to bring the application. The cabinet was again represented by Piet van der Bijl, assisted by a local junior counsel, Gerhard Maritz, their favoured combination to argue security-related cases of this kind. The state president and minister of defence were represented by Pretoria counsel. The respondents' advocates also argued that their respective clients had acted validly in the decision making and issuing of the certificate.

A full bench comprising Judges Mouton, Levy and Hendler presided. In separate concurring judgments, the court unanimously brushed aside the spurious arguments raised about Victoria's standing and rightly found that she had a substantial interest as a widow to bring to justice to those who were responsible for the murder of her husband. The court also found that she would have an interest in proceeding with a private prosecution if the Attorney General declined to prosecute. The certificate deprived her of that right and gave her standing for this reason as well.

All three members of the court found in favour of Victoria and decided to set aside the certificate. It was found that the existence of a report by the Minister of Defence to be considered by the state president in determining whether to grant an indemnity was an objectively justiciable fact. It was necessary that the report meet the requirements of section 103 ter, including factors indicating that the act in question had been done in good faith for the purpose of preventing or suppressing terrorism. The court ruled that, if any of these essentials had not been contained in the report furnished by the minister, then the state president could not validly authorise a certificate to indemnify the murder accused. The court rightly found that the most crucial circumstance in considering an act of murder would be the way in which the killing had taken place. Yet the report submitted to the state president did not contain the medical evidence or the evidence of state witnesses that shed light upon that critical issue.

The court concluded that the state president had not been furnished with a report contemplated by the section that needed to show the circumstances of the killing and set out factors that would show good faith in doing so – or that the act had been done for the specified purposes of the section, to prevent or suppress terrorism. The court concluded that the certificate had not been validly issued, and set it aside. The judgments were handed down on 14 December 1988.

The respondents, including the cabinet of the IG, applied for and were granted leave to appeal against the unanimous decision of the court to set aside the certificate. The appeal was to proceed to the Appeal Court in Bloemfontein. The UN peace plan was implemented the following year and independence arrived before the appeal would be heard. This meant that the appeal did not go ahead, as that court no longer had jurisdiction over Namibia. It would also have served little purpose as the AG issued a directive in the dying days of the peace plan to indemnify all SADF or SWATF members from prosecutions for crimes committed while performing their functions or duties.[43] The defendants could then no longer be prosecuted for the murder.

On Namibia's independence, the Namibian government pursued a policy of national reconciliation based upon the laudable principle of building a united nation in the wake of past divisions and conflict. I was appalled at the grant of a blanket indemnity by the AG

---

43   AG 16 of 1990 dated 9 February 1990.

for all crimes and thought that this could be challenged as a matter of law by the new government, applying principles of customary international law governing conflicts. But there was no appetite for this after independence, given the policy of national reconciliation. Despite this, I remained of the view that there should be some form of accountability – that certain of the worst war crimes should be exposed, and that people should stand trial for them. For me, this one fell squarely within that category.

7

Countering relentless propaganda: Setting up *The Namibian*

The success achieved in the Mariental detainee case – although not reflected in the formal outcome of the case – had much to do with the role of the media in exposing the gross human rights abuse it represented and the activism that followed the exposure.

The sustained efforts by Tony Weaver in particular in skilfully keeping the story alive had been crucial in generating pressure upon the authorities. Gay, a seasoned campaigner, had marshalled her forces in the US, ensuring coverage in the influential *Washington Post* and even having the issue raised in the House of Representatives.

Gwen, too, had played her part. Her reporting in the weekly *Windhoek Observer* was of vital importance locally and her BBC radio broadcasts on the Africa Service enjoyed wide coverage throughout the continent. Her sonorous and well-modulated voice coupled with an easy delivery were especially well suited to radio. Our regular contact and preparation of her defence in the Kempton Park trial had led to a flourishing friendship. We also regularly played social bridge and the foursome often included Tony. We were jointly committed to exposing the apartheid state's abuses in Namibia.

The local media landscape at the time was unpromising for that purpose. With the solitary exception of the *Observer*, media outlets were directly or indirectly owned or controlled by the apartheid state or its local supporters. The state-controlled broadcaster with a single television channel and radio stations in most major languages spoken in Namibia spewed out non-stop propaganda in favour of the apartheid state and the local parties it supported that occupied and benefited from the ethnically based apartheid structures. The local print media also provided relentless propaganda in support of the apartheid state and its locally ordained political groupings.

A new Afrikaans daily, *Die Republikein*, started in the late 1970s. Its initial focus was the internecine struggle for the political soul of local Afrikaners (who were the majority of the whites) when the National Party split. This war of words was waged against its more established rival *Die Suidwester*, the official mouthpiece of the National Party.

The National Party had the monopoly of elected officials voted in by the white electorate. It was the party of apartheid South Africa and was supported by some 80 per cent of local whites. Its local structure had split when Dirk Mudge had led a breakaway faction to form the Republican Party, bent on negotiating with other ethnically based parties to form a tribally based alliance in opposition to Swapo in any future independence election under UN Security Council Resolution 385 and the western proposals to it, which were accepted by South Africa, later resulting in UN Security Council Resolution 435. The Republican Party supported the immediate dismantling of what was known as petty apartheid. These measures included segregated living areas, the prohibition of mixed marriages and mandated separate public amenities, but it espoused an ethnically divided political solution for Namibia – which was the bedrock of apartheid policy. This approach was much too radical for the die-hard Nationalist Party loyalists who wanted to maintain apartheid in its strict form of white superiority and legally mandated segregation. It was backed by its newspaper called *Die Suidwester*. This division had occurred hard on the heels of the Turnhalle initiative, where Mudge had been a principal architect.

The Republican Party formed an alliance with other ethnic-based parties. It was called the DTA (Democratic Turnhalle Alliance) and its newspaper became the official mouthpiece for the DTA. Although some of the petty squabbling with *Die Suidwester* continued for some time, *Die Republikein* soon shifted its focus to non-ethnically based parties that opposed South African rule and especially Swapo. The ethnically based structures and policies it espoused for separate, autonomous, ethnic administrations with profound inequality in access to resources was essentially an apartheid 'lite' programme and understandably found favour with the apartheid state in its political designs for Namibia as a pliable alternative to Swapo. It maintained separate ethnic structures with their own separate schools, and unequal access to resources.

The DTA's mouthpiece fervently supported the South African security establishment in its conducting the war in the north and in its crackdowns upon opponents of Pretoria's sponsored initiatives. It not only lashed out at Swapo and other progressive parties like Swanu and the NNF, but even saw fit to ridicule human rights campaigners who criticised oppressive security force action. It so closely aligned itself with the security establishment that it almost never gave any coverage to security force excesses or atrocities, even when findings to that effect were made in court proceedings – as was proudly acknowledged by its editor at the Shifidi inquest. Koevoet was eulogised by that paper. Some of its key staffers openly associated themselves with Koevoet, even going out on patrols with them to write glowing and uncritical articles about them, even wearing their fatigues. One was reported to have even boasted about killing three 'terrorists' when doing so, although he later denied the claims that had been attributed to him.[44] A photograph of the journalist, Gene

---

44   *The Windhoek Advertiser*, 21 April 1987.

Travers, had appeared in the local press,[45] wearing a Koevoet bush uniform and sporting an automatic rifle in a pose befitting a big game hunter alongside the body of a dead Swapo insurgent. He was defended by the editor of the Sunday *Republikein*, Nic Kruger. When asked about his dress, the editor's response was 'What do you expect a reporter in the operational area to wear – evening dress?'[46]

In the late 1970s, a German supporter of the apartheid state's initiatives in Namibia purchased the John Meinert printing works, which published the small English daily *The Windhoek Advertiser* and the German language *Allgemeine Zeitung*. This acquisition occurred at about the same time as what later became known as the Information Scandal, which involved the purchasing of newspapers and publications with illegal funding from the South African Department of Information as a means of spreading pro-apartheid state propaganda, although it has not been established whether this acquisition formed part of that elaborate illegal scheme. This scandal led to the resignation of John Vorster, the prime minister of South Africa at the time. The editor of the *Advertiser* before the takeover was the fearlessly independent maverick, J.M. (Hannes) Smith. He quit with Gwen to form the *Windhoek Observer*, because of the acquisition.

Smith gave Gwen free rein in her political reporting, which was highly critical of the apartheid state and its initiatives and locally sponsored parties. Gwen also gave considerable coverage to progressive opposition forces to the apartheid state, particularly to Swapo but also to other political and civic groups opposed to the apartheid state, and highlighted human rights abuses. Unlike in South Africa, where the ANC and PAC were prohibited organisations whose leaders could not be quoted, Swapo had not been banned under the Internal Security Act. This was not out of any benevolent predilection for political discourse: anything but. Namibia's international status

---

45   *The Namibian*, 17 April 1987.

46   *The Windhoek Advertiser*, 21 April 1987, quoting Mr Nic Kruger.

constrained and precluded the apartheid state from doing so. It instead turned to other means to curtail and thwart Swapo activity in Namibia. These measures were supported by the DTA and the IG. Special legislation was enacted by the first DTA-led National Assembly in 1981 prohibiting meetings by organisations that included in their aims the armed overthrow of the political order in the country. Unions affiliated to Swapo were prohibited. As is explained elsewhere, this legislation was used to prevent Swapo from holding meetings – at pain of arrest and detention for those who dared defy it.

People engaging in Swapo activism inside Namibia were routinely harassed and detained, often for lengthy periods without charge. It irked the security establishment no end, however, that Gwen quoted Swapo leaders and reported on Swapo activities and the persecution of its members and supporters and gave a voice to internal opposition to its rule.

In about 1984, Smith secured a new business partner in the *Observer*, a local property broker and real estate agent called Thurstan Salt. For the latter, it was a business project that happened to be media related. Smith, on the other hand, was an indefatigable champion of press freedom.

Gwen's continuing coverage of Swapo in the *Observer* spurred the security establishment into action. They laid complaints against some of her reports with the South African Publications Control Board[47] – the censorship body based in Pretoria whose reach, like most security measures, extended to Namibia. Her reporting was not the sole source of complaints, however.

Smith enjoyed notoriety for his back page, where lewd photographs of bare-breasted women in suggestive poses were prominently displayed. This was a feature of that publication. The demand for this seedy offering no doubt accounted for its large sales.

---

47   Under the Publications Act 42 of 1974.

One of the Board's committees duly obliged the security establishment by banning five specific past editions. This was done in May 1984. The grounds raised were predominately security related and concerned Gwen's reports, but also extended to the vulgar back pages. Smith was very concerned about this and consulted me about the bannings. I advised him to appeal against them to the appellate body under that legislation.

The publications committee in question was clearly under the influence of the security establishment and did not take into account Namibia's special status under international law. I warned Smith that if he did not challenge the bannings, more could follow, which in turn could lead to the publication itself becoming banned. This power could be invoked especially in the case of multiple bannings. It was thus imperative to appeal because a permanent prohibition of the publication seemed to be the objective of the security establishment's strategy to silence Gwen (and her coverage of Swapo). Smith said he would revert after speaking to his business partner, Salt.

I heard nothing from Smith until another banning order was published four weeks later in the South African *Government Gazette*. The banning declared two more issues of the *Observer* as undesirable. In the same *Gazette*, a T-shirt was coincidentally also listed as banned. Its inscriptions were telling. On the front of the T-shirt, it proclaimed 'Namibia: South Africa's Vietnam?' and the words 'No win' appeared on the back.

Smith swiftly returned to discuss the latest bannings. I was more emphatic than before in my advice to appeal against them and the earlier bannings because the underlying strategy was now beyond any doubt. Smith still equivocated. I implored him to appeal for the sake of the future of his paper. He said he needed to consult Salt. But, again, he failed to instruct an appeal.

The inevitable occurred a few weeks later when the Publications Control Board issued an order banning the publication (and all future issues) completely. Upon hearing the news, Smith rushed to my office and, despite being almost out of breath, with an extravagant wave of the arm, exhorted, 'Now you can appeal. Please go ahead at once.'

I responded that we would need to act urgently and would get back to him early the next morning about the steps to take.

As I set about researching and planning the steps to appeal to the Publications Appeal Board, also based in Pretoria, I discussed the matter with my senior partner, John Kirkpatrick. He, like all other partners in the firm, was aware that Smith had flouted my advice by failing to instruct appeals against the earlier banning orders. John was adamant that the firm should no longer act for the *Observer* for that reason: 'You simply can't act in the matter after his persistent refusal to follow your earlier advice. This has now occurred because of that failure.'

I replied that I was not sure that I could live with that, and added: 'There's a lot more at stake now than the need to discipline a delinquent client.'

John was unmoved by my entreaty and firmly ruled out the firm's acting any further. He directed me to call Smith to collect his file and take it elsewhere.

I had been made a junior partner of the firm with effect from 1 March that year, together with Hartmut. The corporate culture was well established. No one questioned John's decisions. But I did not agree with this decision. After brooding on the question for an hour or so, I plucked up the courage to return to his office and pointed out that I was now a partner and that, seeing it was a decision of the firm, it should be by majority vote of the partners. I asked for an urgent partners' meeting. Even though entirely unused to his authority being questioned, John's response was to convene a partners' meeting for 7.30 am the following day.

When we met over coffee at the nearby M&Z restaurant the next day, John first concisely stated his position on the issue and invited my response. He then asked the others for their views. Colin du Preez sided with John. Claus Hinrichsen thought an important principle of press freedom was at stake and supported my stance. Hartmut's casting vote went in favour of John. This had taken all of twenty minutes. Even though the outcome disappointed me, I was better able to accept it than a decree by the senior partner to withdraw from that client. Establishing this precedent for deciding matters of principle by majority vote was small comfort in being obliged to relinquish a brief in which I so firmly believed.

Smith was in my office less than an hour later to collect his file as I explained the firm's position and recommended a colleague, Peter Koep. Although his practice was largely commercial, his liberal values meant that he would be prepared to fight the case vigorously. He in turn briefed Bryan O'Linn to argue the appeal. Bryan succeeded in having the permanent ban on the *Observer* overturned in early September 1984. In its ruling, the Appeal Board warned, however, that a total ban would be considered in the future if the *Observer* continued with its favourable comment on Swapo in view of its insurgency activities. The Appeal Board also found that the sexist semi-nude photographs – a hallmark of Smith's journalistic style in challenging conservative norms – to be 'in poor taste, vulgar and irresponsible', and cautioned that a ban on obscenity grounds could arise as well. The paper had a reprieve.

Within the next week, Smith, at Salt's urging and insistence, decided to remove Gwen from political reporting and assigned her to general news. It was suspected that a deal had been struck with the authorities to do so. Gwen declined to accept this demotion. When they refused to reinstate Gwen as political reporter, she walked out and was followed by most of the staff. This happened before the advent of an unfair dismissal regime. Gwen and other staff members were confined to claims for unpaid leave and to their outstanding pay to the date of their walkout. I helped with those claims.

Talk of setting up a newspaper – previously a relatively remote prospect in idle chat between Gwen and myself – immediately took on more urgency. Gwen soon directed enquiries to a wide range of her contacts in both journalism and non-governmental organisations (NGOs) abroad for support to set up a newspaper.

I looked into the legal requirements and some practicalities. The immediate material needs of Gwen and those who had accompanied her in leaving the *Observer* gave added impetus to our efforts. We soon realised that this would take several months. My secretary was about to take a few months' maternity leave and I was able to offer Gwen some temporary work to tide her over financially until we were able to get a newspaper going. After hours, we prepared a funding proposal for the newspaper. I had a little more financial background and put together a budget with projected income and expenditure items. At that stage, almost all journalists were white and most were brought in from South Africa, with few opportunities for black journalists with the local media. We decided to include a major training component for indigenous Namibians in all facets of newspaper production as part of our funding proposal.

One of Gwen's contacts put her in touch with a British NGO that could access EU anti-apartheid funding for the project. Because of my legal background and a smattering of relevant financial knowledge, Gwen asked me to go to London to meet the representative to clinch the deal. She had obtained some funding for my trip. My flights to London were via Johannesburg. I would stay there for an extra night afterwards at my friend Geoff Budlender's home so that I could travel to Gaborone for the day to meet with Aaron Mushimba, a Central Committee member of Swapo, to confirm its backing for the project. This was vital for securing EU funding. The EU was unable to conduct its own assessments inside Namibia, and relied on Swapo and progressive NGOs for the green light when funding organisations to avoid initiatives that directly or indirectly supported the apartheid state or its sponsored initiatives. The trip to London was successful and the required funding was provisionally clinched. Securing the go-ahead from Swapo through Mushimba remained.

On arrival at Sir Seretse Khama Airport, I took a taxi to the President Hotel in Gabarone for our meeting. There, Mushimba was waiting and warmly received me. It was our first meeting and we soon got down to business. He confirmed that Swapo had a very real interest in the establishment of an independent voice in Namibia, critical of the apartheid state, its initiatives and local surrogates in view of the unrelenting pro-apartheid propaganda inside the country. Swapo would give the project its blessing to the EU and also consider further start-up support. I was grateful for the approach. I also reported to him on other matters I was handling, such as detentions and a forthcoming terrorism trial.

Straight after a convivial light lunch, I left for the airport in time for the afternoon flight to Johannesburg. As I entered the small airport, heading for the check-in counter, two men in suits and dark glasses purposefully approached me.

'Are you Mr Smuts?' The one asked with an air of authority.

I answered in the affirmative.

Police identity cards were flashed at me and the two introduced themselves as members of the Botswana Security Police. I was to be held for questioning. Led away to a nearby office within the airport, I was sat down and immediately asked as to the nature of my business with Swapo in Botswana. It was clear that they knew I had travelled to Botswana to meet with a Swapo representative.

Surprised and not a little shaken, but also mystified by this unexpected turn of events, I summoned as much composure as I could and explained that I was merely a Windhoek-based lawyer who handled matters for Swapo, which was entitled to legal representation. I denied that I had committed any conceivable crime in their country. I opened my suitcase to reveal some of the detention files

I had brought along together with the file on the pending prosecution of Swapo operatives on terrorism charges. I explained that Botswana afforded a convenient and a discreet meeting place with exiled leaders because of the handy daily flights to and from Johannesburg and the no-visa requirement. I showed them what the different files entailed and, with growing confidence, added with an air of feigned calm that I could not reveal further details because of attorney–client privilege. I was asked whom I had met at the President Hotel – showing that they knew where I had been. I answered that I met Mushimba and that his details could be confirmed with Swapo's accredited representative in Botswana. They were not surprised by this.

After a few further questions, my interrogators conferred briefly and I was told that I could go. I glanced at my watch and saw that the departure time of my flight had already passed. Reading my thoughts, they rose to their feet and urged me to hurry with them to the departure gate.

'No need,' I said. 'The flight left some time ago.'

'No,' was the quick retort. 'We held it back.'

As they escorted me at pace to the departure gate, they courteously explained that they were being extra vigilant following the relatively recent bombing of an ANC safe house in Gaborone by apartheid state operatives and apologised for the inconvenience they had caused me.

I felt the glare of my fellow passengers as I entered the smallish Fokker aircraft; I was the obvious cause of their delay. I barely had time to get to my seat as the plane, already more than twenty minutes late, lurched forward to taxi to its take-off position.

With funding now secured, the planning could go ahead in earnest.

Gwen had already approached most staff members. They had largely identified themselves when they had walked out of the *Observer* with her. Sue Cullinan was to join the team from South Africa and help with training. One of the founders of the newly established progressive *Weekly Mail* in Johannesburg also regularly travelled to Windhoek to assist us with a range of practical items in the initial stages. *The Weekly Mail* had started in June 1985 and our first issue was planned for 30 August 1985.

We needed to come up with a name for the newspaper. At dinner with Gwen and Sue at the former Gourmet's Inn restaurant at the old swimming pool, we inconclusively bandied names about with each being found wanting until I blurted out '*The Namibian*'. Sue embraced it at once as it was the inverse to the apartheid stalwart '*Die Suidwester*'. By the end of the dinner, it was a done deal. I registered a company, which I called the Free Press of Namibia (Pty) Ltd. It would publish the newspaper. Gwen and I were the directors and the sole shareholder was a non-profit trust I set up and called the Namibian Media Trust. I remained a director for the first few years, but resigned in late 1988 so that I could represent Gwen and the newspaper when charged under the Police Act. (The charges were later dropped.)

The legal requirements of starting a newspaper also required attention. Newspapers had to be registered under the Newspaper and Imprint Act.[48] The Internal Security Act[49] (formerly called the Suppression of Communism Act) prohibited the registration of a newspaper under the Newspaper and Imprint Act unless the proprietor of the newspaper deposited an amount of up to R20 000 (this maximum had, in the interim, been increased in South Africa to R40 000 under an amendment not made applicable in Namibia). The deposit would be forfeited if the minister prohibited the newspaper under the Internal Security Act. The minister's powers in Namibia had been transferred to the IG, installed on 17 June 1985. There was a delay of 21 days in the registration process to enable the police to

---

48   Act 63 of 1971.

49   Act 44 of 1950 (its successor in South Africa, bearing the same name, Act 74 of 1982, was not made applicable to Namibia).

advise the cabinet of the IG on the prospects of closing the paper down for the purpose of the cabinet imposing a high deposit, which would then be forfeited in the event of closure.

I prepared and filed the application for registration more than 21 days before our planned start-up of 30 August 1985. On 15 August, the IG's Department of Civic Affairs and Manpower responded to the application to inform me that 'a deposit of R20 000 must be lodged before registration of *The Namibian* is affected'. My response was that the imposition of that deposit was in conflict with the IG's bill of rights incorporated in its empowering proclamation a few months before. I called upon the cabinet of the IG to reverse its decision. The day before planned publication, the IG reverted to say it persisted in its position to require that deposit. We paid the amount under protest to permit the first publication to proceed and reserved our right to challenge the decision by way of judicial review. Shortly afterwards, we did just that.

In our review application, we did not confine ourselves to the constitutional grounds (of offending the right to freedom of the press embodied in the IG's bill of rights). We also challenged the imposition of the deposit on common law review grounds. These included a claim that the decision was in bad faith or actuated by an improper motive because Gwen had criticised several of the members of the cabinet of the IG, and that they had in turn attacked her. We also pointed out that all other newspapers in Namibia had been required to pay token deposits of R10 only, and that the maximum of R20 000 for *The Namibian* amounted to improper discrimination. We also asserted that the deposit was imposed with an ulterior motive to prevent us from publishing.

The IG opposed the application. The then cabinet chairperson (it rotated), Moses Katjiuongua, made the answering affidavit on behalf of Cabinet. He confirmed that the Cabinet had made the decision to impose the deposit in an awkwardly formulated affidavit. He said that Cabinet was not satisfied that 'the prohibition (of the newspaper) . . . will not at any time in the future become necessary . . .'

One of the principal reasons given for the large deposit (and future potential ban) was articulated thus by him:

> The Cabinet was of the view that unfair attacks on its members will inter alia tend to lower the esteem in which they are held by the public; it will adversely affect their political integrity and their credibility; it will lower the status of the Cabinet as such and ultimately, the Cabinet and its members will be hampered in the performance of its, and their, duties and functions. This, in the view of the Cabinet, is likely to have the effect to endanger the security of the State or the maintenance of public order.

The leap in logic – with the final concluding sentence hardly following what preceded it – was striking.

Katjiuongua also said that 'discrediting and disparaging' the IG would undermine its legitimacy and cause a section of the people of Namibia to 'hold the (Interim) Government in contempt'. And he attached an affidavit by an obscure political scientist from Germany, Henning von Löwis of Menar. This affidavit provided a detailed exposition of Swapo as a 'revolutionary anti-imperialistic national liberation movement' which professed 'a scientific ideology of Marxism-Leninism'. In response to this, we engaged André du Pisani, a respected and knowledgeable academic of local origin, who explained that Von Löwis's analysis ignored historical or political context and was decidedly one-sided, overly simplistic and wrong in several respects (which he carefully listed).

The case was fortunately allocated to Judge Harold Levy, who would not be put off by the scare tactics contained in the cabinet's opposition. And he certainly was not. In his liberal ruling, he stressed the importance of freedom of speech and the press, embracing strong statements to that effect in US case law. He also emphasised that people occupying public office should not be 'too thin-skinned in reference to criticism levelled at them'. If members of the cabinet considered that Gwen's criticism went beyond legal bounds, they could have sued her. But they had not done so. Her attacks were thus not unlawful. And even if they were defamatory, it did not follow that they would constitute a threat to the public order or the security of the state. He found that the justification for the deposit was based on a non sequitur. On the contrary, he said that to stifle just criticism could as likely lead to adverse consequences. He added that it was not open to cabinet members to use their positions to settle personal scores with Gwen – or with anyone else, for that matter. Judge Levy concluded that criticism of members of government could not constitute a danger to the safety of the state. He set aside the imposition of the deposit in these ringing terms.

This outcome, which had come some months after *The Namibian* had been started, was widely welcomed in media circles outside Namibia. Other members of the local media gave it very little coverage.

Although *The Namibian* had been born in a hostile legislative environment, this victory represented a signal to the security establishment, firmly backed by the IG, that future legal steps against *The Namibian* would not go unchallenged and may falter.

Some legal steps did follow – in the form of charges under the Police Act[50] for reports on security force activities, which were used to detain Gwen without trial. Despite the authoritarian legal framework that had severe penalties for the draconian crimes created against the media and reporting, none of the charges against the newspaper and Gwen was ever to stick or even go to trial. They plainly amounted to harassment. Action against the newspaper and Gwen

---

50   Section 27B of the Police Act.

personally was not confined to invoking oppressive laws. There followed a resort to 'dirty tricks' in the form of extrajudicial and criminal measures against *The Namibian*. These included the use of firebombs to set fire to the offices, firing shots at the offices and anonymous death threats against Gwen, myself and other staff members.

It emerged in the judicial inquest into the death of my late friend Anton Lubowski that the resort to dirty tricks of this nature formed part of concerted, state-sponsored and engineered criminal conduct directed at opponents of the apartheid regime by an undercover special SADF unit. Other commissions of inquiry in South Africa revealed that there were other state agencies engaged in similar work.[51] Gwen and *The Namibian* were prominent targets.

The Namibian made a massive difference to human rights reporting and protection. From the first issue, security force excesses received prominent coverage. Following the example of the *Weekly Mail*, Gwen agreed that we also feature a detention barometer in every week's issue, setting out a list of those detained without trial and those whose disappearances were unaccounted for. This led to more detentions being reported and followed up. I have no doubt that the vigilance in relentlessly exposing human rights abuses not only had a chilling effect on security force conduct, but also powerfully promoted the public discourse about the need for real human rights protection in any future order in Namibia and assisted in the burgeoning development of a human rights culture.

The Namibian started as a weekly in 1985. In early 1989 it became a daily. A year or two after that, it became the largest-circulation daily under Gwen's leadership, a status it has consistently retained to date.

As a weekly, it came out on Fridays. In its first year or two, I would go directly from my practice at about 4:30 pm (our firm's official

---

51   Pauw, J. 2017. *Into the Heart of Darkness: Confessions of Apartheid's Assassins*. Jonathan Ball Publishers: Johannesburg.

closing time) on Thursdays and then stay at *The Namibian's* premises, poring over every inch of copy (except for the sports pages) to check that there were no contraventions of the plethora of laws (referred to as a minefield) restricting the publication of stories about the security forces. I would also occasionally pen an editorial on a human-rights-related issue. This would often take until the paper went to bed – to the printing works – at about 11 pm or so. I kept these hours for a year or two to prevent my partners from complaining because this was all in my free time and at no charge to the newspaper.

8

The murder of Immanuel Shifidi

Immanuel Shifidi was one of those very special people one meets in life: a truly kind gentleman, genuinely friendly and a person of principle, experience and humility.

We met in November 1985 shortly after his release from Robben Island, along with other Namibian political prisoners. But we got to know each other closely during the long-running political trial of Frans Angula and six fellow accused as they faced multiple charges under the Terrorism Act. I was their instructing attorney and Shifidi attended every single day of the proceedings in support of the defendants. He soon came to serve as the liaison between me and the relatives of the defendants, to facilitate visits and other matters concerning the defendants' welfare. His quietly efficient and empathetic coordination was a great help, given the number of defendants on trial, as each had relatives who would travel from the northern area to take it in turns to attend. As a former political prisoner he received a small pension through the Council of Churches and devoted his time to assisting where he could.

Shifidi had earlier also approached me to act for his brother, Ferdinand, who had been detained without trial for several months. Ferdinand was later released, never having been charged with any offence.

Facilitating visits for the relatives meant frequent discussions between us to that end. We also often chatted during adjournments about the case so that he could keep relatives informed.

His own trial, several years before, had been far less than fair. He had the distinction of being in the first group charged under the Terrorism Act in 1967, together with Andimba Toivo ya Toivo. The Act authorised indefinite detention without trial, a power the security police exercised extravagantly. During the lengthy period in detention before being charged, access to lawyers or family was specifically precluded.

Torture and abuse invariably occurred during that period and, in his case, was particularly severe. To make matters worse, he was detained far from Namibia after his capture, in Pretoria in South Africa where his trial later took place.

The Act created a very widely defined crime of an 'act of terrorism'. It also cast the burden of proof on an accused to establish his or her innocence. In his case, the fundamental unfairness was compounded by the fact that the Act had been rushed through the South African Parliament after his capture and incarceration in 1966. It had been devised and passed in 1967 to deal with him and fellow PLAN fighters who had initiated the armed struggle in northern Namibia in August 1966. The Act had been backdated so that he and his 36 fellow accused could be charged with the serious crimes created in it (which did not exist as offences at the time they had committed them). To compound it all, the Act also authorised the imposition of the death sentence.

Shifidi had been one of the first Namibians to undergo military training – in his case, at the Ongulumbashe training camp, set up by the first Swapo guerrillas in a remote area of Owambo. The skirmish there, where his fellow defendants were captured on 26 August 1966, signalled the commencement of Namibia's armed struggle for liberation. He was not one of the group leaders, but a loyal team member trained at Ongulumbashe. He was involved in the subsequent armed raid upon the Native Commissioner's compound at Oshikango. Unlike most of the others on trial, he was not captured at Ongulumbashe, but some time later – in the Ondonga area. He had evaded arrest for some three months after the Oshikango attack but was captured after his trusted associate who was looking after his firearm was by chance found out. For his part, he was sentenced to life imprisonment.

Prior to undergoing training at Ongulumbashe, Shifidi had worked as a stevedore contract labourer in Walvis Bay where he, like his fellow Robben Island and lifelong friend, Helao Shituwete, had been OPO supporters, organising fellow workers around labour issues in Walvis Bay.

Despite his unpromising experience with the law, Shifidi relished a court battle. He not only attended every day of the *Angula* trial but all other political cases as well following his release from prison until his death, always on hand to lend enthusiastic support to defendants, their families and the legal team. Ever positive, he managed to maintain his buoyant, indefatigable spirit even when things seemed quite hopeless.

After his release, Shifidi was very active in Swapo and regularly attended meetings and events.

A Swapo rally had been organised for Sunday 30 November 1986 on an open field in the older section of Katutura, known at the time as Ellis Park because it was mostly used for football games. It was not far from where the much-resented, sprawling hostel complex once was – a compound that had housed male migrant workers predominantly from Owambo in degrading and overcrowded conditions. The complex had recently been dramatically demolished by way of an implosion at the instance of the IG in a flourish of publicity aimed at gaining some credibility by trying to distance itself from apartheid practices. What had been widely known as the 'hostel', or 'omkomupandu' in Oshiwambo, was a prominent symbol of those practices. If anything, the gesture had backfired and was derisively labelled an empty publicity stunt by many activists and Katutura residents alike. Many thought that the demolition was wasteful, and that the structures could rather have been rehabilitated and put to public use with at least a section being retained as a reminder of those inhuman conditions.

Katutura is the large township on the outskirts of Windhoek where black people were resettled after being forcibly removed in 1959 from what was known as the Old Location, closer to central Windhoek, and its segregated white suburbs. This had been one of the more significant moments in Namibia's political history. The forced removals had galvanised massive political resistance around the issue. There had been a defiance campaign when the proposed removals were announced. Public transport was boycotted, as were beer halls. Demonstrations followed. These peaceful protests led to confrontation between demonstrators and the police, and were brutally put down. At least 11 people were killed when the South African Police fired into crowds on 10 and 11 December 1959. Homes in the Old Location were flattened to make way for a new whites-only suburb, exultantly named Pioneer's Park, bearing a striking resemblance to the apartheid regime's demolition a few years before of Sophiatown in Johannesburg, the forced removal of its inhabitants and the creation of the white suburb of Triomf (meaning 'triumph') in its wake.

The forced removals from the Old Location had a profound political impact. Support surged for the recently formed Swapo, which had originally been established as the OPO shortly before but had changed its name to Swapo in 1959. There was also a groundswell of support for the other resistance organisation called Swanu, which was predominantly Herero. Both had been active in resisting the removals, and had gained much stature and momentum as a result.

The Swapo rally in Katutura on 30 November 1986 got off to a belated start. Chaired by Dan Tjongarero, it was also slow going as the first speaker's address in English was translated into Oshiwambo and then Afrikaans, sentence by sentence.

As usual, Immanuel Shifidi was in attendance – leaning against a pickup on the western fringes of the gathered crowd, wearing a *Namibian* T-shirt calling for the immediate implementation of UN Security Council Resolution 435 – when a small pickup pulled up nearby. A group of 30–40 men purposefully approached it. They each grabbed a rudimentary weapon from the open load bay and made for the assembled crowd with pace, brandishing their weapons – bows and arrows, assegais, traditional knives and knobkieries. They quickly descended on those attending the meeting, lashing out indiscriminately as they surged towards the open area and the podium. Shifidi was one of the first people in their path. A sharp object, most likely a traditional knife, punctured his chest. He slowly slumped to the ground, partially propped up by the pickup he had been leaning against, bleeding profusely from his chest wound and also from another to his forehead. *The Namibian*'s photographer, John Liebenberg, was positioned nearby to cover the rally. He saw what happened and rushed to Shifidi's assistance, calling for help. The driver of another small pickup came forward and rushed Shifidi to the nearby Katutura Hospital.

Shifidi was pronounced dead upon arrival.

Pandemonium broke out as the group of armed men ploughed into the crowd, wielding their weapons. Most attending the rally rapidly dispersed while Swapo marshals on duty at the rally pursued the disruptors. This was the cue for heavily armed members of the police's specialist Task Force Unit (formerly known as the riot squad) to arrive on the scene in Casspirs. The Task Force Unit was essentially a paramilitary unit of the police used in urban areas to quell political protest and activities. Notoriously heavy-handed, they soon ran amok, immediately dispersing those who remained as well as those trying to flee, firing teargas indiscriminately at them and at anyone else on the streets in the area. Live rounds were also fired; one person was struck and badly injured. Children, who would customarily play in the streets at that time on a Sunday afternoon, were not spared. The task force members also lashed out with their sjamboks (crude, sturdy, whip-like devices) against everyone in the area. There was total havoc as people were chased from the streets.

Several frightened people took refuge in St Michaels, the nearby Anglican Church. A shaken church elder phoned Bishop James, who in turn immediately contacted me.

'There are some very bad things happening right now in Katutura. I have just had a call from St Michael's. People are sheltering in the church from police violence. Would you please come with me to the church? We need to speak to the people, address their fears, find out the cause and see what we can do.'

As we cautiously approached St Michael's, the streets of Katutura were eerily quiet and deserted except for the menacing presence of Casspirs manned by heavily armed task force policemen in their camouflage fatigues, accentuating the contrast between the powerful and impenetrable proportions of those vehicles and the humble homes that densely lined the streets.

About 30–40 people, including young children, were huddled in a group in the front pews of the church. As Bishop James entered the church, his reassuring presence did much to alleviate the tense atmosphere. He had that effect upon people. I had also witnessed this in outlying and vulnerable parishes in war-torn Owambo. They spoke to us of the Swapo rally that had been broken up, and relayed rumours of at least one dead and several others injured as a group of assailants had marauded through the gathering.

We listened to a few accounts. Some of those who spoke to us had been lightly injured after being struck by hurtling teargas canisters or sjamboks. Everyone was traumatised.

After a while, the Casspirs moved out of the area. We encouraged everyone to go home, as it seemed safe to do so.

Once outside, a youth activist rushed up to us and announced: 'The Casspirs are moving to other parts of Katutura instead of returning to the [nearby] police station.' This, he added, was ominous, as the task force members seemed in a particularly rampant mood.

We decided to take a wide detour through Katutura, past the football stadium, before making our way home. We would return via an area popularly known as Donkerhoek, where many activists lived. At first, all remained ominously quiet for a Sunday afternoon: no sign of any police vehicles. But as we turned east into Claudius Kanduvazu Street and started the gradual incline towards Donkerhoek (loosely known as Owambo Location because people had initially been resettled in areas of Katutura on an ethnic basis in accordance with apartheid policies), we saw a Casspir some distance ahead of us. It was travelling quite slowly in the same direction. Teargas canisters were being randomly fired at people's homes. The compact, standard houses in that part of Katutura, built on small plots and very close to the street, were easy targets in this exercise. The area was several kilometres from where the rally had been disrupted. There were no signs of any protest in the area, and no justification for the task force's presence there, let alone for this gratuitous police violence meted out to that targeted segment of the community.

Bishop James exclaimed in horror as this scene unfolded in front of us: 'Oh no! This is truly shocking. Look at how they are carrying on. Very dangerous. Please slow down and keep a safe distance from those violent hooligans.'

I had not heard Bishop James ever use such disparaging language.

Worse was to follow. The Casspir drew to a halt in the middle of the street outside the house of Frans Kambangula, one of Katutura's most prominent Swapo leadership figures. His home would have been well known to the security police and their task force counter-

184

parts as activists often met there – and would often have been under surveillance when doing so.

I recognised the distinctive Walvis Bay number plates of an old Mercedes-Benz parked across the road from Kambangula's house. It belonged to another high-profile member of Swapo's leadership and former Robben Island prisoner, Nathaniel Maxuilili. It, too, was no doubt familiar to the police as he was continually under surveillance and constantly harassed. He had travelled from Walvis Bay to attend and speak at the meeting. Two of the policemen effortlessly descended from their high perch on the Casspir and set about smashing Maxuilili's car windscreen and windows with truncheons and rocks picked up from the open area next to the vehicle. Their task completed, they clambered back up into the Casspir. As it slowly pulled off, more teargas was fired into Kambangula's home and the neighbouring homes, as if to round off the wanton violence visited upon those prominent activists.

We watched aghast, astounded by the aggression and the sheer scale of its brazen execution, and made sure to maintain a safe distance from the Casspir, which eventually headed to the Katutura Police Station.

Not long after returning home, Dan Tjongarero called with the news of Immanuel Shifidi's death and spoke of how the meeting had been disrupted. He suspected foul play on the part of the security forces and asked me to assist in establishing the truth so that justice could be done and Shifidi's killers brought to book. He also wanted to find out who had been behind the violent disruption directed at Swapo supporters and the organisation. I asked Dan to try to get hold of Shifidi's brother, Ferdinand, and his daughter, Hilda. We agreed to meet at my office the next morning.

It was a busy evening. I also spoke to John Liebenberg, who provided his account of events. There were several calls from other activists who were all in shock at the news of Shifidi's death.

First thing the next morning I contacted the state pathologist –
Dr Jan Botha, a competent and approachable professional – and
asked about the cause of death and when he planned to conduct the
post mortem examination. He invited me to meet him straight away
at the mortuary for me to identify Shifidi and for him to explain the
wounds and cause of death. I had previously been to the mortuary
to attend a post mortem examination of a detainee who had died in
detention. I thought I would be prepared for this visit. But it was different, more personal. Dr Botha explained that the death had been
caused by a stab wound to Shifidi's chest. He showed me that the
visible wound to Shifidi's forehead was not from a gunshot (as had
been thought by John Liebenberg) but was rather the result of a forcible blow to his head from a blunt object like a kierie. His findings
appeared entirely correct and there was no need to engage our own
forensic pathologist to observe the post mortem.

Dan and Niko Bessinger were waiting for me on my return to the
office. I reported on my mortuary visit and Dr Botha's assessment of
the cause of death. Dan had managed to get hold of Hilda so that
she could formally identify her father.

Dan and Niko had come armed with a copy of the Afrikaans morning daily newspaper, *Die Republikein* – the official mouthpiece of the
DTA and the IG, which was dominated by the DTA. Its uncritical
support for the security forces was reflected in its reporting. It also
went out of its way to discredit and belittle critics of human rights
abuses by the security forces by venomously lampooning them in
its cartoons, which were skilfully drawn by its most ardent Koevoet
supporter, Gene Travers, and also sneeringly referred to by its editor,
Des Erasmus, in his regular column, written under a pseudonym.

The newspaper gave prominent coverage to the events of the previous afternoon. Its banner headline on the front page proclaimed
(as translated) 'Chaos erupts at meeting'. The thrust of the report
was that mayhem had resulted at the meeting when elements of the

assembled Swapo supporters had violently turned on one another, resulting in two deaths – including that of a child killed in the stampede that followed – and widespread injuries. It claimed that it was only after police intervention that order had been restored.

The leader page of the newspaper featured an editorial on the subject under the heading 'Swapo'. Freely translated, it stated:

> The so-called factions (schools of thought) within the party can indeed have far-reaching consequences.
>
> When Swapo wanted to hold a meeting in Windhoek yesterday, it ended up in fighting [bakleiery] where people lost their lives and many were injured and is indeed a demonstration that there are different schools of thought within Swapo. There are members of the internal wing that flutter around like doves of peace in an attempt to garner political support, and there is the external wing that inflames violence with their smoke signals. This necessarily leads to tension within the party, especially when a moment of truth arrives like yesterday afternoon's meeting in Katutura. This time Swapo will have to do more than their traditional accusation that the police were responsible for the violence; on the contrary, this time the police acted to contain the spread of violence after it spontaneously burst out among Swapo members.

The report of two deaths was incorrect. The only casualty, apart from the truth, was Shifidi.

Dan said that he had received reports from the Swapo marshals on duty at the meeting that one or more of the assailants were thought to be attached to the security forces – in particular, 101 Battalion of the South West Africa Territory Force (SWATF), based at Oluno, near Ondangwa. With the exception of officers who were mostly white, it comprised Oshiwambo-speaking troops who had volunteered to fight for the South African forces, as well as some former Swapo insurgents who had been captured and 'turned around' in captivity. I had already received information to that effect earlier that morning from Thomas Haipinge, a security guard working at our building, who was coincidentally a Swapo marshal in his spare time.

Dan said there had been some other ominous incidents. Both he and Niko had received anonymous threats of death, and violence and disruption, before the meeting. Swapo rallies were usually preceded by barbeques (commonly known as Swapo braais) the night before. At the get-together held on the preceding Friday evening, some Swapo supporters on the fringes of the event had been attacked. When the hue and cry had gone up, the assailants had fled.

I reminded Dan and Niko of an incident at the Catholic Corpus Christi procession earlier that year. Invoking apartheid legislation, the procession was initially banned by the IG for two reasons. It was said that it was, in fact, a Swapo march masquerading as a church event and that the march could lead to violence because of other elements who opposed Swapo. We had successfully challenged the ban, which was overturned by the courts. During the ensuing procession, some marchers were assaulted by a small group of individuals, one of whom was reputed to be a DTA office bearer. One of the victims had told me that he had also seen a submachine gun on the seat of a nearby pickup used by those who had disrupted the march. Even though the procession had been closely monitored by the security police, no one was ever arrested or charged with the assaults.

Not surprisingly, there was growing distrust of the security forces and a belief in their involvement in attacks on Swapo and other activist groups seen to be aligned to Swapo.

Dan and Niko suspected complicity on the part of the security forces in the violent and unlawful conduct directed at opponents of the regime, especially at the weekend's rally. They pointed to that morning's editorial in *Die Republikein* and its coverage of the event.

They strongly suspected that the disruption had been staged by the security establishment as a plan to justify a fresh clampdown on Swapo and, more specifically, as part of a strategy to ban Swapo meetings on the pretext that their members were unruly and violent, incapable of peaceful political discourse. This would warrant a ban by the IG to prevent violence at future gatherings, given what had been so assertively expressed in their mouthpiece that morning.

Earlier that year (on 25 March 1986), we had succeeded in securing a court ruling that had effectively emasculated legislation directed at preventing Swapo from holding meetings in its own name. That case had been primarily handled by Hartmut, although Hosea and I had also assisted. Nathaniel Maxuilili, Jerry Ekandjo and Frans Kambangula had been charged with contravening the Prohibition and Notification of Meetings Act of 1981. This law had been enacted at the instance of the South African security establishment in 1981 by the previous National Assembly, also comprising a coalition of anti-Swapo parties led by the DTA. It prohibited the arranging and holding of meetings for any organisation 'which propagates . . . the overthrow of any . . . authority . . . or the bringing about of a political, social or economic change by . . . violence or intimidation or forcible means'.[52]

Although not mentioned by name in the legislation, it was obviously aimed at preventing Swapo from holding lawful meetings. Swapo's armed struggle against South African rule had started in 1966 and later intensified considerably from the mid- to late 1970s following Angola's independence, which had meant that Swapo was able to base military activities on a wider front from Angola.

The indictment against Maxuilili, Ekandjo and Kambangula claimed that they had organised a meeting on 21 April 1985 for Swapo and that, by doing so, they had contravened the Act because Swapo's Constitution and Political Programme propagated the violent over-

---

52   Section 2.

throw of the existing authorities (in South West Africa). Hartmut had engaged skilful counsel, Ian Farlam, assisted by Jeremy Gauntlett, to object against the charge sheet on the grounds that the section offended against the bill of rights in the establishing proclamation of the then IG in June 1985. Other grounds were also raised in support of the objection.

A full bench of the High Court was assembled to hear the argument. It included the liberal Harold Levy, who struck down the charge sheet on behalf of a unanimous court. He reasoned that section 2 could only hit an organisation that had as its sole objective the violent overthrow of the existing order. He referred to Swapo's constitution and found that none of its objectives included a violent overthrow. The listed objectives were all peaceful and permissible. The Political Programme, also relied upon by the prosecution, referred to armed struggle as 'the main form of our liberation activity'. But Judge Levy found that there was no statement in it that specifically provided for the overthrow of the authorities by violent means. He also found that the programme made mention of other activities, such as reconstruction of the economy, education, health and social welfare. Judge Levy concluded that, because the Act was directed at organisations that have as their sole and only object the violent overthrow of authority, the charge sheet did not disclose an offence against our clients – and quashed the charges.

This victory had far-reaching implications. Since its adoption in 1981, the Act had been utilised to prevent Swapo from lawfully holding meetings. It could no longer do so after 25 March 1986, much to the consternation of the security force establishment and the IG.

The rally at which Shifidi had been killed was one of the first major public meetings organised by Swapo following this seminal court victory.

Dan and Niko were convinced that the violent disruption of the meeting had been deliberately devised to rationalise new legislative measures directed at preventing Swapo from holding future meetings. If we could show that there had been security force involvement in the disruption, this capricious design may yet be thwarted and certainly exposed.

I asked them to obtain information about the assailants' security force allegiance and supply us with names or any further details. Dan dropped by later that day to tell me that he had obtained confirmation from a Swapo marshal that some of the assailants were members of 101 Battalion. A few names were even supplied to him. He called a press conference later that afternoon where Niko claimed that members of 101 Battalion had been involved in disrupting the rally as a pretext to justify the heavy-handed police intervention. Dan expanded upon that theme by adding that this was part of a strategy to discredit Swapo and claim that it is a 'danger to the public'. Although not mentioning *Die Republikein* by name, he criticised the integrity of its press coverage and its objectivity. He pointed out that, even though it did not have any reporters at the meeting, it had seen fit to make far-reaching factual assertions about it. He joined the call by the Council of Churches for a judicial inquiry into Shifidi's death and the events surrounding it as Swapo had no confidence at all in any investigation carried out by the security forces, given the strong suspicion of their involvement in those very events and the bias they had shown in their handling of the situation.

The front-page lead story in the next day's *Republikein* carried a denial by the police of any involvement when the Swapo meeting had 'descended into chaos'. It did so in the context of debunking Dan's claims before mentioning them.

The day after Dan's press conference, he was approached by Colonel Jumbo Smit, a senior member of the criminal investigation division of the police and overall head of its investigation into Shifidi's murder. He demanded that Dan provide all information of alleged security force involvement, including any names of members of

101 Battalion. Dan declined to make a statement to him and referred Smit to me. I explained to Smit in his follow-up visit to my office that we suspected complicity by 101 Battalion or Koevoet in Shifidi's death. He then demanded names from me so that he could investigate the matter further. I said I would get back to him on that. Dan and I both had the feeling that the police seemed more interested in establishing precisely what we knew than in taking our allegations seriously and the need to investigate them properly. These fears subsequently turned out to be well founded at the inquest held in June/July the following year.

In the days that followed, I provided three names of suspected 101 Battalion members involved in the disruption to Col. Smit. After receiving no feedback from him, I subsequently met with the then Deputy Attorney-General (the deputy head of prosecutions) to enquire about the outcome of the police investigation and was told that the investigation could not come up with any suspect and that an inquest would be held at some unspecified date in the future. This came as no surprise, given Smit's dismissive attitude and visible irritation at the suggestion of any security force complicity.

Despite being on record for clients in my meetings with the Deputy Attorney-General and Smit, I was quite remarkably not informed about the date of the inquest. I only found out about it when Ferdinand Shifidi came to my office on the afternoon of 28 June 1987, the day before the inquest was due to start. He had heard about it from Hilda, who had received a subpoena a few days before that. Ferdinand had immediately travelled from the north for the inquest and expected me to be ready for the proceedings. He brought Hilda to my office the next morning and we made our way together to the Windhoek Magistrate's Court to seek a brief postponement so that we could prepare for it.

Windhoek's Chief Magistrate, Frikkie Truter, was the presiding officer. At the very outset, I rose to apply for a postponement, complaining that I had not been formally informed of the date by the authorities and had only heard from Ferdinand the previous afternoon and had only been able to meet with Hilda that morning. I called Hilda to give evidence to confirm that. The prosecutor leading the evidence at the inquest had, before the start, also declined to provide me with the affidavits of witnesses. I asked for an order directing that these be given to us, as well as for a postponement to enable us to prepare for the inquest.

Truter was initially reluctant to provide access to the affidavits. I emphasised that the purpose of the exercise was to obtain the truth – and that we would assist him in that process and be better equipped to do so if we had access to the statements and assess whether we would want to apply to call any witnesses. After listening carefully, Truter granted a postponement and also directed that we receive the statements. The inquest was postponed to 8 July 1987. I was able to brief a formidable legal team to represent the family, led by local senior counsel, Bryan O'Linn, assisted by a competent junior counsel and my friend, Theo Frank.

Dr Jan Botha was called first to provide his medical evidence, which meticulously detailed the injuries to Shifidi and lucidly explained the cause of death.

The next witness, Colonel Nel, was the local branch commander of the Security Police. He had been at the rally in an unmarked car to observe the proceedings. If Bryan had a specialised skill, it was cross-examining security policemen. In that respect, he had no equal in Namibia and few in Southern Africa. There was little subtlety to his cross-examination. He pounced upon any inconsistency or equivocation, and invariably ended up pulverising even the most hardened security policeman into submission. Bryan hailed from the small town of Omaruru and had started out as a policeman. He soon worked his way up to the rank of detective sergeant before leaving police work to study law in South Africa. He returned to practise at the bar and became a highly thought of and courageous counsel and human rights advocate, fearlessly taking on the security establishment in trials of dissidents in a career spanning many years. Under his leadership, the Bar Council frequently spoke out against the ever-increasing abuses of human rights and inroads into the rule of law in the 1980s.

Although Colonel Nel had been on duty at the rally, he was unable to provide any detail of the disruption because, so he said, he was there merely to monitor the speakers. His concentration, he explained, had been solely fixed on the makeshift stage and nowhere else. He disputed Bryan's assertion that, as a senior police officer, he also had a duty to prevent the commission of crimes such as murder and assault from taking place. He said his function was rather to monitor and observe the proceedings and nothing else. This attitude reflected the position of the police in northern Namibia, where very few policemen saw it as their purpose to perform usual police functions. Even the few deployed in that capacity seemed to regard their role as supportive of counterinsurgency initiatives and activities, rather than possibly performing any service to the community living there.

Nel said that there had been three groups of two security policemen each in unmarked cars at the rally. Although that was the official count, I suspected that there had been at least an unofficial fourth group, which included a former journalist whom many of us suspected to be an undercover security police operative. Such a small contingent was most unusual and, with hindsight, highly suspicious. Meetings of this kind were more commonly teeming with both security police in plain clothes and even more members of the task force in their camouflage fatigues, brazenly brandishing their weaponry for all to see. One would typically feel almost surrounded by them at events like these. This was even the case at the funerals of activists I had attended.

As was the practice, at least one group of security policemen had

had a video camera aimed at the crowd and the stage to record the proceedings. When Colonel Nel was asked about the whereabouts of that footage, his response was that video recorder had curiously been turned off at the time of the disruption. His only explanation for this most unlikely scenario was that the recorder was periodically switched on and off. When Bryan sought to press him on this issue and the failure on the part of the security police to do anything at all to address the criminal conduct that had occurred, the Magistrate intervened to put an end to this line of enquiry. He took a very narrow view of the ambit of an inquest, saying that it was not an enquiry into police conduct but into the cause of death of the deceased. He ruled that this line of questioning was not relevant and confined Bryan to establishing whether or not the video footage existed. Nel's unhelpful answer was that there was no footage at all and that, when the violent disruption had occurred, he and his detachment had beat a hasty retreat as stones had been thrown at their vehicles. He had then summoned the Task Force to deal with the ensuing mayhem.

We had been told that one of the suspected members of 101 Battalion involved in the disruption, Martin Iipinge, had been injured in the fracas and had been admitted to Katutura State Hospital. One of the Swapo marshals on duty at the rally had told Dan that he had recognised Iipinge as one of the assailants, both at the meeting and at the hospital afterwards. After the marshal had questioned Iipinge in the hospital, the hospital authorities had immediately moved him to another ward. In our investigation, we could find no trace at all of his admission to the hospital under that name.

Bryan asked Nel whether the security police would not have investigated how Iipinge could have disappeared without a trace from the hospital. Nel said he was unaware of him and had not done any investigation at the hospital. He also claimed to be unaware of the attack at the Swapo braai on the previous Friday evening. This was hardly credible as events of that nature were more often than not also

195

under surveillance by his branch. His evidence was evasive and vague in the extreme. It raised more questions than answers. His denial of any video footage was unconvincing, as was his blinkered viewing of the events. It spoke rather of concealing evidence and a cover-up.

The next witnesses were more predictable. Mr April Uirab, who lived close to the point where the assailants had assembled, described a group of at least 25 – armed with bows and arrows, assegais, knobkieries, pangas and knives – charging towards the crowd. He said he would be unable to identify them individually as he had only momentarily seen them. He did see Shifidi being attacked and slump to the ground next to a pickup. He said that Shifidi had been unarmed and minding his own business at the time of the attack.

John Liebenberg and Jean Sutherland testified about what they had seen. It was along similar lines. Evidence to like effect was also given by two other people who had attended the rally.

The proceedings took a different turn when the official police investigating officer, Warrant Officer Xoagub, was called. He attributed the failure to identify and charge any suspects in connection with Shifidi's death to obstacles he encountered. Uppermost on his list had been the lack of cooperation he had received from me and members of the community. This theme was later expanded upon by Smit in his evidence, accusing me of obstructing the police in its murder investigation by discouraging members of Swapo's leadership and rank and file from making statements to the police. He was later constrained to qualify much of that under cross-examination when confronted with correspondence in which I had supplied him of the names of three potential suspects.

Xoagub's evidence painted a pitiful picture of police work. He claimed to be unaware of the attack at the Swapo braai. He also claimed ignorance of vigilante attacks upon the Corpus Christi procession and a recent attack upon a Swapo leadership figure, Joshua Hoebeb. He had also failed to follow up a number of extremely obvious leads. These even included going to the hospital to interview any of the injured straight after he had become involved with the investigation. Some had remained there until the Friday that followed the incident. He had effectively worked on the investigation from the Tuesday (2 December). He was unable to explain why he had not gone to the hospital shortly afterwards and had only proceeded there on the Friday, by which time all those injured had been discharged. And worse still, he had only made inquiries about the identities of those hospitalised a month later, in January 1987, and obtained a list of 22 such people then. Not surprisingly, he was unable to trace the whereabouts of Martin Iipinge.

When asked about repeated allegations about the involvement of members of 101 Battalion, he said that he was too junior to confront other elements in the security forces about allegations of that nature. It was not his role, but rather the responsibility of his senior, Smit. He himself made no investigation of his own about the names supplied to the police by my firm. In his cross-examination, Bryan repeatedly put to Xoagub that the police investigation had been pathetic.

The thrust of Col. Smit's evidence-in-chief was the obstruction he had experienced, primarily from me. According to him, no one who had attended the meeting wanted to come forward without first speaking to us and, after doing so, they would then decline to make a statement. He also implied that we had been responsible for the obstruction his investigation encountered at the hospital when seeking names of those admitted, long after they had been discharged. He found it necessary to complain to the Deputy Attorney-General about this. When asked about his enquiries to 101 Battalion following the letters I had sent, containing three names of alleged members of the Battalion, he replied that he had written a letter to the battalion's commanding officer, who had replied that not one of them was a member of his battalion or had been. This was all he had done in that regard. No further enquiries of any nature were made.

At the outset of Smit's cross-examination, Bryan put it to him that there was widespread distrust of police investigations when allegations were raised concerning involvement of the security forces in criminal conduct against activists. Smit denied there was a basis for this and reiterated that there had, instead, been a deliberate obstruction of his investigation. Bryan then listed instances where police investigations had failed to come up with suspects in cases where crimes had been committed against activists. He referred to the death of Johannes Kakuva in detention a few years before and the assaults at the Corpus Christi procession. None of these had resulted in prosecution. Smit started to stumble with unsatisfactory answers and soon found himself floundering when Bryan moved to the manifold failures on the part of the police to follow obvious and very basic leads in their investigation of Shifidi's murder.

Smit conceded that he had known of the attack at the Swapo braai on the preceding Friday night but had failed to inform Xoagub of this fact. He could not explain why a junior detective was tasked to investigate the murder. Nor could he answer why heavily armed Task Force members in Casspirs had failed to arrest anyone brandishing spears, pangas, assegais and knobkieries. His responses about the failure to visit any of the injured in hospital were similarly unsatisfactory and were described by Bryan as scandalous. Smit said that subsequent enquiries to the hospital superintendent had not been helpful, with the latter refusing to provide medical records to him. After conceding that he was aware of his power to subpoena that information, he failed to explain why he had failed to do so.

Smit was also asked whether he had investigated the conduct of Task Force members that day. He was referred to press reports of teargas being fired indiscriminately and assaults by its members in Casspirs. He said that was not what he had established. John's evidence, supported by a photograph showing Task Force members taunting members of the community by raising a Swapo flag high from a

Casspir when forcibly dispersing people at the rally, was put to him. He saw absolutely no need to investigate their conduct, however.

After a series of evasive answers in cross-examination concerning possible Koevoet and security force involvement, the magistrate intervened and, to a hushed courtroom, pointedly asked Smit whether security force members could have been used in the attack on the fateful day. Smit denied this but could not justify this statement.

At the end of Smit's evidence, an affidavit by the officer commanding of 101 Battalion, Colonel Welgemoed, was handed in. He referred to the four names Smit supplied to him and denied that any of them had ever been part of his unit. He added that a strikingly similar name to one, Immanual Amukwaya, had previously been a member of the unit, but had left on 31 October 1986 after resigning on 17 October 1986, a month before the fateful meeting and killing.

At our request, the prosecutor leading the evidence called Mr Des Erasmus, editor of *Die Republikein*, to give evidence. Our request was motivated by his editorial in which had stated as a fact that the violent disruption of the rally had been the consequence of Swapo infighting.

Erasmus acknowledged that he authored the editorial – and had written it on the same Sunday evening of the killing. He had not been at the meeting. Nor had he attended a subsequent police press conference. He said he had sent two senior reporters, Gene Travers and André de Bruin, to attend, cover the rally and the subsequent media briefing, and report back. He said that they had gone back to Katutura after hearing that there had been violence there. They were, he said, the source of the factual statement concerning Swapo infighting contained in his editorial and of the assertion that Swapo would once again come with accusations of police complicity – and that this time the police were indeed required to intervene. It was put to him that a responsible editor would have awaited an investigation before expressing this editorial opinion. He said that there was only one conclusion to be drawn from the information supplied to him by his reporters, and that was why he had written that editorial then. He strenuously stated that he would not spread untruths (now termed 'fake news') through an editorial.

Bryan also put to him that when shocking ('opspraakwekkende') cases of security force abuses had been exposed, not a word of these had been reported in his newspaper. He was unrepentant in his response, retorting that it was 'actually his choice as to what should be placed in his newspaper'. Bryan went further and suggested to him that his newspaper's reporting regularly amounted to a 'totale verswyging' (total concealment) of the truth. He objected to that description, and the attack inherent in it against his newspaper and the integrity of those involved in it.

Erasmus was also asked about the commentary that appeared in his publication under the name of 'Kerneels gooi korrels en krummels' ('Kerneels scatters kernels and crumbs'). He acknowledged that he was the author of that regular column. Shortly after the incident, he penned a piece under the heading 'Shots (of air) and toy guns' ('Windskote en popgewere'). The text included: 'Something to giggle about is Dan Tjongarero and Niko Bessinger's shooting with words ['geskietery met woorde'] after Swapo's little thing ['dingetjie'] of Sunday in Katutura'. We had felt that this piece was denigrating and in appalling taste on behalf of Shifidi's family. Bryan raised it. But Erasmus expressed no regret and said it was intended to refer to Dan and Niko's reaction afterwards.

One of *Die Republikein's* reporters, André de Bruin, was then called. He materially contradicted Erasmus and candidly pointed out that he and Travers had not attended the rally at all (which also accorded with Dan's recollection) and had only driven to Katutura after being tipped off about an outbreak of violence (no doubt by police sources as Travers in particular was close to the security police and to Koevoet). De Bruin said he had only taken photographs while Travers had taken notes. They had first gone to the Katutura Police Station and then tried to interview some of the injured at the hospital – with more success than John Liebenberg. He confirmed that he and Travers had attended the police press conference afterwards. He denied that his source had informed him that the fighting had been between different factions of Swapo or that there was Swapo infighting. When pressed on this subject, he became evasive and Bryan put to him that he was involved in a cover-up and was refusing to tell the truth to the inquest.

This evidence (especially by Erasmus) represents a low point for journalism in Namibia, particularly in view of what was subsequently established. Travers and De Bruin are now deceased. Erasmus, although long since retired, continued to contribute reports and columns for *Die Republikein* until very recently up to his death in his 80s. None of these journalists has, to my knowledge, ever expressed any regret for or even properly acknowledged their shamefully misleading reporting of Shifidi's death and their complicity in a cover-up.

The final witness, Bernardt Shiimi, was called on the last day scheduled for the hearing. He had been at the rally and spoke of a white pickup speeding suspiciously away from the scene after picking up two black men near to where Shifidi had been slain. This had occurred shortly after the violence had broken out. He spoke of confusion as Swapo marshals had chased after some of the disruptors. The pickup driver was also a black man but Shiimi did not note down the vehicle's registration number.

All this evidence had taken a few days. It had received wide coverage and excited considerable interest. Many Swapo supporters and sympathisers who had filled the court each day felt we had made much progress by exposing a hopelessly inadequate police investigation. I was frustrated that no concrete evidence had emerged concerning the identity and origin of those who had broken up the meeting and any possible involvement or collusion on the part of the security forces.

At the end of the day preceding Shiimi's evidence, Hosea received a very promising lead concerning 101 Battalion involvement. His close friend Akapandi John Endjala had heard from his younger brother who lived in their home village in northern Namibia that the latter had bussed some 101 Battalion members to Windhoek to disrupt the rally. His younger brother may be willing to talk to Hosea. Because of surveillance, we felt that Hosea should proceed to the Ondangwa area very early the next day with Akapandi for fear that this key witness could be got to ahead of us. Hosea would aim to speak to him on the same afternoon, write up an affidavit overnight and have it signed off first thing the following morning.

We did not think Hosea's absence during Shiimi's evidence would be noticed as he and I had been alternating as instructing attorney during the proceedings. We waited for Shiimi's evidence to be completed before broaching the question of a postponement with the prosecutor for the purpose of obtaining evidence, which we said had very recently come to light. We intimated that we needed a few days but dared not say more for fear of revealing any indication of the identity and location of our witness or the nature of his testimony. The prosecutor, who had become increasingly collegial in the course of the proceedings, agreed not to oppose our application for a brief adjournment. We jointly approached the Magistrate in chambers to say that a day or two was needed to investigate a lead that might result in us applying to call one or more witnesses. Without demur, the Magistrate granted an adjournment until the following Tuesday (14 July).

Hosea had, in the meantime, discreetly and expeditiously driven to the Ondangwa area to meet Martin Endjala well before the curfew. He was overwhelmed by Martin's account. Hosea transcribed his detailed notes overnight into an affidavit and very early the next morning took Endjala to a bank manager as commissioner of oaths to swear to the handwritten affidavit, signed shortly after the bank opened for business on 10 July. Hosea headed straight back to Windhoek, armed with the explosive affidavit. His evident delight at this breakthrough on his return was more than justified.

Martin Endjala drove small to medium-sized busses for a living. During the last week of November 1986, he had been approached by Jacob Thomas, a member of 101 Battalion, for a bus to transport soldiers to a course in Okahandja, the seat of a large military base about 80 km north of Windhoek at the end of the month. On Saturday 29 November 1986, Endjala had arrived at the 101 Battalion base and been paid in full by a uniformed white officer to transport 27 men to Okahandja and back. Another bus driver had been engaged to take another group of 27 soldiers. Later that day, they had set out on the road south. The soldiers had been dressed in civilian attire and had with them a large supply of basic weapons in the form of bows and arrows, knives and knobkieries.

Upon reaching Okahandja, Thomas explained to Endjala that it was not clear at which military base they would sleep and that they should press on to Windhoek. It was then that he disclosed that they were actually travelling south to attend a Swapo rally to be held in Windhoek the next day. When arriving at a base in Windhoek, they had been accompanied by a military motorcyclist in uniform to yet another base, only to be told that the soldiers would in fact be sleeping over at a base just outside Okahandja. After dropping them off, Endjala had agreed with Thomas to meet the following day.

On that fateful day, he had accompanied Thomas to the rally. They had positioned themselves near the stage. While standing there, they had been joined by some of the accompanying soldiers, including Nangolo Josef who said that his group had arrived at the meeting in a Ford pickup, parked on the western side of the open area (as had been identified by John Liebenberg). Josef said that the others had remained at the pickup and he had then left to join them.

One of the group had come across from the pickup to Thomas

and Endjala and said they should now leave the meeting as 'trouble' was about to start. Endjala had left at once in the company of his assistant driver and Thomas. They had driven directly to the agreed rendezvous under the Swawek Bridge nearby Katutura on the national road to Okahandja. On arriving there, Endjala had recognised a white Ford pickup, waiting under the bridge. The leader of the group from 101 Battalion, known only to him as Kashiimbi, had been behind the wheel. A few members of the group had been sitting in the back of the pickup. Another vehicle had soon joined them – a beige Toyota 4×4 pickup driven by a white man in the company of another. Several members of the group had been on the back of that pickup, all in civilian clothes. Endjala had recognised one of the white men as an officer he had seen at the headquarters of 101 Battalion's near Oluno, when he had been paid.

When they had arrived back at the military base near Okahandja, it had been established that three members of the original group were missing. The white officer in the beige pickup had returned to Windhoek and later returned with two men. It was said that one remained missing.

A celebratory braai had been held and attended by about six white officers. Some members of the group had complained of injuries they had received from the Swapo marshals and said if it had not been for the appearance of police in Casspirs, they would have feared for their lives at the hands of the Swapo marshals. They had said it was a good thing that the plan was for them to run towards the police station as the police intervention had saved them.

Endjala concluded by referring to their return to Ondangwa on the Monday morning. He had dropped the soldiers off in Oluno, and not at the military base. He had been unaware of their plan and had merely been engaged to transport them. Some time afterwards, he had heard from Thomas that the missing soldier had since returned to the base. Thomas had been killed in action in May 1987, but

Kashiimbi was still in the service of 101 Battalion with the rank of corporal.

This testimony was groundbreaking. We had not yet encountered such graphic evidence of direct complicity on the part of the security forces in criminal conduct against opponents of the apartheid state and its local surrogates.

At almost the same time as this breakthrough, Dan had burst into my office, his face brimming with satisfaction. He had finally been able to trace Shilongo Iipumbu, the Swapo marshal on duty at the rally who had identified Martin Iipinge by name as part of 101 Battalion. He had spoken to Dan at the meeting and to fellow marshals in the days that followed. But Dan had been unable to locate him straight afterwards when I had asked to see him to take a full statement from him. Dan had kept up his search for Iipumbu but was repeatedly told that he had suddenly left for northern Namibia. Everyone had assumed that he had gone into exile following the rally as nothing had been heard from him for some time.

Iipumbu was in the north for several months after the incident and returned to Windhoek following the publicity generated by the inquest. Dan said he had useful information. As this was a significant development, I called Hartmut to join us to share in the news. Dan said that Iipumbu had been able to note down the vehicle registration number of the suspicious Ford pickup that had featured in many accounts as being the repository for the weapons used by the assailants in their attack and for their speedy getaway. Hartmut undertook to make an enquiry at the registering office about the ownership of the vehicle as soon as it opened the following morning and to take a full statement from Iipumbu.

Iipumbu's affidavit shed more light on the events of that day. As everyone was gathering before the rally had started, he had been approached for a Swapo poster by a group of three men. He had recognised one of them as a member of 101 Battalion. He had seen him in uniform when visiting the northern areas. Iipumbu had told a fellow Swapo marshal, Axel Johannes, and said they should keep an eye on the group. Johannes had thought one of the others may have been a member of Koevoet.

Iipumbu and Johannes had followed the group to the western side of the open area in the vicinity of the Lutheran Church and spotted a white Ford pickup there. They had seen a larger group coming from that direction towards the pickup and open area where the rally had been held. Iipumbu had seen them grab knobkieries and bows and arrows from the Ford pickup. He had immediately suspected foul play and made a note of the vehicle's registration number, SW 60175. He had made his way quickly to the podium to inform Dan of his concerns. Dan had said he would make an urgent announcement to alert the crowd to be vigilant as soon as the translation of the last portion of the speaker's address was completed. Before Dan could do so, the group had ploughed violently into the crowd. Chaos had erupted as people had fled in different directions.

Iipumbu had then turned from the podium, ran towards the Ford pickup and spotted about ten weapon-bearing assailants fleeing the scene, chased by Swapo marshals, running towards the Katutura shopping centre and the police station. Iipumbu had joined their pursuit, running past Shifidi whom he saw slumped motionless against a pickup as well as another person who had an arrow protruding from his leg. As they were receiving attention, he had continued to give chase.

The police had suddenly appeared in force and shot and injured one of the marshals. (This had been announced at the time. The police's excuse for firing live rounds was that he was carrying a mock AK-47 rifle made of wood, which was mistaken for the real thing. I have seen several of these replicas, which Swapo marshals ostentatiously sported. Even to my untrained eye, they were not remotely the real thing.) The shooting of the marshal had had the effect, no doubt intended, of the pursuit being instantly abandoned and allowing the assailants to slip away. Iipumbu had returned to the injured to see if he could help. Police reinforcements in Casspirs had then arrived, firing teargas and rubber bullets at the dispersing crowd and beating people with sjamboks as they scattered for safety and cover.

On the following day (Monday, 1 December 1986), Iipumbu had gone to visit the injured in hospital. He had recognised one of the group of three who had approached him before the rally among those who had been injured, and asked him who he was. The response had been Martin Iipinge. Iipumbu had asked him where he worked. The evasive answer had been that he did not work in Windhoek, but had travelled for the meeting. Iipumbu had reported the information to his colleagues, who in turn had passed it on to Dan. When Iipumbu had called at the hospital to visit the injured the following day, Iipinge was no longer in the ward. Iipumbu had left Windhoek soon afterwards.

Hartmut's enquiry at the vehicle registering authority had revealed that a vehicle bearing that registration number was reflected as belonging to the South African Police, care of Police Headquarters, Windhoek, even though the vehicle was listed as a Datsun and not a Ford.

Hartmut had meticulously minuted Iipumbu's affidavit and attached the damning evidence from the registration authority bearing those ownership details, together with a few photographs taken by John Liebenberg to illustrate the various key points in Iipumbu's affidavit.

Armed with the incriminating evidence in the two affidavits, Hosea, Hartmut and I accompanied Bryan to the acting Attorney-General, Estienne Pretorius. Bryan had contacted him beforehand about the meeting and insisted that Brigadier Piet Fouché, the overall head of criminal investigation be present rather than Smit as we had no confidence in the latter. (Fouché was widely respected as a detective and had not to our knowledge been involved with the security branch in their highly politicised work and their excesses. He later became the first Inspector-General of the Namibian Police at independence. I was consulted about that appointment and had supported it.)

Fouché was present at the meeting. Pretorius was most perturbed by what was contained in the affidavits and said as much. He assured us that a further investigation would proceed at the highest level and that the perpetrators, no matter what rank, would be brought to book. Fouché said little during the meeting but undertook to oversee the further investigation and assured us that he too would do so without fear or favour. He asked for our cooperation, especially in approaching Martin Endjala, and asked if Hosea could accompany him or one of his officers for the purpose of identifying a key suspect, Kashiimbi.

It was a positive meeting and we agreed to assist. Although Hartmut, Hosea and I were slightly sceptical that the real suspects would ever be charged, Bryan was more confident. He knew both Fouché and Pretorius and respected their professionalism. We felt that even if the main culprits were ultimately not charged, it would be more than likely that prosecuted subordinates would end up fingering them.

Hosea left for Ondangwa the next morning to meet Detective Inspector Oswald Theart, a thoroughly professional detective nominated by Fouché to accompany Hosea to get Martin Endjala to identify Kashiimbi for the latter's arrest. The plan was to do so at Kashiimbi's residence before he reported to the base the following morning. By the time they arrived at his home with Endjala, Kashiimbi had already left. They proceeded to the base, armed with a warrant for Kashiimbi's arrest. The Officer Commanding 101 Battalion refused to permit Theart to carry out the arrest on the base and ordered them to leave. Theart was infuriated and in Hosea's presence reported this to Fouché, who was likewise displeased at this deliberate defiance of the law.

The stakes had suddenly increased. We now knew that something would happen.

In the meantime, the inquest had again been postponed to 21 July so that the statements could be finalised and to accommodate our meeting with the acting Attorney-General. When the inquest finally resumed, Truter read the affidavits of Endjala and Iipumbu into the record and made his formal finding, required by the inquest legislation, that the cause of Shifidi's death had been massive bleeding as a result of his artery being severed by a sharp object, such as a knife, which constituted an offence on the part of unknown persons as 'part of a group operation to disrupt a political meeting.' He said that it was not possible to identify the culprits but referred the matter to the Attorney-General for further investigation and to determine whether to prosecute.

It seemed from all the evidence at our disposal that Shifidi was probably not personally targeted but happened to be at the wrong place at the wrong time.

That was the end of the inquest.

It came as an anticlimax, of course, following all the frenetic activity over the previous days and the preceding cover-up of multilayered complicity, but it was strictly speaking the correct ruling according to that legislation. It was now up to the new police investigation and Attorney-General to charge those responsible.

Several months passed before I received an off-the-record indication that a prosecution would go ahead; 1987 came to a close without any concrete indication of who would be charged and when. I had by then given six months' notice of my resignation from Lorentz and Bone, to leave the firm on 29 February 1988 to set up the Legal Assistance Centre, Namibia's first public interest law firm. I would do so as an advocate but first needed to do pupillage lasting four months, starting on 1 March 1988. The centre would commence its operations upon completion of this period in early July 1988.

During the first month of my pupillage in March 1988, Pretorius, now installed as Attorney-General, decided that six defendants would stand trial for Shifidi's murder and on a further charge of public violence. Indictments were served. The six were due to answer to the charges in court on 21 March 1988. Their identities were revealing: Colonel J.H. Vorster, the head of military intelligence at SWATF Headquarters in Windhoek; Colonel W.H. Welgemoed, the Officer Commanding 101 Battalion; Commandant A.J. Botes of SWATF Headquarters (presumably also of intelligence); Lieutenant N.J. Prinsloo of 101 Battalion; Eusebius Kashiimbi, a corporal of 101 Battalion; and Rifleman Steven Festus of that battalion. This was indeed dramatic, demonstrating that the prosecution's case was what we had all along suspected – an operation by the South African military to break up the Swapo rally violently, planned and approved high up.

Surprisingly there were no police accomplices, despite indications of their complicity, including supplying the vehicle and facilitating the escape of the perpetrators from the meeting (as well as the inexplicable dearth of evidence in their investigation for who had been involved).

What followed was even more dramatic, however. It seemed unthinkable.

On the morning the accused were scheduled to appear, the South African state president, P.W. Botha, intervened in the trial. A certificate at his instance under section 103 ter of the Defence Act to stop the proceedings was handed up in court. It was signed by the AG this time and not the cabinet of the IG. It stated that the president had authorised him to do so, and ordered that the criminal trial not proceed. The section empowered the state president to direct the minister of justice (whose powers were delegated to the AG) to stop court proceedings 'instituted by reason of an act done, commanded, ordered or directed in good faith for the purpose of or in connection with the prevention or suppression of terrorism in an operational area'.

Commenting to the media, the AG, Louis Pienaar, himself a qualified lawyer, inexplicably said that the certificate in no way interfered with the independence of the courts as the parties were free to test the certificate in court and the courts would then decide if President Botha had acted within the law. The Bar Council, chaired by Bryan, condemned the certificate as a 'flagrant interference in the normal process of the law.' It also expressed its incredulity and shock that the decision could have been taken. In his statement, the IG's minister of justice, Fanuel Kozonguizi, said that the Cabinet had previously indicated that it would not want to be part of the issuing of certificates under section 103 ter (as had occurred in the murder trial of Frans Uapota's alleged killers) and stressed that the Cabinet had not been involved in this decision and would prefer that the law take its normal course. He expressed his support for the Attorney-General's decision to prosecute the military defendants and his confidence in the courts to determine the guilt or innocence of those accused. The Council of Churches of Namibia also condemned the issuing of the certificate, as did Swapo.

Hosea called me to discuss this shock development. We agreed that it should be challenged. He would advise Hilda as next of kin of her options and convey my views to her. He and Hartmut prepared a brief for Jeremy Gauntlett, assisted by Les Rose-Innes, to prepare an application to court to set aside the certificate and for the criminal trial to continue. They quickly set about this and the application was completed by 29 March 1988.

The issuing of the certificate was challenged on several grounds including that a football field in a suburb of Windhoek where a lawful political meeting was being held could not qualify as an operational area for the purpose of section 103 ter. It was also contended that there was no factual basis for the president to have properly been of the opinion that the violent disruption of the meeting and the killing of Shifidi could have been in good faith or for the purposes of or in connection with preventing or suppressing terrorism or that it was in the national interest that the prosecution be stopped.

The state president, the AG and South African minister of defence opposed the application to set aside the certificate that stopped the murder trial. Once again, they all denied that Hilda had standing to bring the challenge. It was especially astonishing that the AG himself took issue with her standing after his earlier media statement when issuing the certificate, that it could be challenged in court in support of his equally astounding assertion that the independence of the courts was not affected by the certificate. If she could not challenge it, then who on earth could do so? Adding insult to injury, they saw fit even to dispute that Hilda was in fact Shifidi's daughter – an issue never raised at the inquest. This spurious tactic was easily addressed. Her birth and baptismal certificates clearly showed that he was her father and an affidavit from his sister confirmed that.

The AG said that he had no discretion on the issuing of the certificate once the resident had decided to issue it.

State President P.W. Botha himself made an affidavit opposing the application. He contended that the entire territory of Namibia was an operational area for the purposes of the Defence Act and that he had formed the opinion that what had occurred on the fateful day was advised, commanded, ordered, directed or done in an operational area in good faith to suppress or prevent terrorism. He gave no reasons for this opinion. Instead, he said that, under section 103 ter, he was not obliged to give reasons when ordering a certificate. It emerged that he had not initially been inclined to authorise the issuing of a certificate. But, after an additional memorandum had been submitted by Brigadier Van Vuuren stating that it would not be in the national interest for the prosecution to continue, he had decided that the certificate should be issued. He refused to disclose the contents of that memorandum on the grounds of state privilege – also his basis to

212

refuse copies of the report he had received from the minister of defence to motivate the issuing of a certificate. Significantly, he declined to say which further considerations had induced him to change his mind about the issue. He did mention, though, that the intended prosecution could demoralise the military and undermine its effectiveness were it to proceed.

The case was heard by a full bench on 12 August 1988. Judge President Berker presided. Judges Harold Levy and Johan Strydom made up the complement of three judges. Jeremy's cogent arguments attacking the certificate were well received. The judges seemed dismayed by the unchallenged inquest evidence to the effect that a group of soldiers in civilian clothes, wielding an assortment of weapons, deliberately and violently disrupted a lawful political meeting, perpetrating serious assaults and causing the death of Shifidi.

The evidence pointed to a planned operation on instructions and with the knowledge of those holding positions of command in the military. Their concerns about this were demonstrated in the many questions they posed to the respondents' counsel during argument.

At the conclusion of argument, judgment was reserved.

The judgments took several months to finalise and were handed down on 20 March 1989. The court swept aside the certificate and found that it was no bar for the continuation of the prosecution.

Each judge wrote a separate judgment. Harold Levy dealt with the challenge on Hilda's standing and roundly rejected it. He also found that the president and those advising him had not placed any facts to show how a football field where a lawful political meeting was held in a suburb of Windhoek could possibly be an operational area. This requirement of the section had not been met. The certificate was invalid for this reason alone. He also found that the report provided to the minister of defence by a certain M.F. Ackerman, chief legal advisor, created a totally wrong impression of the events and amounted to a distortion. No reasonable person, if apprised of the true facts, could have come to the opinion that the soldiers' conduct was in good faith in suppressing or preventing terrorism.

Judge Strydom agreed that the certificate should be set aside, but advanced different reasons. In a carefully reasoned ruling, he referred to the undisputed fact that some 50 members of 101 Battalion were ordered to disrupt a legal meeting and to assault those attending it in the circumstances established at the inquest.

He concluded: 'However one looks at the evidence, it is extremely difficult to credit those responsible for the operation having bona fide intended to suppress and prevent thereby acts of terrorism . . .' He pointed out that the section required the state president to come to the conclusion 'that the conduct ordered was bona fide and was for the prevention and suppression of terrorism'. This would need to be established before an opinion as to whether preventing the trial from proceeding was in the national interest. He was satisfied that the 'discretion exercised by the [state president] was so unreasonable as to give rise to an inference that he did not apply his mind to the facts and circumstances of this case, and to what is required by s103 ter (4), when he opined that the act ordered by members of the Defence Force, and executed by such members, was so ordered to prevent or suppress terrorism'.

The Judge President agreed with the result proposed by his two colleagues and added some reasons of his own in his concurring opinion.

Within days of the ruling, the respondents brought an application for leave to appeal. It was heard and granted on 17 April 1989. The appeal was directed to the Appellate Division of South Africa, then the highest court of appeal for cases arising in Namibia.

Events also overtook this appeal. UN Security Council Resolution 435 was implemented on 1 April 1989. The peace process and election under UN supervision took place over the ensuing months and, like the appeal in Victoria Mweuhanga's case, it would not be heard before independence. As a result, the accused in this case also never stood trial. A component of the peace plan was a widely worded indemnity proclamation that would provide a shield against prosecution for a criminal act of violence like this, as determined by the AG. In the dying days of the peace plan, the AG published a notice under the proclamation granting amnesty to all members of the SADF and SWATF (as well as the police, which included Koevoet) for criminal conduct that occurred in the course of their duties and functions.[53]

Shifidi's killers thus escaped prosecution even though it could be argued that their criminal conduct went outside the scope of their duties or functions under the Defence Act. The extradition of those in South Africa could thus have been sought after independence, but the new government declined to investigate doing this because of its policy of national reconciliation, which was said to preclude a prosecution of this kind and presumably because it was thought by many that the notice under the amnesty proclamation was also a bar. I have never shared either view.

One can speculate as to what was contained in Brigadier Van Vuuren's report that had caused P.W. Botha to change his mind and order the certificate. I suspect that Van Vuuren may have alerted Botha to the risk of officers higher up than the colonels – as well as others within the security establishment – being implicated, especially given the overt political purpose of violently disrupting the rally and the political mileage to be gained by the security establishment and its political allies in the IG who were uneasy about Swapo being able to hold meetings lawfully after our court victory in the *Maxuilili* case.

The memory of Immanuel Shifidi lives on, though. Within months, if not days, of his death, the community renamed the open area where

---

53   In Government Notice AG 16 of 9 February 1990 (Gazette 5894), the AG declared a general amnesty in respect of persons 'who while they were members of the SADF, including SWATF, in the performance of their duties and functions in the territory, have performed . . . any act which amounts to a criminal offence . . .'

he was slain as Shifidi Square. The recently founded and highly effective national student movement, NANSO, with strong representation in schools throughout the country and especially in Katutura, initiated a move to rename a school in Katutura as the Immanuel Shifidi Secondary School. The idea caught on quickly with students at the school and their parents. The community effectively unilaterally brought about the change of name. In the face of the widespread support for the name change and its exclusive use by most connected to the school, the IG was eventually begrudgingly obliged to accept the new name. It rightfully remains.

9

A ruthlessly enforced curfew

Within three months of his appointment as first AG in 1977, Judge M.T. Steyn, clothed with wide legislative and executive powers, issued the Security Districts Proclamation, AG 9 of 1977 (AG 9). It provided the legal framework for the effective state of martial law in the northern regions. When issuing AG 9 in 1977, the AG simultaneously declared Owambo, Kavango and Eastern Caprivi as security districts. AG 9 soon became notorious for its sweeping powers of arrest and detention accorded to the security forces in security districts. Less discussed was section 3 of AG 9, which gave the AG wide powers to issue orders restricting movement and activities in security districts.

In June 1978, the AG issued the first of two orders under section 3. These would together constitute the legal basis for the curfew imposed on Owambo. The first order prohibited any vehicle movement at night in Owambo, except with the written permission of a peace officer or officer of the security forces. The second order followed a year later in June 1979. It prohibited any person from being 'at any place in the district of Owambo outside the boundary of a stand, lot or site or other place intended for human habitation, at any time during the night without permission' of a peace officer or security force officer.

Contravening the curfew constituted a crime, as did any act of obstructing, restricting or hindering members of the security forces in the exercise of their powers, duties or functions under AG 9. It was ruthlessly enforced, often with fatal consequences. Those who ventured in vehicles or even moved on foot at night were frequently shot at, mostly without prior warning. Many innocent people were killed in this way. The ban on movement at night was also the source of severe hardship and suffering. In the case of medical emergencies, the wait until sunrise could and sometimes did have grave consequences too.

By the mid-1980s, I was travelling to the northern area of Owambo for work with increasing frequency. As more people became aware of the possibility of legal redress, more cases of security force atrocities were reported, requiring more visits to consult clients and witnesses. The deep-seated disaffection with the curfew and its inhumane application in Owambo was a recurring theme on most visits. There were regular instances of security force excesses under the cloak of the curfew. A particular spate of unjustified shootings at civilians, especially just after dusk and also later at night during 1986, caused mounting resentment.

Church and community leaders bitterly complained about its effects whenever I travelled to the north.

The then secretary of the ethnically constituted Legislative Assembly for Owambos, Oswald Shivute, increasingly contacted Hosea and me as well as *The Namibian* about security force excesses in the area. Many residents would call upon his offices to complain about security force atrocities. Most of those complaints centred on the application of the curfew.

During the 1980s, August was the confirmation season in Owambo for the Anglican Church. In fact, it usually took about six weeks for Bishop James to complete his round of annual confirmation services there. That time of the year was presumably chosen for sound practical reasons. The comparatively mild climate then meant that very long confirmation services – at the best of times constituting a test of endurance, going on for well over four hours – were more manageable for all concerned. The curfew dictated a starting time that was not too early as several of the congregants would need to travel considerable distances to their churches on foot and could not commence that trek until after sunrise. This would be too much in the blistering heat of the summer months.

And so it was that any discussion with Bishop James during August 1986 about human rights matters meant meeting up with him in the north.

The confirmation service at the Ondangwa parish coincided with some of my other commitments at that time. Bishop James had suggested I arrive at the church four hours after the designated starting time. It turned out to be an optimistic projection. About three quarters of an hour later, James' jubilant procession emerged from the church and he stationed himself near the entrance to greet the appreciative departing congregants. It was a significant event in that church's calendar – confirmations and the annual visit of their highly popular and respected bishop to their parish. Bishop James called me over to be present while he greeted each congregant, introducing me as well. After the customary pleasantries were exchanged, the subject often shifted to hardships caused by security force elements in their respective areas. Most of these concerned the curfew.

A mini feast had been prepared for the bishop at the home of Mr Eliakim and Mrs Elizabeth Namundjebo. Upon their invitation, I accompanied him to our gracious hosts. The conversation soon turned to the curfew and more recent incidents where security force elements had indiscriminately fired at people moving after dusk. I related the latest complaints referred by Oswald Shivute, who was becoming a vital conduit of instructions to Hosea and myself on human rights abuses in the north.

I enquired from Bishop James whether the time had not arrived for us to tackle the curfew head-on in court together, instead of each time seeking to address individual problems caused by it. His whole face instantly lit up. I explained that it would be a tough challenge as the recognised grounds under common law to take on subordinate legislation were very confined and that the court would in all likelihood be disinclined to assist us in what would be perceived to be a serious challenge to the status quo and what was widely considered to be a vital cog in the military occupation of the northern war zone of Owambo. The curfew notice was subordinate legislation because it was proclaimed by an official (the AG) under powers conferred upon that position under a law, as opposed to being the outcome of a deliberative legislative process. It could be challenged on the grounds that the terms of the curfew exceeded the powers granted to the official under the empowering law. And it could also be tackled on grounds of gross unreasonableness or being void for vagueness or enacted in bad faith. It was going to be a long shot as those who determined unreasonableness (the judges) would have little appreciation for the circumstances there, never having set foot in the north.

Even if unsuccessful in terms of the court outcome, it could possibly result in an amelioration of the curfew by an amendment to the notices. And at the very least, it may even be applied less ruthlessly by enforcing some accountability in court and exposing the appalling abuses which the curfew facilitated.

I asked him if he would be prepared to be an applicant again.

Before I would reach the end of my justification for legal intervention, Bishop James was beaming and could hardly contain his enthusiasm. His immediate response was, 'Where can I sign? Where can I sign? Now. Please let me sign up at once.' He then resumed in a more serious tone: 'Nothing would give me more pleasure. I'll make a point to see Bishop Kleopas [Dumeni] about this tomorrow.'

Bishop Dumeni, who headed the largest denomination, the Evan-

gelical Lutheran Church in Namibia (ELCIN), was based near Ondangwa at Oniipa, some 15 km southeast.

I undertook to approach Bishop Haushiku of the Catholic Church
upon my return to Windhoek. He too was excited at the prospect of
taking on the curfew in court.

A few days later, Bishop Dumeni unexpectedly arrived at my office.
He felt so strongly about mounting a challenge to the curfew that he
wanted to convey his instruction and emphatic support for it to me
in person.

I had already brainstormed about the basis for a challenge with
Hosea and enlisted Jeremy Gauntlett's help to settle our application.
It was to be brought by the three bishops in their personal capacities.
Bishop Dumeni lived in the north and the other two bishops spent
much of their time there in the course of their pastoral duties, despite
being based in Windhoek. Their respective churches would be applicants too, representing the communities whose lives were imperilled
by it and also because of the way in which the curfew affected church
activities – ruling out evening and early morning services and cur-
tailing meetings and activities. These had always been the lifeblood
of the churches, like midnight services at Easter and Christmas,
evening services and bible study groups, youth activities and the like.

Hosea and I also felt that the reference in the curfew notice to a
'stand, lot or other place intended for human habitation' defied application to the actual circumstances of more than 80 per cent of the
people of the area who did not live in the designated and demarcated
sites in the townships of Oshakati, Ongwediva and Ondangwa.

The rest of Owambo was communal land with portions allocated
to family units by local headmen and women. These homes in the
rural areas would usually comprise a unit of several structures or
dwelling quarters in close proximity. Mostly, but not always, this unit
would be surrounded by a fence. We referred in detail to this type
of home unit in the application by the term for it in Oshindongo,

'egumbo'. We pointed out that these land allocations were not formally surveyed and not always clearly demarcated. It was also not clear where human habitation ended and areas for stock and other purposes and mahango fields started within the allocated portion. We also pointed out that a person's entitlement was not confined to their allotted area and could extend to certain communal areas, such as grazing areas and meeting places.

We also made it clear that toilet facilities were often not found within the egumbo area. This was because almost all rural areas were at that time not yet served by waterborne sewerage. Most residents were then obliged to perform natural functions in the bush, invariably outside and some distance from the egumbo or in a toilet constructed some distance from the egumbo. We contended that the notice was grossly unreasonable on this ground alone. It was thus unlawful to leave the egumbo to go to the toilet at night. Even though we facetiously called this our 'shit' point, I felt it was a particularly compelling one, demonstrating how unreasonable the curfew was.

Another powerful point we raised was that the system of exemption was incapable of execution. In the case of medical emergencies like births, illnesses or injuries, people would be obliged to contravene the curfew to obtain permission. This would place their lives in danger as security force elements readily fired at moving vehicles without first attempting to enquire about the purpose of travel. Furthermore, the distances people would need to travel to the nearest military or police base to secure permission may be considerable, compounding this very real risk.

We gave the example of one of Hosea's clients, Petrus Nataneal, who had been shot and injured at his home at dusk when venturing to the boundary of his small allotment of land to speak to his neighbour from the adjacent allotment. He was said to be in breach of the curfew.

These issues were articulated in Bishop James's affidavit, superbly settled by Jeremy. The other two bishops confirmed his statement and joined the application in their personal capacities and on behalf of their churches.

The cabinet of the IG (which had been installed the previous year with limited powers), the AG and the South African minister of defence were cited as respondents. They all opposed the application and were separately represented in their opposition.

The chairperson of the cabinet, Dirk Mudge, made an affidavit, strenuously opposing the application. A number of further affidavits were attached to his in support of the contentions he advanced. There was, of course, the usual point-taking contesting the standing of the churches – whether they could sue as institutions. This had by now become a customary tactic employed by the lawyers who represented governmental parties in security-related cases – even where life-and-death issues were raised, as was the case in this application. Mudge conceded that toilet facilities may not be within what he crudely described as the 'kraal enclosure' but asserted that inhabitants made use of 'alternative arrangements', without specifying what on earth they were. He also said that the curfew did not result in any 'apparently insurmountable problems'.

Even though he accepted that the terms 'erf, lot or site' did not accurately reflect the description of homes in rural areas of Owambo, Mudge contended that the notice was sufficiently clear for people to understand. In support of this statement, he attached affidavits from some well-known DTA-supporting headmen and the head of Etango, euphemistically termed a cultural organisation that operated under the patronage of the security forces and the IG and engaged in propaganda dissemination directed at discrediting Swapo and supporting the security forces. They said they understood the operation of the curfew.

Mudge also said that the curfew was absolutely necessary to combat Swapo's insurgency in the area. This statement was supported by affidavits provided by senior South African military officers, explaining that most acts of insurgency were perpetrated under the cover of darkness.

Mudge also said that the exemption system worked well and that no instances of hardships in that regard had been recorded. Nor had there been complaints about the operation of the curfew. It strained belief that he could have made these two statements. I was always inundated with complaints about the curfew – a consistent feature of any visit to the north. And I had also heard of difficulties arising in cases of medical emergencies. It simply served to demonstrate how out of touch members of the IG were of the actual situation in Owambo, becoming victims of their own propaganda relentlessly spewed out in their newspapers and in the broadcast media controlled by the apartheid state.

The South African officer commanding of the military forces in the Owambo area made an affidavit in opposition to the challenge on behalf of the minister of defence and AG. He was equally cavalier in asserting that the use of toilet facilities created no problem at all with the application of the curfew provisions. He said that this was demonstrated by the fact that we had not referred to any incidents of people being 'disturbed' by security force members when relieving themselves. He echoed Mudge's unsupported statement that 'alternative arrangements' were utilised, also not remotely alluding to what these were. He also said that cases of medical emergencies reported at military bases resulted in assistance. Only vehicles not stopping at roadblocks would be fired upon and those engaging in movement at night would first be challenged by soldiers. In the case of a medical emergency, permission for night movement would be granted. Like Mudge, he contended that the curfew was vital for the security forces to combat the armed insurgency of Swapo, providing extensive details through his senior staff officer for operations of those activities in a separate affidavit. These scare tactics would bear fruit.

After detailed discussions about the opposition to our application with Jeremy as well as with Hosea and Bishop James, we decided to consult a range of people to refute the three key elements raised in opposition to the application. The first of these concerned the demarcation of egumbos. Both Mudge and the military asserted that they were without exception fenced in and that the language employed in the notice adequately covered them.

The next aspect was the crucial toilet point – to refute the unsupported claim that unexplained 'alternative arrangements' were made and to show that the location of toilet facilities or the places where people would relieve themselves were some distance away and often outside fenced premises and would result in a breach of the curfew when doing so after sunset.

The final focus would be on the system of exemption – to show that it was both unworkable and caused severe hardship.

On the first (and second issue), we decided to engage my old friend Kerry McNamara, an outstanding and visionary architect, as an independent expert. He had lived in Owambo in the late 1960s, supervising the construction of the Ongwediva Training College and other school buildings. His acute powers of professional observation, combined with his sense of humanity and how he socially connected with people, had meant that he had developed a special interest in and understanding of rural housing in the area. He had become particularly interested in the layout of egumbos and other structures and how the spaces were occupied and worked for their inhabitants. He was tasked to explain to the court how dwellings outside the small designated urban areas were erected and occupied. He agreed to travel with me in a small chartered plane on 20 October 1986 to the north for the day to refresh himself on rural housing and describe the dwelling and settlement types as an independent expert. This he did adeptly, aided by Jeremy's deft touches.

Another friend, Tony Figueira, one of Namibia's foremost photographers, accompanied us that day to help with photographs to illustrate the points Kerry would make. We took a number of photographs from the air. We also travelled around for several hours observing settlement types and speaking to occupants about the use of space.

During the previous week Hosea and I had spent three days in Owambo, travelling over 450 km within the area, consulting with a number of witnesses and observing egumbos. These witnesses included Ben Kathindi, who was born and raised in Owambo. He had completed a degree in architecture at Howard University in the US the year before and was then working as an in-house architect for ELCIN (one of the applicants, headed by Bishop Dumeni) and was based at Oniipa in Owambo. Ben confirmed that numerous egumbos were without exterior walls or fences to surround them for varying reasons, including poverty, the duration of the structures and personal preferences. Some residents would move their egumbos after some years. The resulting new egumbo may also be without a surrounding fence for some time until other structures were completed during that transitional phase. Ben also pointed out that in cases where egumbos have toilets, these are situated some distance from the egumbo for obvious reasons of sanitation. In the case of his own family's egumbo, situated some 16 km from Oniipa, the toilet was 80 paces outside the fenced-off egumbo.

Oswald Shivute also made an affidavit, confirming that he received numerous complaints of a serious nature concerning the operation of the curfew. He confirmed that the residents were unclear about what was meant by its terms. In the course of 1985, he received 106 serious complaints and had recorded 58 by mid-October 1986. He also said that he himself had been fired upon at dusk in 1978 while travelling in his motor vehicle in western Owambo. There had been no warning whatsoever. One of the shots narrowly missed him and another shaved the skin of an occupant in his car.

In the course of our travels within Owambo the previous week, I observed and photographed several instances of egumbos which were not surrounded by fences or stockades. I also documented where these egumbos were encountered. I also observed toilets at considerable distances from egumbos and paced those distances myself for the sake of accuracy and photographed them. In two instances, these distances were 45 and 60 paces. In some instances there was partial fencing, also photographed and locations given.

I also attached copies of four recent inquests obtained at the Ondangwa magistrate's office where the curfew had led to the deaths of four ordinary citizens (not alleged to be insurgents). (Inquest investigations are to be conducted into all deaths that are not the result of natural causes and which are not yet the subject of criminal investigation). In two of the cases, the 'challenge' made to the deceased persons was stated to be merely the word 'ila' which simply means the injunction 'come'. This could never have been understood by anyone conversant with the local Oshiwambo dialects as a challenge or to serve any identificatory purpose.

Hosea and I also consulted Solly Amadhila, a specialist paediatrician practising in Owambo. Like Ben, he was born and raised there. He had attended medical school in South Africa and successfully completed his specialisation as a paediatrician at Stellenbosch University. He was then the only paediatrician for the whole of Owambo; he treated both in-patients and out-patients at the Oshakati State Hospital and at Onandjokwe Hospital near Oniipa. A truly impressive professional, Solly accepted that some patients may approach military guards and receive medical treatment as a result – as was said on behalf of the minister of defence. But he disputed the statement that the curfew had no 'inhibitory effect on the movement of the local population in situations of medical emergencies'. Solly said the contrary was, in fact, his experience. The curfew did indeed have a detrimental and inhibitory effect upon the people of Owambo in seeking and obtaining medical assistance for emergency cases at night.

Solly sketched the harm in delaying medical treatment, especially in the case of children where the harm is exacerbated and where dramatic changes in condition can quickly occur in the space of hours. Postponing treatment can be prejudicial and, in some cases, fatal. This was also the case in obstetrics, where 'high-risk' expectant mothers need to be admitted to hospital when going into labour. He proceeded to list complications that can arise, and had arisen in his experience. He said that the cause of many children handicapped by injury at birth had been home births of 'high-risk' pregnancies: labour had commenced at night and the mother had been compelled to give birth at home because of the curfew. He had encountered many such cases, both as a paediatrician and, prior to that, as a medical officer at Oshakati State Hospital.

Solly also stressed that sick children required healthcare service on a 24-hour basis. For instance, in cases of gastroenteritis – then a leading cause of child mortality in Owambo – deaths could frequently be prevented by prompt medical treatment, such as placing a child patient on a drip. He gave other compelling examples where delays in treatment were gravely prejudicial and could even be fatal.

The point about the unstated 'alternative arrangements' for relieving oneself at night within an egumbo was not only factually denied by Ben Kathindi – we also obtained an affidavit from Dr Kenneth Abrahams, a general practitioner in Windhoek, about that assertion being wholly improbable. Unlike his white colleagues in Windhoek, Kenneth was always available to assist in matters medical when it came to evidence in human rights cases. His support was vital, as is demonstrated by an instance that arose when he was away from his practice.

About a year or so before the curfew challenge, one of Hartmut's clients – Alun Roberts, an anti-apartheid activist from England – had been arrested and detained by the security police near Arandis while trying to obtain information about Rössing Uranium for purposes of a campaign against companies investing in Namibia. His parents were besides themselves with worry because he had a chronic medical condition – severe asthma, I think – which required regular medication. Hartmut approached the security police on that score. They said they would see to it that a district surgeon would visit and treat Alun. This, of course, was unacceptable in view of what had happened to Steve Biko: South African district surgeons had acted grossly unprofessionally, and had effectively facilitated the fatal assaults that had led to Biko's death. We certainly had no confidence in a state-employed district surgeon. We insisted that a private doctor should see him. After making extensive and repeated representations to the AG's office on the subject, the security police eventually relented under directive from the AG's office and agreed that a private doctor could see him.

This was a breakthrough. Hartmut asked me to approach my own doctor, who refused point-blank to see Alun. I tried to reason with him, explaining that it set an important precedent and that Alun's parents were desperate with anxiety. All to no avail: he did not want to get involved.

My secretary then contacted every general practitioner's practice listed in the Windhoek telephone directory – all white – to enquire whether the doctor would be prepared – for reward – to treat a detainee patient. The answer was a uniformly resounding no.[54]

Through the Council of Churches, we obtained the name of Dr Varavia, a South African doctor of Indian origin who would consult Alun. He travelled to Windhoek that weekend to see Alun, who was

---

54   Two black doctors, who had started to practise in Katatura, then unknown to me but whom I came to know shortly afterwards, were not listed then. The chronic shortage of black medical practioners at the time, was, according to Solly Amadhila, to be ascribed to two fundamental factors – Bantu education and the fact that it was almost impossible for African students from Namibia (as opposed to those classified as 'Coloured') to gain admission to the medical schools at Wits and UCT. The black section at the University of Natal was the only realistic possibility at the time.

in reasonable health and had access to his medication. His grateful parents were enormously relieved.

After qualifying as a doctor at the University of Cape Town, Kenneth Abrahams completed a postgraduate diploma in tropical medicine and health at the University of Liverpool and qualified as a doctor of medicine in occupational health in Sweden. He returned from exile and set up a general practice in Khomasdal, a residential area designated for coloured people during the times of segregated areas. He explained that it is dangerous to the health of communities to perform natural functions in close proximity to living quarters where no waterborne sewerage is available. In the absence of running water, he pointed out that it was inconceivable that appropriate and satisfactory 'alternative' arrangements could be made. Buckets and other receptacles kept inside an egumbo would, given the hot, humid conditions in the summer months, constitute a serious threat to the health of communities. If they leaked or were knocked over they would attract flies and disease, including highly contagious ones like cholera, typhoid, hepatitis, dysentery, poliomyelitis, intestinal parasites and worms, and gastroenteritis. Constructing 'drops' just outside an egumbo in close proximity to the living quarters would give rise to similar threats to health.

After completing Dr Abrahams's affidavit, we had, I firmly believed, comprehensively refuted all the points raised in defence of the curfew. This would place the court under pressure.

Judge President Berker assembled a full court comprising five judges to sit on the matter – a first. Support for the challenge had swelled in the weeks that had quickly passed since its genesis. Many travelled from Owambo for the hearing on 29 October 1986. The public gallery was packed to capacity long before the designated starting time. The kindly Registrar moved the proceedings to C court, which had an upstairs gallery – no doubt a remnant of the early years when people were racially segregated when attending court. The larger courtroom was still hopelessly insufficient and overflowed into the foyer.

The arguments were long and replete with laborious references to the dry detail of the legal requirements of subordinate legislation and its interpretation. This did not deter attendance over the two full days of argument. The proceedings even spilled over into a third day. The IG was separately represented in court to the South African minister of defence and the AG. Both teams heavily played their trump card – the necessity of the curfew to combat insurgency effectively. Without it, they said there would be mayhem and a dramatic escalation in insurgency and loss of life. They also each took considerable time addressing the legal issues raised in the application.

At the conclusion of the hearing, judgment was reserved. As we were packing away our papers, the senior counsel representing the AG, Johan Conradie called me aside with a friendly gesture.

Highly regarded as an advocate, he was soon afterwards appointed as a judge in Cape Town and later also served in the court of appeal in South Africa with distinction. His address had been clinical, not as long as counsel representing the IG's address, and made far less dramatic reference to scare tactics, being more focused on legal points. He put out his hand and congratulated me on the set of papers we had put together. He magnanimously added that, whatever the court outcome, my clients had been truly well served and that I had highlighted extremely important issues affecting the community in the north. He expressed the hope that, at the very least, the curfew should in the future be applied more humanely.

On 16 January 1987, the Judge President, for a unanimous court, rejected the application. In the introductory section of background facts, the court's ruling referred to the efforts of the security forces to curb Swapo insurgency in Owambo, explaining that heavily armed insurgents infiltrated the area from Angola, planting mines on roads and footpaths, committing acts of sabotage and killing civilians who did not cooperate with them. It was stressed that most of this activity occurred under the cover of darkness. For this reason, the court found that it was necessary to control the movement of people and the curfew had been promulgated 'to protect the local population and to maintain law and order'.

Once these sentiments were expressed – so wholly out of touch with those in whose interest it was claimed that the curfew was enacted to protect – it became clear where the court was headed. The court found that the power to declare a curfew fell within the wide powers accorded to the AG to make laws for the country. The wording of the curfew was within the mandate given to the AG to restrict travel and movement at night. The fact that the restriction upon movement could be relaxed upon application to the security forces meant that it was not unreasonable. The court failed, however, to deal with the fact that the system of relaxation was not capable of implementation, and the practical problems we had set out in such detail. There was also no mention of medical emergencies in the court's judgment at all and nothing of the reality for those who experienced the curfew on a daily basis.

In turning to our point that the wording rendered the curfew a nullity on grounds of unreasonableness because of the toilet point, the court accepted the unsubstantiated assertion by Mudge and the military of 'alternative measures' without even remotely referring to the comprehensive refutation of that unspecified assertion.

The court concluded that the wording of the curfew was 'clear and certainly not unreasonable'. An added aside was that relieving oneself is part of human habitation and having to do so was not hit by the curfew and that people could relieve themselves without first obtaining permission. The court pointed out that people were not ordered to stay within the confines of walls or fences and that the measure had been 'framed' by the lawgiver 'fully aware of the practice of local inhabitants'. A fiction if ever there was one.

The application was dismissed with costs.[55]

---

55   It is reported as *Kauluma and others v Cabinet for the Interim Government of SWA and others* 1988 (2) SA 512 (SWA).

The result was unsurprising. But what was shocking was the failure to refer to any one of the detailed affidavits cataloguing the myriad of problems and the injustice brought about by the curfew. There was not even the faintest allusion to hardship or even inconvenience caused by the curfew – not even in passing.

In this brief whitewash by the court, none of the manifold manifestations of unreasonableness was acknowledged or even as much as mentioned, except the glib reference to the toilet point.

The groundswell of resentment against the curfew on the part of those affected by it had galvanised unprecedented support for the application. *The Namibian's* coverage of the case had no doubt assisted, as well as the churches' having fervently embraced the challenge. This case, more than any other I had been involved in before or since, had ignited a sense of purpose to bring accountability through the courts for injustice experienced in the daily lives of more than half the country's population. Even though there was no trace of an acknowledgement of any injustice by the court, this did not detract from the advance it represented for the development of a rights culture.

Some more tangible, beneficial consequences of the case emerged. Even though the curfew remained firmly intact, there were far fewer cases of security force elements shooting at civilians at night without prior warning. This no doubt saved lives and prevented serious injury to many. But it was still rigidly applied, except for the stretch of road between Ongwediva and Oshakati and within those urban areas. It remained in force until 20 February 1989 on the eve of the implementation of the UN peace plan under Resolution 435 implemented on 1 April 1989. It was briefly imposed again a few weeks later on 11 April 1989,[56] however, when hostilities resumed on 1 April, until their cessation a couple of weeks after that.

---

56   *The Namibian*, 11 April 1989.

10

'We pray that these tragedies
will come to an end': Setting up the
Legal Assistance Centre

Human rights work grew exponentially in the years that followed the case of the Mariental detainees. A number of factors accounted for this. The wide publicity the case enjoyed led to others coming forward when their loved ones were picked up or went missing, or when they were on the receiving end themselves of security force abuses. There was also more activism around human rights. The churches had become more involved. The close alliance I had forged with the bishops of the three main churches representing people in Owambo had meant that priests were more actively encouraged to assist their congregants whose rights had been trampled on. The increase in human rights work snowballed as I came to know and work more closely with so many brave members of the clergy from the three main churches in the northern areas of the country.

A growing number of cases was also referred to us by the then secretary of the ethnically constituted legislative assembly for Owambos, Oswald Shivute. He increasingly utilised his position to receive complaints about atrocities perpetrated by the security forces.

Following the release in 1985 of the Namibian political prisoners who had been held on Robben Island, three of their number (Ben Ulenga, John Pandeni and Petrus Iilonga) spearheaded the rapid growth of a new union movement. Their focus was not only to secure better employment conditions and strive for rights at the workplace, but also centred on mobilising the disenfranchised workforce around political issues. The lack of both employment rights and the related rights of political participation meant that the assertion of worker rights became politicised and union members and their leadership were routinely subjected to harassment, including arrests and detentions. Migrant workers employed in the urban centres and on the mines in central and southern Namibia would return to their homes in Owambo on their annual leave and be subjected to human rights abuses during those visits. Their family members who lived in the north would be continually subjected to abuses as well. This concerned the unions and their leadership. Human rights abuses became increasingly commonplace in urban areas as well.

Labour law had been the primary focus of my postgraduate studies. My special interest in workplace rights coupled with their close connection with human rights meant that I worked closely with the union movement. Those rights took on far greater significance than would otherwise be the case in any more normalised society because of the prior prohibition upon black unions and the complete lack of employment rights, compounded by the absence of any real political rights for the black workforce. I represented the new unions in getting established and in their ensuing disputes with employers, with the sole exception of disputes that the Mine Workers Union of Namibia (MUN) had with the mining houses represented by my firm.

The union work was both demanding and dynamic. During this time, I was able to assist the first of these progressive unions (the Namibia Food and Allied Workers Union) secure its registration with the authorities. This in turn enabled the union to represent its members in their disputes and in negotiations with employers. This was a major step forward and had not occurred previously for the black workforce. The registration of the other progressive unions followed, including MUN, the Metal and Allied Namibian Workers Union (MANWU) and the Namibia Public Workers Union (NAPWU), all affiliated to the National Union of Namibian Workers (NUNW).

It was also during this time in the mid-1980s that students in Namibia became more active and better organised. A dynamic student movement was formed, called the Namibian National Students Organisation (NANSO). Under the impressive leadership of Paul Kalenga and a core group of committed fellow student leaders, it soon made rapid advances throughout the country. I worked very closely with that body in the ensuing years. Its effectiveness meant that the organisation itself, as well as its individual members, soon faced harassment from the security police. This took on various forms and included detentions. So, too, were their activities subjected to surveillance.

NANSO was extremely effective in mobilising the youth in Namibia, especially at high school level on matters directly affecting them, such as the hated system of Bantu education with its ethnic basis and appalling structural inequality, and the proximity of SADF military bases to schools in northern Namibia. Student activism in South Africa also had an impact, contributing to the increase in mobilisation and greater assertiveness. After all, similar issues faced students in both countries.

Namibia did not have its own university yet. Namibians pursuing university studies would, in many instances, go to South African universities. The black universities in South Africa during the 1980s where many Namibian students enrolled were focal points of resistance to the apartheid state. Many young Namibians also went in increasing numbers into exile to pursue their studies. In the mid-1980s, the Academy was started in central Windhoek at premises which would later house the Polytechnic (now the Namibian University of Science and Technology). The Academy offered a limited number of university degree courses and soon called itself the University of Namibia. Together with a number of high schools, it would become a flashpoint of student unrest during the mid- to late 1980s.

I not only represented NANSO and many of its students when they needed representation, but I also became involved in some of their initiatives. One of these was resisting conscription for young Namibians of colour who were selectively enlisted along ethnic lines into the newly established South West Africa Territory Force (SWATF), which formed part of the SADF. At this time, ethnically based units for volunteers had already been established in Owambo (known as 101 Battalion or Owambo Battalion); a similar unit existed in the Kavango region. There were very few employment opportunities for school leavers in those areas. As a result, there was no shortage of recruits for those battalions. There was also 911 Battalion in the central areas, which likewise initially relied upon volunteers with a deliberate ethnic composition, drawing upon Herero, Nama-Damara and Tswana-speaking volunteers as well as those drawn from the coloured community and Rehoboth Basters.

In the early 1980s, selective conscription of black Namibians was introduced in the central and southern regions. It was vehemently opposed by progressive students and parents. One of our clients was the father of a conscript, Eduard Binga. He contested the power to conscript his son as an indigenous Namibian as part of the SWATF or SADF on the grounds that the South African authorities or their local appointees had no power under international law to call up indigenous Namibians for military service.

It was argued that the League of Nations Mandate had been terminated and that it was not competent for the South African government to legislate for Namibia. It was argued in the alternative that, even if the mandate were still in existence, conscripting indigenous Namibians into the South African military would conflict with the terms of that mandate. The challenge was dismissed by a full bench of three judges in mid-1984.[57] That decision was confirmed on appeal to the Appeal Court in Bloemfontein.[58]

In the meantime, ethnically based conscription continued. NANSO vehemently opposed it, encouraging resistance among students in high schools, especially in the central, western and southern regions as the pupils in those schools were those being called up. I supported them in doing so. I spoke at workshops to discuss the issue and also did so at one of their well-attended annual national conventions at Döbra, near Windhoek. These interventions were most challenging. This was because it was a crime to call upon or encourage conscripts to refuse to report. This crime was created in the Defence Act.[59] Its sweep was breathtakingly wide. It prohibited anyone from using 'any language or doing any act or thing with the intent to recommend to, encourage, aid, incite, instigate, suggest to or otherwise cause any other person or persons in general to refuse or fail to render any service' under the Defence Act. This provision had of course been introduced to target anti-conscription activities. The maximum penalties for contravening it were heavy – a fine of R5 000 or six years imprisonment, or both the fine and imprisonment.

It was obviously difficult to have a candid (or any) discussion of the issue in view of this draconian provision. I would usually preface any discussion on the issue by first quoting this section and warning the students to be careful not to contravene it. I would then add that my input was not aimed at contravening the section. It was rather to inform them about the latest atrocities perpetrated by the military against Namibian civilians in the north of the country and to emphasise the ethnic nature of the call-up, placing this within the divide and rule policies and structures created by the apartheid state in Namibia. I would then exhort the students to debate the issue carefully before making their own choices and to understand the

---

57   *Binga v Administrator-General for SWA* 1984 (3) SA 949 (SWA).

58   *Binga v Cabinet for SWA* 1988 (3) SA 155 (AD).

59   Act 44 of 1957.

options open to them. It was a tight balancing act. I knew that there would be security force informants at most meetings. I stuck to the facts of cases – both current and previous ones involving the military – and explained the military's role in perpetrating atrocities.

The focus was upon the role of the military and the divisive nature of an ethnically based call-up. It was then for students to make up their own minds. It was of course a close call and I probably only escaped prosecution because that would certainly serve to draw far more adverse attention to the issue, which the authorities preferred to avoid because my defence would include asserting that the war was unjust, with extensive reference to cases illustrating this. But that was the nature of my practice during the 1980s – continually navigating my way through a myriad of treacherous laws that were aggressively and at times deviously enforced. These talks also served to advance a human rights agenda, which was a conscious aim.

The sheer volume of work had become overwhelming by the mid-1980s. The nature and logistics of the work had become increasingly difficult to accommodate within the constraints of a commercial law practice. Travelling the considerable distance to the northern areas took time. It was over 700 km to Okatana in Owambo where I frequently stayed, and I would often proceed further from there to sites of atrocities. The curfew in Owambo compounded matters, as did the condition and safety of roads off the bitumen-surfaced national road.

There were also no lawyers in full-time practice north of Tsumeb, where more than half the population of the country lived. And those lawyers in Tsumeb, like most of their counterparts elsewhere, were not prepared to take on human rights work – and, in most cases, were openly hostile to it.

A number of foreign and non-governmental organisations (NGOs) that supported community work in Namibia were concerned about the lack of legal access for those in the northern areas. One of these organisations, the Ford Foundation, took the lead and arranged a visit to Namibia by Geoff Budlender, one of the founders of the South African Legal Resources Centre (LRC) that had been set up some seven or eight years before and had by then made a massive difference to the legal landscape within the apartheid state. A number of meetings were arranged for Geoff with the few progressive lawyers in practice in Namibia, community organisations and church groups about the need to set up a public interest legal practice in Namibia. I was one of those invited to meet him. I was eager to hear about the work of the LRC and how it worked with community-based advice offices to make the law more accessible – and particularly how impact litigation was utilised to make a difference in the lives of the oppressed communities that the LRC served.

I strongly supported the idea of establishing a public interest law firm, or setting up advice offices, or both. I suggested to Geoff that a public interest law office in Namibia should preferably be headed by a black Namibian. This was rather difficult at the time. Hosea was still doing his articles. Other black law graduates at that time did not have an interest in being based in the north and doing work of that nature. I promised my support for whichever structure could be set up from my position in my law firm. As at 1985, there was only one black Namibian lawyer in private practice. (He was at the bar.) Hosea and Fonny Karuihe were both then doing their articles of clerkship.

After returning to Johannesburg, Geoff recommended that I should be approached to set up such an office. I was invited to visit the LRC in Johannesburg to see first-hand how the LRC went about its work. That visit was followed by others. On each occasion I enjoyed the warm hospitality of Geoff as well as the LRC national director, Arthur Chaskalson, and his gracious wife Lorraine. Both Geoff and Arthur generously gave up their weekends to spend hours providing invaluable advice about the numerous facets of setting up a public interest law centre under apartheid rule.

During the course of 1986, I made the decision to set up an advice office in the northern war zone. I had at first thought that I and other lawyers at my firm could service an advice office staffed by full-time paralegals at a reduced professional rate. Much of the preparatory and investigative work in cases would be done by paralegals drawn from the area and trained to do so. They would be guided by the lawyers in my firm.

Establishing a centre of this nature would, however, prove to be a difficult task. The only commercial office space available would be in the garrisoned (and predominantly white) towns of Ondangwa or Oshakati, where security force personnel resided and military bases were located. That would obviously not work at all.

Those towns were heavily fortified behind perimeter fences. Anyone entering these towns needed to pass through military check-points manned by armed soldiers who subjected local citizens to humiliating body searches and abuse. Oswald informed me that Peter Kalangula, the head of the ethnically based administration for Owambos, would make an office available to us within their building complex in Ondangwa. This would also not work for us as we could not be associated with an ethnically based structure that formed part of the apartheid policies imposed upon Namibia.

The churches, which firmly supported our work, were not in a position to provide office space. They were also reluctant to do so within any of their existing structures as this would create a danger-ous security risk for any complex we used. There were sound reasons for these fears. The printing press of ELCIN had been bombed on no fewer than three occasions before this. The print works put out a monthly newspaper called *Omukwetu*, which increasingly carried news of security force atrocities and human rights abuses. It irked the security establishment. It was widely believed that the mortar attacks on its print works had been perpetrated by the military because of the critical content of the newspaper.

Not long before, a Catholic church at Omuulukila in western Owambo had also been bombed. I happened to be visiting the area and staying at Anamalenge, about 20 km from the destroyed church. I was in the area to consult Josef Katofa and follow up other recent disappearances in the district. Upon the urging of the Catholic priests, I visited the church. It had been totally destroyed, except for a section of the wall that housed the box for the holy sacraments – which had miraculously remained unscathed. Despite a denial, it was widely believed to be the work of the military.

In spite of being targeted in this way, and after much discussion and deliberation, Bishop Dumeni and his leadership were prepared to permit us to construct our own building within the large ELCIN compound at Ongwediva. This was a perfect solution. It is located in central Owambo. A condition was that the offices would need to be some distance from the other buildings within the compound for safety reasons – so that if the offices were subjected to a mortar attack, other buildings would hopefully not be destroyed. This was a courageous step by ELCIN and was the culmination of the relationship of trust I had built up with the churches.

International church and aid organisations in Sweden, Norway and Denmark that received considerable financial support from their respective governments enthusiastically supported the idea and were prepared to fund it. Erecting a building to house the centre and a nearby accommodation facility for visiting lawyers would take more than another year to plan and complete. This all entailed an unusual planning brief for my architect friend, Kerry McNamara. The centre's filing room was to be constructed to withstand a mortar attack so that all records would remain intact. The nearby accommodation facility for attending lawyers was erected a safe distance away from the office in case of a bombing.

While this office was being constructed during 1987, it became increasingly clear to me that it would be difficult to supervise and service that office from within a commercial law firm and that a separate public interest law firm would also need to be established, based at the seat of the courts in Windhoek.

I discussed this with Hosea, who said he would leave with me. My partnership agreement required me to give six months' notice, to coincide with the end of either August or February. I resigned in early August 1987 to leave on 29 February 1988.

After consulting widely, I decided to call the public interest law firm the Legal Assistance Centre (LAC). The centre being built at Ongwediva was to be called the Human Rights Centre (HRC), each to be funded and governed by separate trusts.

I set up a trust, the Legal Assistance Trust, to fund and supervise the operations of the LAC. Geoff's advice was that the trust should include senior and respected lawyers. This, he said, would provide pivotal protection to the LAC. Geoff said that having someone of Arthur's standing had provided much-needed protection for the LRC. Without Arthur, Geoff was convinced that the LRC would not have survived. Not having a figure of Arthur's immense standing to lead the LAC to shield it from adverse concerted action from the apartheid state, and being a junior lawyer with other junior lawyers and paralegals, I would need the support of senior lawyers of standing in the trust. I asked John Kirkpatrick to chair it and he agreed to do so. I also asked my friend at the local bar, Theo Frank, and Jeremy Gauntlett from Cape Town, who had assisted in so many cases in Namibia. Geoff was also prepared to join the trust. He provided invaluable guidance and counsel during the difficult initial months: a fine lawyer with excellent judgement, a master of tactics and legal strategy with a cool head. John resigned within the first year, however, and a retired judge, Ken Bethune, took his place. He served the LAC with wisdom and dedication until his death some eight years later.

The HRC needed to be a separate entity. For reasons relating to the regulation of legal practice, it could only form part of the public interest law firm if the staff were supervised by a practising lawyer on a full-time basis. This was not possible at the time. It was funded and established by a separate trust called the Human Rights Trust. Its trustees were Bishops Kauluma, Haushiku and Dumeni, and me. After independence, we were able to amalgamate the two trusts.

I decided to start the LAC as an advocate. I had increasingly wanted to argue cases myself in the superior courts. As an attorney, I did not have the right of audience because of the English-type bifurcated bar inherited from South Africa, which limited that to advocates. I needed to complete pupillage for four months and pass the national bar exam set and supervised by the South African bar, to which the bar in Namibia was affiliated. The offices would open at the beginning of July 1988.

Shortly before I left, Hosea informed me that my former firm had offered him a partnership after hearing that he intended to join the centre. He felt he should accept it and I was constrained to agree. The centre was a highly risky enterprise and he rightly pointed out that I could always practise as an advocate on my own if the centre were to be closed by the authorities – a very real risk. The firm's attitude towards my departure had been less than supportive. He was under-standably concerned that he would not be taken back in that event. I completely respected his decision and supported it. A partnership offer was a momentous achievement and I was delighted for him. Hosea was elected as a trustee of the LAC upon John's resignation and loy-ally served the Centre for more than twenty years in that capacity.

With Hosea no longer available, I needed to find one or two attor-neys to join the centre. There were no other progressive lawyers locally who were available – black or white – so I approached Geoff Budlender and one or two other activist lawyers in South Africa for recommendations. After the first state of emergency had been de-clared in South Africa, Fink Haysom, who worked at the centre for Applied Legal Studies attached to Wits University, had organised an emergency workshop for South African lawyers to share experiences and network. He had kindly invited me to this worthwhile event. Even though the legal framework of the South African state of emergency differed from the oppressive legal order in Namibia, strategies for addressing detentions and their conditions, and for mounting challenges to their legality – as well as restrictions upon meetings, assembly, speech and movement – meant that there was much to learn. And I did. Fink prophetically said that there was much to learn from our brushes with the raw power of the security establishment in the northern war zone when hearing about Koevoet and its brazen illegal conduct – that this could be the shape of things to come in South Africa. Unbeknown to both of us at the time, the former Koevoet operative, Eugene de Kock, had only months before been put in charge of the lethal covert state assassination unit based at Vlakplaas.

Contacts made at this workshop helped with the search for lawyers for the LAC. Andrew Corbett had recently qualified at a progressive Cape Town firm and was recommended. He was excited by the prospect of helping to build a new public interest law firm in our hostile environment and agreed to start in early July 1988 when we open our doors for business. He in turn recommended another recently qualified lawyer, Michaela Clayton, who also signed up to join at the same time.

In the meantime, addressing the many practical details was all-consuming – office accommodation in Windhoek was not easy to come by and the Catholic church accommodated us for the first three or four years. I also frequently travelled to and from Ongwediva to oversee the building of the Human Rights Centre. Hosea helped me to identify and appoint three paralegals to run that office. Karl Ndoroma was one of them. A former Mariental detainee, Ben Ausiku was another. They in turn worked with a committee drawn from the local community to plan for the opening of the Human Rights Centre on 8 July 1988.

The ELCIN compound at Ongwediva where the HRC had been built had a hall that doubled as a place of worship. It could comfortably seat more than 500 people. The three bishops agreed to lead a multidenominational service in the hall to celebrate the opening of the HRC (and the LAC) on 8 July 1988. Clergy from each of the churches were invited to attend.

I also invited diplomats based in South Africa. They would not usually travel to the war zone as this may be seen as recognition of SADF's role there, but were prepared to do so for the opening of a human rights centre. Their presence and visible support was crucial for our protection. The Swedish ambassador, as well as senior officials from the US, British, Canadian and Norwegian missions in South Africa, attended, as did Geoff and a prominent member of South Africa's opposition who had raised human rights abuses in Namibia. But the real focus was on the community living in the area and the church leaders there. Parish priests came from across Owambo, no doubt encouraged by their bishops who led the service.

Prominent business leaders in the north were also invited. These included Frans Indongo, who donated a head of cattle for the feast after the opening ceremony. Although we had met briefly some years before, he had a short time before the opening impressed me by transporting people himself from his area to see me about a human rights abuse. He had patiently waited for them to consult and then taken them home again.

The hall was packed to capacity, with several people standing outside and lining the walls inside on the sides and at the back. Some members of the media were also there. Gwen led a strong contingent from *The Namibian*, which gave the event wide coverage in the next issue of 15 July 1988. The other newspapers, mostly supporters of the security establishment, were noticeable in their absence. But very significantly, reporters from both the television and Radio Owambo service of the state broadcaster attended and provided extensive coverage of the event on Radio Owambo, which broadcast the entire proceedings live on their service. The tight control on news and content on radio was primarily exercised over the English and Afrikaans services, which the minders could easily monitor and control.

During the early 1980s, Radio Owambo was widely detested for broadcasting propaganda. There had, however, been a gradual and subtle shift in reporting and spontaneous commentary concerning atrocities and human rights abuses in the late 1980s as they became more common and as the listenership thirsted for more coverage of those incidents and news of those from their communities who had been caught up in them. These were often through live call-ins or written messages broadcast on the morning chat show. Many of my friends from the north felt that the live broadcast of the opening of the HRC was the culmination of this trend of incremental reporting of human rights issues, and was a turning point. It certainly took a great deal of courage for those reporters to do so. The decision would certainly have been made in Oshakati by local reporters who increasingly understood the mood of people in the area.

All three bishops played a part in the service. Bishop Dumeni did a welcoming and led the prayers, Bishop James delivered the main address and Bonafatius Haushiku, the Catholic bishop, delivered a vote of thanks and a benediction at the end.

Bishop James, in this moving address, described the occasion as 'history in the making' and said that the history of Namibia 'will record that this centre was born in a period of lawlessness and disrespect for human rights and values'. He spoke of the system of rule as being 'inhuman' and 'barbaric'.

Bishop James was also very gracious towards me in his address. As was reported in *The Namibian*:

Bishop Kauluma emphasised that the establishment of the Human Rights Centre had come at a time when the 'the need for it has been heightened by the war situation in which human rights, freedom and dignity of persons continue to be violated and abused.

We hope and pray that with the work of this new centre these tragedies will come to an end, and that legal advice will be available to all the people of this region who may need it, and to those who may come from other parts of the country seeking the same.'

He urged members of the public to make use of the centre 'which has been established with the purpose of upholding your human rights and dignity'.

I had carefully prepared my short address in advance, because half was in Oshikwanyama and I was not confident enough to speak off the cuff in that language. (I had by then been taking Oshikwanyama lessons with Sally Kauluma, Bishop James's erudite wife. This had been vital. In those days, the medium of instruction in primary schools in Owambo was the vernacular and Afrikaans in high schools as part of Bantu education. A working knowledge of a local dialect was essential for working in the area. I had asked Sally to include the idiomatic use of language in her excellent classes – teaching a language where no textbook had as yet been written – given my deeply held belief that understanding the idiom of a language assists greatly in understanding the people who speak it.)

I gave an explanation of how the centre would work, and introduced the paralegals who would work there and the Windhoek-based lawyers who would service the centre. The first part of my talk was in English, with my friend, unionist and former Robben Islander John Pandeni doing a simultaneous translation into Oshiwambo in his booming baritone, perfectly suited to the occasion. I surprised many in the gathering and also, as I subsequently repeatedly heard for several years to come, listeners of the live broadcast when I switched into Oshikwanyama halfway through until the end of my address. John then switched to providing a running English translation for the benefit of the invited quests from abroad.

The HRC and the LAC were soon inundated with masses of work – mostly human rights violations reported to the HRC.

Given the diplomatic presence at the opening ceremony, the usual heavy security force presence was absent. But we knew this uneasy calm would soon dissipate after the departure of the diplomats. The hostility we all felt from the authorities and especially the security establishment seemed to simmer below the surface but boiled over barely a month after we had opened office.

On Saturday 13 August 1988, I received a call from one of the HRC paralegals. Ben Ausiku from Outapi informed me about an incident in which the South African military had destroyed a cuca shop in that area, killing three people and detaining seven others. He sought advice about how to follow up his investigation on Monday 15 August. I was concerned when I received no feedback from him that Monday afternoon or on the following morning. Instead, I received a call late on Tuesday morning (16 August) that he and the HRC's coordinator (Philip Mwandingi), who had joined him on Monday morning, had been picked up and detained by the security forces on the Monday afternoon. I asked Andrew Corbett to make urgent enquiries so that we could prepare an urgent application for their release.

The third paralegal, Karel Ndoroma, was attending a course in advice office work arranged by the Black Sash in South Africa. The detentions not only deprived Ben and Philip of their liberty, of course, but also meant that the HRC had to close temporarily, cutting off legal access in the area.

What made matters worse was the denial we received that the security forces were detaining them – a very worrying and ominous development. Our concern for their personal safety intensified. Andrew and I set about putting together an urgent application. I also decided to travel to the north to investigate their disappearances personally in view of the denials of their detention.

Sick with worry, I issued a statement on Tuesday, expressing our grave concern as to their fate in the face of denials of their detention and deploring the fact that they had been picked up while going about their human rights work, investigating an atrocity. We called for their release and demanded immediate access to them.

Our urgent application was finalised and I was about to travel to the north when I received a call late on Wednesday evening that they had been released by the military at the Ruacana base late that afternoon. Ben and Philip were safe and had not been harmed. It was a massive relief. I was overwhelmed by the support we had received throughout the country – especially in the north, as well as from diplomats and friends of the centre outside the country.

The HRC reopened its doors on the following day 18 August. Ben and Philip were never charged with any offence. And those whose detention they were investigating were also released not too long afterwards.

The challenges that faced the LAC and HRC not only arose from the very hostile environment with peace a very remote prospect at that time, but also took on manifold other forms. The sheer volume of work was overwhelming from the very first days. This was compounded by the vast distances to be travelled by all of us involved.

The paralegals at the HRC travelled extensively to follow up and investigate several of the serious human rights abuses reported to that office. We as the LAC's lawyers regularly travelled by car to the HRC (a distance of over 700 km each way) to service that office.

The overwhelming majority of cases handled in the first year of the LAC concerned human rights abuses reported at the HRC. Many of these resulted in civil actions for damages for victims suing for assaults and damage to property experienced at the hands of the security forces.

In the first year alone, we instituted 236 claims for damages against the security forces.

After the first few months, the apartheid state came up with a strategy directed at effectively closing down the centre. The government defendants in the claims were the South African minister of defence (representing the military) and Cabinet of the IG (later replaced by the Administrator-General when the IG was disbanded shortly before the implementation of UN Security Council Resolution 435 on 1 April 1989) as responsible for the police, because Koevoet was a unit of the police. These government defendants came up with a new defence to these claims after a few months by denying that attorneys in the service of the LAC were legally authorised to conduct litigation on behalf of clients under the rules governing the practice of lawyers. In some cases, special punitive costs against the lawyers themselves were also sought.

The purpose behind taking this point was to prevent the LAC from acting on behalf of any clients at all. If the point succeeded, it would mean that the centre's attorneys could not legally represent clients in litigation. It was thus aimed at closing down the LAC as a public interest law firm. A truly shocking development.

It was entirely unexpected. Long before the centre opened, I had approached the Law Society to exempt LAC attorneys from certain restrictive rules applicable to attorneys. I did so on the advice of Geoff Budlender of the LRC. The same legislation governed lawyers in South Africa. I was able to forward copies of the exemptions granted in South Africa where the organised profession had been facilitating towards the establishment of the LRC and its operations. These useful precedents had persuaded the local Law Society at the time to grant similar exemptions.

The Government Attorney, however, took this point upon a narrow, formalistic reading of the regulations governing attorneys, that those employed by a centre like ours were not entitled to sign legal process and represent clients in court. This point had not been taken at any stage in South Africa where the LRC had been operating for some seven or eight years by then.

Arthur Chaskalson was horrified by this turn of events and agreed to represent us in our challenge to this. He did so at no charge to the centre. Acting upon his advice, we brought an application to declare that our attorneys were entitled to represent clients of the centre, provided that no charge was made for those services.

This application was strenuously opposed by the AG and South African minister of defence. It was eventually heard on 28 August 1989. A full bench of Judge President Berker and Judges Strydom and Hendler was to hear the challenge. Arthur's address emphasised from its outset the importance of the right to counsel and how fundamental this was to a fair trial and to a legal system supposedly based upon those principles. His compelling eloquence soon struck a chord with the court. Each of the three judges was aghast and appalled at the stance taken by the government defendants.

After a while and in the full flow of Arthur's erudition, the Judge President interrupted him, sternly turned to counsel representing the defendants, and pointedly enquired, 'Mr Van der Bijl, how can it be in the public interest to silence this centre which provides legal access to people who would not otherwise have access to the courts?'

It was evident from their body language that the two other judges shared the underlying concern.

Mr Van der Bijl piously mumbled in response that his client was merely upholding the strict letter of the law.

The Judge President responded that if his clients were to have concerns about legality, then the rules needed to be changed. He asked Van der Bijl if he had not engaged us about finding a way to resolve the dispute. Inexplicably, Van der Bijl answered that there had been settlement discussions. Arthur swung around to me in evident surprise at this assertion and I indicated that it was entirely baseless.

There had, of course, been not the slightest settlement overture. On the contrary, Chris Brandt of the Government Attorney had conceded to one of our attorneys that this defence had been invoked because of the sheer number of the human rights claims.

Arthur indicated to the court that we were unaware of any settlement discussions.

The Judge President, visibly frustrated at Van der Bijl's response, announced that he would adjourn the court to permit the parties the opportunity to explore a resolution. In the ensuing adjournment, Arthur declined to engage in discussions with Van der Bijl and asked Jeremy Gauntlett, his co-counsel in the matter, to do so. Jeremy had extensive discussions with both Van der Bijl and his junior, Gerhard Maritz, and an agreement was eventually reached in which the Government defendants agreed to drop their special defence and not to raise it again. We agreed to approach the Law Society within a month to request appropriate changes to the rules governing attorneys where required. I do not recall any amendments to any laws being required, demonstrating yet another sterile resort to formalism to frustrate real justice.

This was a massive victory. We all felt that we should win the case as the point was transparently bad, based on a formalistic approach in the face of the fundamental right to representation. That the court would plainly have none of it soon became evident during argument. The support for the centre expressed by the court was heartening. The fact that the UN peace plan was well underway and seemed irrevocably so, together with the presence in court of several international observers and representatives from the UN, probably also played a part. The case even received coverage in the *New York Times*.[60]

The outcome of the case, widely viewed as a significant win for

---

60   *New York Times*, 20 August 1989.

the LAC, enhanced the LAC's standing, with its existence enjoying approval of the court. Despite this, our attorneys Andrew and Michaela were not made to feel welcome when attending the Law Society AGM soon afterwards. Indeed, a past president of the society referred to the LAC at that occasion as an 'onding' in Afrikaans – a pejorative term meaning an undesirable thing or phenomenon. But no resolution was adopted. Support from the profession was in sparse supply. I had applied for membership of the Society of Advocates in 1988. After successfully completing my pupillage, I had met the requirements for membership except for not having chambers where bar members practised. Arthur had remained a prominent member of the bar and strongly advised me to join and participate within its structures. I had not expected much debate on the issue, given Arthur's eminent precedent. But my membership application was opposed and the bar was split on political lines. My membership was eventually carried by a majority of one, much to Bryan O'Linn's frustration as he had tried to steer the issue on grounds of principle and access to the courts. He said afterwards that, had the split been equal, it would have given him much pleasure to use his casting vote as chairperson. This had been surprising as the Bar Council had been vocal in its condemnation of human rights abuses. Much of that had to do with Bryan's leadership and forceful character.

The hostile reception from the establishment and the legal profession was not replicated in the communities around Namibia. Shortly after the official opening of the HRC, a delegation from the Kavango region came to see me about opening an advice office in Rundu. Within months we opened an office there manned by Ambrosius Haingura. This was replicated in Tsumeb with Nico Kaiyamo and in Walvis Bay under Wilfried Emvula. The latter office presented its own set of challenges. The South African government had a few years before it decided to administer Walvis Bay separately from the rest of Namibia – as part of the Cape Province because of a nineteenth century treaty between the colonial powers of South Africa and Germany. Administering Walvis Bay as part of the Cape Province meant that South African law applied, which differed in some respects from the rest of Namibia where some of the more racially discriminatory laws had been repealed. Different security laws had been enacted in the past years in South Africa, which had not been applied to Namibia. The Cape High Court exercised jurisdiction and no longer the High Court in Windhoek. This all fortunately came to an end upon the incorporation of Walvis Bay into Namibia in 1994 after democracy had come to South Africa.

Although much of the first year or so was a battle to survive for the LAC, the tumultuous events of the implementation of the UN peace plan placed heavy yet exhilarating demands upon the centre. These included making urgent representations concerning the massacre of Swapo insurgents after their incursion on 1 April 1989, making an input on the repeal of discriminatory laws to precede the UN supervised election, a similar input on the proposed registration and later electoral legislation, and then monitoring the process. A most unusual brief and one of the highlights of my career was representing all of the prisoners in the political section of the Windhoek Prison to argue for their release under the peace plan (which provided for the release of political prisoners). The then chairperson of the European Human Rights Commission, Prof. Carl Nørgaard, was the eminent jurist selected by the UN to make the determination. He found in favour of the prisoners I represented.

I had acted for the majority of the political prisoners in their trials and later forged a close relationship with the rest of them when I represented twelve of the group when they went on a hunger strike in September 1986 in an attempt to improve subhuman conditions of imprisonment. These conditions included only one 30-minute visit per month and receiving only one letter per month. The hunger strike ended after twelve days when some concessions were eventually made by the authorities. It became tense during the latter part of the hunger strike. One prisoner had already been admitted to hospital and the others were becoming weaker; the IG remained resolved not to give an inch. Negotiations were tense, with neither side wanting to climb down from their positions. When it did end, a closer bond had developed between us as well as a much-improved relationship with the prison authorities, who had expressed appreciation to me afterwards for my role in resolving an issue that was developing into an unmanageable nightmare for them. Sadly, I was out of the country briefly on the day of their release. A few days later I accompanied a US observer group to the north and the former political prisoners arranged a braai at the HRC for me. I had come to know all of them behind bars. It took time for the reality of meeting them as free people to sink in, an emotional moment for all of us. That meeting, including the gracious speech made by the most senior in their number, Petrus Bernadinus Shekutambah, counts as the most moving moment of my professional life.

With the attainment of independence on 21 March 1990, the traditional workload of the centre fortunately changed. No longer primarily preoccupied with investigating human rights atrocities, representing victims of those abuses and assisting our clients by creating more space within which they could operate, the centre geared itself to adapt to the new challenges of nation building. The focus shifted to the new right-giving Constitution to ensure that the rights enshrined in it would have meaning for the people of Namibia. In doing so, the Centre continued to represent vulnerable and disadvantaged communities, asserting their rights. The centre expanded its civic education, however, to explain the Constitution at school and community level. Labour work likewise expanded, as did a newly established land rights component and a highly effective gender equality project. A juvenile justice project soon followed.

At its core, the centre, through these and other activities, aimed at consolidating the gains of our hard-won independence and assisting in fostering the development of a rights culture and respect for human rights.

Shortly after independence, I stood down as director of the LAC. Andrew took the reins for the next eight years or so, to be succeeded by Clement Daniels who, as a final-year student at the University of the Western Cape, had helped me to found the centre. One of the students we had funded through our scholarship programme set up in our first year, Norman Tjombe, took over from Clement. The current director is the first woman to hold the position – Toni Hancox continues the work of the centre with vigour and enthusiasm.

The centre has become part of civil society in Namibia and remains the only public interest law firm. In 1997, it was awarded UNICEF's highest honour, the Maurice Pate Award, for its outstanding contribution to the cause of human rights.[61] Its work goes on.

---

61   *The Namibian*, 11 June 1997.

11

The Interim Government
and human rights

The surprising thing about the imminent abandonment of the
Constitution – that lengthy document so top-heavy with ringing
preambles, so glutinously coated with abstract principles of right
and justice and obligation, so ribboned with guarantees to minori-
ties and special interests, so honeycombed with promises of life
and liberty and happiness for all, so stiff with austere legalism,
so sweetened with the codes of civility, that Constitution painstakingly fabricated and assembled over several weeks in panelled,
chandeliered halls and flourished in triumph at the climax – the
surprising thing was not that it was about to be ceremoniously
tossed out of the window, but that it had taken such a comparatively long time for that to happen.

Shiva Naipaul, *A Hot Country*[62]

In the midst of the dark days in the 1980s, there was a very brief
glimmer of hope for positive change in the unpromising legal landscape when, in June 1985, the IG was installed. It was made up of
parties that had participated in the South African-sponsored internal
initiative known as the Multi-Party Conference (MPC). On 18 April
1984, the MPC adopted a bill of rights – aimed at protecting most
civil and political rights, including the rights to life, liberty, a fair trial,
freedom of movement, peaceful assembly, express political activity
and freedom of expression.

---

62   Abacus, 1983.

In June the following year, the MPC formed the IG. In its empowering proclamation[63] was their bill of rights, which the participating parties had adopted the previous year. The proclamation expressly precluded the IG from passing any law that infringed the rights set out in their bill of rights, offering the tantalising prospect of relying upon the promise of a new order where governmental conduct was subject to entrenched rights, given the professed commitment to upholding and respecting the fundamental rights set out in such unequivocal terms.

It only took a few weeks for that promise to be exposed as a cynical and empty publicity stunt. It came in the *Katofa* case, which set in train a pattern consistently followed in every subsequent court challenge – and there were many – where the IG's bill of rights was invoked. Each time, the response was a vehement disclaimer, with the IG denying that its bill could be relied upon because prior legislation was invoked and that its bill only applied to the IG passing new laws.

After *Katofa*, the IG opposed legal access for detainees in *Akweenda*. It acted against the right to freedom of expression in imposing in the maximum deposit on *The Namibian* for improper motives. The IG rubber-stamped the South African president's banning of the murder trial of the alleged killers of Frans Uapota and afterwards strenuously opposed Victoria Mweuhanga's quest for justice when seeking to set aside that ban. It opposed the challenge to the curfew and also acted similarly in several other instances not included in the book. These include two separate bans of marches only to be overturned by the courts. Furthermore, the challenge to the LAC operating as a law firm was done in its name (as well as that of the South African minister of fefence). Not only did the IG oppose the invocation of its own bill of rights in court when acting in terms of the draconian legislation it inherited, but it proceeded to pass its own legislation, ironically called

---

63   Proclamation R101 of 1985, 17 June 1985 in Gazette 9790.

the Protection of Human Rights Act,[64] which was found in its key provision to impermissibly infringe fundamental rights in its bill and was struck down by the courts.[65]

The IG also did nothing to rein in the excesses of the South African security establishment, including Koevoet. On the contrary, the IG and its mouthpiece *Die Republikein* lavished praise on that lawless unit as well as on the SADF and SWATF. The IG, after all, held office at their pleasure (given the dominance of the military within the South African government) and duly obliged its masters when required, rubber-stamping countless infringements of human rights.

The empty commitment to protecting human rights was not confined to challenges in the courts. One of the members of the IG, Moses Katjioungua,[66] strenuously tried to get the IG to dismantle the ethnically based government structures set out in AG 8 of 1980. The IG's unofficial leader, Dirk Mudge, thwarted this and said it was a constitutional matter to be determined by a constitutional council and promptly proposed – no doubt at Pretoria's bidding – that this body be presided over by Piet van der Bijl, whose principal claim to fame was drafting right-depriving, repressive, security legislation. He was removed from the post before he could take office after Katjioungua took his cabinet colleagues to court to set it aside and Van der Bijl returned to Pretoria. Although maintaining a subservience to the security establishment, the IG's worst legacy and disgrace was its complicity in the continuation of the appalling inequality in expenditure on education and other services on ethnic lines, despite having some power over purse strings. As I have pointed out, under the IG's tenure ten times more was spent on the education of white children than on those in Owambo. It was certainly within its power to ameliorate this inequality. Yet it did nothing to do so.

---

64   Act 16 of 1988.

65   *Namibia National Students' Organisation (Nanso) and others v Speaker of the National Assembly for South West Africa and others* 1990 (1) SA 617 (SWA).

66   Together with cabinet colleague, Andrew Matjila.

Turning its back on its own bill of rights and its complicity in abuses tarnished the IG's credibility, but fortunately did not undermine growing enthusiasm for the notion of asserting rights in court. The reverse occurred: an ever-increasing appreciation for the value of the real protection of rights in a meaningful manner became a permanent fixture in political discourse, the country having experienced the illusion of it under the IG. Despite the IG's comprehensive failure to uphold rights, a human rights culture was taking root.

12

A decade of electric shock torture

A common thread that would weave its way through most accounts given by the political detainees I encountered was that of the electric shock treatment meted out to them as one of the forms of torture and abuse endured during their detention. It was usually at the hands of the security police and Koevoet. Those captured or picked up by Koevoet in northern Namibia faced more crude brutality and would count themselves fortunate if they survived to tell the tale.

From my first detainee client – Axel Johannes, a senior Swapo figure – in my first months as an articled clerk in early 1980 to the dying months of the South African occupation in January 1990, electric shock treatment was a recurring detainee complaint.

During this decade, whenever the spectre of electric shock treatment was raised, it was always met with vehement denials. Under oath, senior police officers would express their horror that this form of abuse of detainees could even be suggested of them. Those denials would invariably carry the day. The testimony of political detainees – already at a disadvantage because of the charges levelled against them and with no medical or other corroboration for their claim of having undergone electric shocks – would prove to be no match for the well-rehearsed, pious proclamations of innocence and outrage by senior and junior police officers alike at the very thought that they would engage in or even abide treatment of that nature.

The problem was that electric shock torture – for that is what it is – would frequently leave little trace if skilfully applied. Medical experts advised us that small burn marks would be left on the flesh where the electric current had been applied. These marks would mostly disappear quite soon afterwards – within days – even though the pain at the time would have been excruciating.

The problem perennially faced by political detainees was that they would have no access to lawyers, independent medical practitioners or, of course, their families for months and sometimes even longer after being tortured. (After winning the *Akweenda* case, which meant access after 30 days for detainees held under AG 9, the security forces switched to invoking the Terrorism Act, which permitted indefinite detention without charge and without access.) By the time detainees could consult us, any physical trace of electric shocks and most other torture would usually be long gone.

Without corroborating evidence, our clients would have little prospect of persuading courts that an admission or confession extracted from them was not freely or voluntarily made or succeeding with a civil claim for damages.

In the mid-1980s, and especially after the first state of emergency was declared in South Africa, there was widespread detention of dissidents. Abuse of detainees was also the order of the day there. The same security police were involved, after all.

Even after the installation of the IG in Namibia in June 1985, the security police remained under the effective command of Pretoria until independence.

During the state of emergency in South Africa, innovative human rights lawyers invoked a remedy recognised in English commercial cases, especially for breaches of copyright, known as the *Anton Piller* order. It took its name from the landmark ruling written by Lord

Denning, which established the remedy.[67] It entailed obtaining an order from a judge in secret (*in camera*) without notice to the affected party. The order would authorise the sheriff to enter premises to search for and attach items or documents in possession of a defendant where a claimant has a right to them or, importantly for our cases, for them to be preserved and produced in evidence in an intended claim.[68] This remedy had proven to be crucial in instances where copyright had been infringed, for instance where recorded music and films were illicitly reproduced on a large scale – a practice that became known as bootlegging.

It is obviously an extraordinary remedy because it is granted without notice to a defendant and affords the right to enter the latter's premises and search for items without prior notice or the right to be heard for a defendant. The remedy requires that an applicant must have a cause of action to be pursued against the named defendant. Secondly, the applicant would need to make out a case that the defendant has specific items or documents in the latter's possession constituting vital evidence in substantiation of the claim. In the third instance, there would need to be a well-founded apprehension that the evidence may be destroyed, hidden or spirited away by the time the case comes to trial and if notice of the application were to be given.[69]

In the late 1980s, lawyers in South Africa applied for *Anton Piller* orders to search police stations for torture equipment.[70] The first application in the Eastern Cape came before a conservative judge, who refused it.[71] Word soon spread about the use of the remedy in

---

67 *Anton Piller KG v Manufacturing Processes Ltd and Others* 1976 RPC 719 ([1976] 1 All ER 779).

68 As neatly explained by Clive Plasket in *The Final Word on Anton Piller Orders against the Police* (1992) 4 SAJHR 569 with reference to *Jafta v Minister of Law and Order* 1991 (2) SA 286 (A).

69 *Shoba v Officer Cammanding, Temporary Police Camp, Wagendrift Dam and Another* 1995 (4) SA 1 (A).

70 *Plasket* at 570-1.

71 *Ex parte Matshini* 1986 (3) SA 605 (E). See further Plasket at 570-1.

this context. One of the talented human rights lawyers who initially invoked it, Clive Plasket (now an outstanding judge in South Africa), was generous in sharing his experience and providing advice to others about making use of the remedy.

In August 1989, Wilibard Nambinga, of the Kuisebmund township, was arrested and detained by the Walvis Bay police. He complained to the LAC advice office in Walvis Bay that he had been given electric shocks. Our coordinator of that office, Wilfried Emvula, contacted LAC attorney Andrew Corbett about it. Andrew in turn spoke to Clive Plasket and secured helpful advice about bringing an *Anton Piller* application. This had to be done in the High Court in Cape Town because Walvis Bay was then being administered as part of the Cape Province of South Africa.

After we had discussed the case, Andrew prepared the application, travelled to Cape Town and obtained an *Anton Piller* order authorising the Deputy Sheriff of Walvis Bay to search the Walvis Bay Police Station. Andrew and another attorney nominated by us, Hosea Angula and Mr Nambinga were authorised by the order to accompany the Deputy Sheriff in that search.

Nambinga had in the application described how he had been blindfolded and taken to an office at the Walvis Bay Police Station for interrogation up a flight of stairs. A brown canvas-type bag was put over his head in the office. It was wet and more water was applied to it. He was forced to strip naked. The interrogation proceeded and electric shocks were applied to his genitals. This obviously caused him severe pain.

Armed with the court order, Andrew then proceeded to Walvis Bay together with Hosea to meet Attie Barnard, the experienced Deputy Sheriff for Walvis Bay. The latter had no prior inkling of the nature of the order. After meeting up with him in Walvis Bay, the order was handed over to him and its purpose explained. The searching party arrived at the police station at about 5:30 pm. It was a Friday afternoon.

There was only a duty sergeant at the charge office. The more senior officers, already on weekend mode, were contacted at the local golf club where they were relaxing over a few drinks at its nineteenth hole. The few who responded took about half an hour to arrive at the police station. In the meantime, Barnard instructed that no one could leave the premises until their arrival.

The officers were visibly taken aback at the terms of the order and begrudgingly remained in attendance while the Deputy Sheriff commenced the search in the stipulated presence of Andrew, Hosea and Nambinga, to the evident discomfort of the officers.

The offices near the charge office threw up nothing. Across the internal courtyard was an office up a flight of stairs. The police officers were asked who used it and what it was used for. They said they did not know. It was locked and the Deputy Sheriff asked for the keys. They said they did not know where they were kept and that it may take some time to find them. The Deputy Sheriff, at Andrew's insistence, said he would wait until the keys were located. It did in fact take some time for the keys to emerge. During this time, one or two of the senior officers quietly slipped away.

The ranking officer remaining was Lieutenant Loubser, deeply disliked by the community in Kuisebmund for his heavy-handed tactics against activists. He had been the investigating officer in a lengthy political trial held in Walvis Bay where fourteen young activists had been charged with public violence the previous year. These charges had arisen from student unrest in 1988. Michaela and I had represented those defendants in that trial. Our clients had been badly treated prior to and during the trial. At the forefront of the nastiness was Loubser. He was particularly unpleasant to our clients, and even to us, throughout the duration of the trial.

In the preceding years in Walvis Bay, the police had routinely harassed activists and especially the Swapo leader Nathaniel Maxuilili and those they saw as sympathetic to or supportive of human rights, such as the Anglican and Catholic priests, Mike Yates and Hermann Klein-Hitpass, respectively. The police went so far as to plant uncut diamonds in a parcel sent by Mike, by obtaining access to the post office overnight to do so, and then to arrest and charge him with illicit dealing in diamonds. This is illustrative of the dirty tricks to which the police would stoop to harass those perceived as thorns in the flesh of the apartheid state. Mike was arrested on this trumped-up charge. It was eventually rightly thrown out in court, but after much anguish and stress to Mike and his wife, Dee-Dee. A senior officer a few years ago contacted Yates from South Africa to confess to this and apologise to him for this dastardly act and for the harm it had caused Mike and his family.

Back to the search of the office up the stairs at the back of the police station. The office had its windows blacked out – often a sign of a torture chamber. A brown, army-type canvas bag was soon found – perfectly matching Nambinga's account. Shortly afterwards, an antiquated, manually operated telephone with two wires was dis-covered in the office. Loubser was asked what it was used for. Those instruments had not been in use in Walvis Bay for far more than a decade or two. He said he didn't know. When asked again what the office was used for, he eventually stammered 'special operations', but declined to elaborate. Andrew enquired whether the wires were live. One of the policemen in attendance, who had presumably not been involved in administering electric shocks, stepped forward to check. He touched the wires and exclaimed loudly in pain as he was thrown backwards to the floor by the impact of the shock.

The Deputy Sheriff attached the old manual phone and the canvas device.

An elated Andrew excitedly recounted these events by phone straight afterwards and in more detail the next day in Windhoek. It was a major breakthrough. We knew that electric shock treatment would at last be conclusively established.

It came as no surprise that Nambinga's civil claim for damages afterwards became settled in his favour.

A few months later a client in Katima Mulilo, Shadrack Mwilima, also claimed to have undergone electric shock treatment at the hands of the police. He had been incarcerated in December 1989 following his arrest on suspicion of the murder of a policeman named Khama near that town. Mwilima was picked up with a fellow activist for questioning. Shortly after his arrest, some policemen came for Mwilima where he was held in the cells at the Katima Mulilo Police Station. He was bundled into the back of an enclosed police pickup and taken to another building some distance away. He was able to work out that he was close to the Zambezi River. He was taken inside this building, which was used as an office. He was met there by two white plainclothes policemen. They questioned him about the murder weapon used in the murder of Khama.

The policemen then placed towelling rags around his handcuffed wrists and blindfolded him with a grey plastic bag over his head. The bag had a drawstring, which was tightened. A stick was thrust behind his knees and in front of his elbows, trapping his legs and forcing him into a crouching position. The policemen then lifted him and placed him so that the stick rested on two supporting objects, resulting in him becoming suspended in mid-air. Two wires were attached to the smallest fingers on each hand. He was pushed backwards and forwards like a pendulum – a technique the policemen proudly boasted to be the helicopter method. His interrogation continued with electric shocks being applied. This continued for some time. The pain he experienced from the shocks was exacerbated by his enforced position. The stick constrained his limbs from jerking when the shocks were applied. The wires were moved to apply shocks all over his body – his legs, upper body and ears. His estimate of the duration of the interrogation in this manner was about 45 minutes. At its end, he needed to be carried out by the police and was dumped in the back of the police pickup. He was left to lie in the back of the police vehicle for some time after returning to Katima Mulilo Police Station. Some days later, he was released on bail. No charges were ever made against him.

After his release, he reported his torture to a Swapo legal officer at the Swapo regional election office. The officer put Mwilima in touch with us. Andrew hastened to Katima Mulilo and took a statement from him.

After Andrew's return to Windhoek, we prepared an *Anton Piller* application, which I moved in court on 25 January 1990 – less than two months before independence.

The order was granted and Andrew returned to Katima Mulilo accompanied by a local attorney, Dirk Conradie, and Clement Daniels from our office – who were all authorised by the court order to be in attendance, with Mwilima, when it was executed.

The building in question turned out to have been used by SADF military intelligence prior to their withdrawal during the UN peace plan. The Security Police presumably took it over. In striking similarity to the Walvis Bay incident, the keys for the building could also inexplicably not be found. But Dirk Conradie, of slight build, managed to climb through one of the windows. A search revealed a stick closely resembling the proportions and description given by Mwilima. It was attached and provided important corroboration for his version. His case too became settled.

The right-giving Constitution that came into force upon independence on 21 March 1990 should have ensured that electric shock torture was to be something of the past. But that was not the case. Old police habits die hard.

Another *Anton Piller* order obtained by us at the LAC in June 1991 revealed that three stock theft suspects had been subjected to electric shock treatment in a back office at the Windhoek Police Station. The ensuing search, again involving Andrew, delivered electric shock torture equipment in the form of a briefcase with a wired-up handle in the back office described by the victims in the application. One of the two Deputy Inspector-Generals of the Namibian Police, General Poole, came to see me after the case and assured me that this practice would not recur. He said he was appalled by it and would personally see to it that it would be totally rooted out.

After that, there were thankfully no further reports of electric shocks administered to people in police custody until the widespread detentions that followed the state of emergency declared in the then Caprivi region following the separatist armed insurrection which had occurred there in 1999.

13

'Serious war crimes':
A calamitous start to the
UN peace plan

Windhoek would virtually close down from mid-December until after New Year during the 1970s and 1980s. Most businesses and firms would shut up shop within varying degrees of proximity to Christmas, and reopen shortly after New Year. Nothing would happen over that period – by consensus, a time of a total inactivity. But not in 1988. Out of nowhere, the story broke on 14 December of a breakthrough agreement on independence for Namibia reached in Brazzaville, Congo, between South Africa, Angola and Cuba.[72] Although this had not taken place in sleepy Windhoek, it heralded the start of frenetic activity that would only abate at independence some fifteen months later.

In a US-brokered deal that had been painstakingly negotiated over several months, it was agreed that the UN peace plan set out in Resolution 435 would be implemented on 1 April 1989. The accord also included a phased withdrawal of 50 000 Cuban troops from Angola, which the Reagan administration had rigidly advocated since assuming office nearly eight years before and had now achieved in its dying days in office. The accord was followed by a ceremonial signing in New York on 22 December 1988.

---

72   *New York Times*, 14 December 1988.

There had been sporadic flurries of prior diplomatic initiatives directed at implementing the peace plan after South Africa had turned its back on it in 1978 with Operation Reindeer. But all of these had come to nought. The drawn-out talks preceding the accord had not held much hope of a breakthrough. The unthinkable, however, occurred in December 1988 and certainly took me by surprise. I tempered my excitement in view of previous disappointments. There was always the risk that the South African security establishment, no doubt disturbed by the spectre of free elections in Namibia, would find a way to scupper things again.

This time, the climate for peace was more promising. Recent developments would coalesce, favouring an international settlement. One of the single most significant developments had been the statesmanship of Mikhail Gorbachev, which meant that the Cold War would no longer dictate foreign policy in Africa and no longer justify hawks in the US and UK governments in supporting South Africa's stalling tactics to deny independence for Namibia. The US and UK governments' underlying basis for resisting even tougher sanctions and more pressure upon South Africa, which were increasingly taking their toll, now fell away. The cost of the war had also placed a strain on South Africa's economy, together with its lack of decisive success in prosecuting the war. These were also factors.

Very soon and from early January 1989, UN personnel and foreign diplomats and journalists started to converge upon Windhoek. The IG's term of office was to end on 1 March 1989 and the AG was to reassume full powers in advance of the implementation date of 1 April.

The UN peace plan in a nutshell provided for a ceasefire and confinement of Swapo and SADF troops to base, the return of Swapo exiles, the phased withdrawal of SADF troops, the repeal of discriminatory laws, the release of political prisoners whose characterisation would be determined by an international expert advising the

UN Special Representative, and the holding of an election for a constituent assembly to draw up a Constitution for an independent Namibia by a two-thirds majority. Supervision of the entire process was to be by the UN Special Representative, assisted by the UN Transitional Assistance Group (UNTAG). The process was to take a year and be completed by 1 April 1990.

As the start-up date of 1 April 1989 rapidly approached, it became clear that UNTAG was not sufficiently deployed to supervise and oversee the process. Few police and military observers were in place, especially in the outlying northern areas that mattered most. It was to prove a logistical challenge to deploy observers, as events soon demonstrated.

Anton Lubowski invited me to a meeting in Harare on 1 April to discuss the implementation of the peace plan. It involved the Swapo leadership, progressive foreign and local NGOs, and church leaders. I declined the invitation because I was concerned that there could be problems with the commencement of the peace plan, which would require my presence at home.

As I stood on the fringes, observing a Swapo rally in Katutura on the afternoon of 1 April, the mood was almost festive, celebrating the start of the long-awaited implementation of the peace plan. UN observers with their blue insignia were in attendance and, despite plenty of plainclothes security police being unsubtle about their presence, the atmosphere was peaceful. As all was going well at the rally, I slipped away after a while and had returned home by the late afternoon. I was greeted by my phone ringing. The paralegals at the Human Rights Centre (HRC) had been frantically trying to reach me. Despite the ceasefire, hostilities had flared up in the northern war zone. A group of about 30 people, mostly children, had arrived at the HRC late that afternoon. Extremely frightened, they had sought refuge and asked to spend the night there. They had fled from the Okahenge area in the district of Endola, where large-scale fighting had erupted in the early afternoon. Their accounts spoke of a security force massacre of a group of Swapo insurgents who had infiltrated the area.

I urged the HRC workers to provide them the necessary shelter and proceed to the area to investigate matters first thing the next morning. A number of activists contacted me that evening with similar reports. A meeting was convened at my house the next day, Sunday 2 April. Student, union, church and Swapo Youth League leaders gathered for the meeting. I had by then received two updates from the HRC workers following their fact-finding work. It seemed that the ceasefire had collapsed on its first day and there were reports of human rights violations. It was decided that I would travel the next morning to investigate, with LAC staff lawyer Michaela Clayton and paralegals Pero Nampila and Ono Angula.

We set off in a single-engine air charter flight at first light the next morning (Monday 3 April). The Ondangwa military airbase, which accommodated civilian aircraft at one end, was a hive of military activity with much movement of aircraft and helicopters. It was back on a war footing. Small helicopter gunships and larger helicopters were urgently buzzing around. As we left our aircraft and made our way to Karl Ndoroma, who had come to collect us, a military ambulance rushed to meet a landing helicopter.

Karl took us straight to Okahenge, the scene of the first hostilities on 1 April. He had met with local residents the day before, who were awaiting us. The homestead belonging to Jacob Wedenge was closest to the scene of the fighting and had been partially destroyed in the course of the clash. Three brick structures had been razed to the ground and their contents totally destroyed. We interviewed Jesiah Wedenge, an articulate high-school student aged approximately eighteen. At about 10 am on the morning of 1 April, he had first seen a large number of footprints nearby. Soon afterwards, a Swapo guerrilla in uniform had emerged from the nearby bush and introduced himself as Simon. He had explained that the guerrillas were 'no longer making war' as there was now a ceasefire. He was, however, armed with an SKS rifle. They would also not be seeking food from residents this time, as they had brought their own supplies.

Jesiah took us to a small clearing in the surrounding bush close to where the group of guerrillas had been attacked. Strewn around were numerous partially consumed cans of Danish pork loaf and other cans with labels in what resembled Russian script. Although Simon had not spelled out their purpose in coming to the area, he had been in a relaxed frame of mind and assured Jesiah that the guerrillas were not 'troubled'.

Some hours later, at approximately 1:20 pm, Jesiah was walking back home from his neighbour and noticed an unusual plume of smoke, like those emitted by smoke grenades to alert ground or air support to a location. In less than ten minutes, heavy gunfire deafeningly erupted with the arrival of two helicopters (one big and one small, presumably a Puma and an Alouette). Jesiah and others in their homestead had scrambled for cover, seeking safety under their beds, and were fortunately unscathed despite the three separate rooms in their homestead complex being destroyed in the heavy gunfire.

There were numerous spent shells lying around, including those from RPGs and SKS and AK-47 rifles, as well as those from R4 rifles, used by the security forces at the nearby scene of the engagement. Karel, a former PLAN officer, was able to make these identifications. There were also several large spent shells, approximately 20 mm in diameter, apparently the type shot from large firearms housed in helicopters or mounted on Casspirs.

The partially consumed tins of food suggested that the guerrillas were having a meal when they had been attacked. This was confirmed by another nearby resident, a woman who noticed when fetching water that the guerrillas were eating and resting when Casspirs and helicopters had arrived and the firing had started. We also saw a replica of a medical kit. Most of the supplies were of Dutch origin. There were also numerous pairs of underwear at the scene. A short distance away, Jesiah pointed out the remains of a belt with an engraved hammer and sickle, and a comb with the name Paulus Kashona inscribed on it.

Jesiah said that no UN personnel had come to the scene or approached him afterwards to find out what happened. Only a group of journalists had called there shortly before us.

We then went to nearby Endola to see Pastor Thomas Ndiwaka-lunga, the resident ELCIN clergyman. He said that he and Dr Nestor Shivute of the Oshakati State Hospital had seen the bodies of 33 guerrillas on Saturday 1 April at Okahenge. The security forces present would not allow them to approach the bodies. He had heard from residents that the guerrillas had entered the area overnight and reportedly said that they were waiting for a command as to where to report to be monitored by UNTAG, and, stating that they were not there to continue fighting.

On Sunday 2 April between 11 am and 12 noon, fighting had also erupted in the vicinity of Ondeshifilwa, about 10 km northwest of Endola. Pastor Ndiwakalunga discovered 21 corpses at Ondeshifilwa a few hours before seeing us on Monday 3 April, and accompanied us to the site.

At a clearing in the bush at Ondeshifilwa at the large, shallow shona, we saw the corpses for ourselves. I went closer to take photographs of the pitiful sight of 21 corpses piled together without any dignity afforded to those in death. Decomposition had already started to set in, given the heat and humidity in the slightly more than 24 hours following their death. It was comfortably more than 35 degrees at about 3 pm when we were there. Even as a layperson, it was clear to me that several had been shot in their heads, some seemingly at close range – although I could not say for certain.

I realised that I was being watched from a Casspir on the edge of the clearing, parked under a tree. I called Michaela closer. The others had stayed at the vehicle while I had walked over to the bodies to have a closer look. I embraced her and asked her not to be offended as I hastily removed the film, and dropped it discreetly down the front of her blouse, took another spool from my pocket, and turned to take a few more shorts of the dreadful scene. We rejoined the others, who had remained at the vehicle some 30 to 40 metres away. A petrified Pero would not speak again until we landed in Windhoek about three hours later. Karel said the Koevoet members had had their automatic rifles trained on me as I approached the bodies to take my first set of photos, which had distressed Pero.

Pastor Ndiwakalungu complained that he had waited the whole of the previous day at Okahenge for the UN to arrive, to brief them. But they had failed to turn up. No UN personnel had approached him on that day either. Nor had any been to the area to speak to anyone else. Residents in the area spoke of a group of about 70 guerrillas who had come to the area during the night of 31 March or early hours of 1 April. It would appear that the total of 54 bodies he had seen were from this group.

The HRC workers had also received reports of three battles about 10 km east of Outapi in western Owambo on the Sunday, with witnesses seeing about twenty corpses afterwards being taken away and buried in a mass grave at the Outapi military base.

I had seen and heard enough to proceed to the local Security Police headquarters at Oshakati. Colonel Nel, head of the Security Branch there, agreed to see Michaela and me. We requested access to the two guerrillas who had been captured. This was declined after speaking to his superior, Brig. Nel (of *Mushimba* notoriety). A laborious reference to Proclamation AG 9 was provided as the reason, saying that only the AG could authorise access. Colonel Nel was however prepared to confirm that only two prisoners had been taken at that time (4 pm on Monday 3 April). Upon further questioning, he confirmed that they had both been captured on Saturday 1 April. This meant that no captives were taken on Sunday despite several deaths in encounters (in the subsequent 48 hours). This he confirmed. And in response to a further question, he also said he would have been informed had any more captives been taken on the Monday by the time we saw him. He declined to provide the total numbers of those killed or injured. He was not authorised to do so but said an official press release would be forthcoming later (which put the total, as at Monday 3 April, at 140 killed).

After this terse question and answer session, I summoned all the gravitas I could and pertinently pointed out to him in Afrikaans: 'In view of what we have seen and heard, I must formally point out that summary executions and a policy not to take prisoners would amount to a serious war crime. I'll be expressing my grave concern about this to the UN as a matter of urgency. I am giving you notice as of now, 4 pm on 3 April, of my intention to do so and I'll confirm to the UN that I have done so as of this moment. This is now a matter of record and I'll also confirm this to you in writing.'

I added that, given UN involvement, there would be far less scope for indemnities and the customary cover-up. I cannot recall ever addressing a senior security police officer in this way. The circumstances called for it.

A frosty and sullen look was the sole response.

As we rushed to the airport, I made notes about precisely what was said and checked the details with Michaela. The military activity at the airport seemed even more frenzied as we boarded our small plane. Pero had still not spoken a word since the traumatic visit to Ondeshifilwa. As soon as the small plane settled at its cruising altitude, I furiously set about writing a report for the UN Special Representative, Mr Martti Ahtisaari. Michaela, shaken and drained by the day's events, stoically assisted as we recorded the events. I would finalise the report that evening and it was completed early the next morning.

We were able to deliver it to Mr Ahtisaari personally at Eros Airport as he was about to fly to the north that morning at about 9 am. He was accompanied by the head of the UN military component, General Prem Chand, to investigate what had happened.

In our report, we concluded that 60–70 guerrillas had been present at Okahenge on 1 April. They had not been seen before in the area and had presumably infiltrated the area from Angola the previous night. (Okahenge is a mere 15 km from the Angolan border.) The skirmish at Okahenge did not appear to have been initiated by the guerrillas. On the contrary, indications were that they were not in the area with hostile intentions, even though they were armed.

We also stated that there had been fighting in the Ondeshifilwa area on 2 April and that 21 corpses were discovered in a nearby clearing the next morning. There were no signs of fighting where they were discovered, but there were nearby. It seemed that the bodies had been unceremoniously dumped in a group together there after the engagement. We expressed concern that the bodies had been left to decompose and by reports of mass graves elsewhere. The guerrilla death toll had on Monday afternoon been later announced as 140.

We recorded our meeting and sent an urgent letter to the security forces, calling upon them to observe the provisions of the Inquest Act, observe basic human decency in dealing with corpses, and allow families to bury their dead with dignity.

We concluded:

> We wish to express our gravest concern at the fact that so few people are being taken prisoner, and we are obliged, most regrettably, to infer from the circumstances that there would appear to be a policy of not taking any further prisoners after allegedly capturing the first two guerrillas.

We also expressed our concern at the role of UNTAG. We referred to their failure to investigate the matter by not having approached key witnesses from the area. We also saw little, if any, evidence of a UN presence in northern Namibia and questioned whether UN police and military observers were accompanying the security forces and properly monitoring their conduct in the area:

> If the UN is not monitoring and observing security force action, we urge the Special Representative as a matter of utmost urgency to ensure that same is done forthwith. We point out that there has already been an extremely excessive loss of life and that further excessive casualties may be curbed by the timely and most urgent intervention by the Special Representative. We are accordingly concerned that the obligations of the UN in terms of Resolution 435 . . . are not being fully complied with. We respectfully consider that the compliance with these are imperative to avoid further loss of life.

I faxed a copy of the report to Gay McDougall in Washington. Her organisation had put together a Commission on Independence for Namibia comprising a number of eminent American diplomats, academics, civil rights lawyers and former politicians. The Commission had a permanent presence in Namibia throughout the process and sent three observer missions of distinguished Americans at different stages of the process. The LAC worked closely with the Commission in pursuing its mandate. It was my special privilege to accompany all three delegations on their respective visits to northern areas. One included George McGovern, whose hero status for me was further enhanced by his humility and warmth.

Gay provided our report to the UN delegations of the frontline states in New York. They in turn urgently circulated it to Security Council members and the UN Secretary General.

The concerns expressed about a policy of taking no prisoners received wide publicity in the media and were, to my knowledge, urgently taken up diplomatically with the South African government by a number of governments. The South African government had made much fuss about Swapo breaching the letter and spirit of the ceasefire agreement by sending a large group of armed guerrillas into Namibia. The high moral ground of a ceasefire breach enjoyed by South Africa, however, was soon surrendered by the excessive (and disproportionate) response that seemed to me to amount to a serious breach of international law.

The ratio of prisoners taken to fatalities at the time of the report was 1:70 (2 prisoners were captured to 140 killed at that stage). This ratio changed radically over the days and weeks that followed our report. By the time the ceasefire was finally restored several weeks later, the total number of Swapo fatalities stood at 316, with at least 31 prisoners. This meant that, after our report, 176 guerrillas had been slain and 29 taken prisoner.[73] The ratio of prisoners to those killed had changed from 1:70 to 1:6 after our report. I believe that our urgent intervention assisted in galvanising diplomatic pressure, which ameliorated the scale of human rights abuses and saved several lives. A total of 27 security force members were said to have lost their lives – the highest death toll in the war since the carnage at Cassinga.

Two days after our visit and report, I received a coded confidential message from the HRC that at least one Swapo guerrilla wanted to hand himself over to the UN. I was told that there were others in a similar position. Our intervention was sought to achieve this. We urgently met Cedric Thornberry, chief director in Ahtisaari's office. We called upon the UN to set up a mechanism as a matter of utmost urgency to enable PLAN fighters to report to assembly points under UNTAG supervision for repatriation to their bases in Angola to

---

73   Thornberry, C. 2004. *A Nation Is Born*. Gamsberg Macmillan: Windhoek, pp. 125–126.

avoid further loss of life. Thornberry was sympathetic to our request and favoured the idea but said that the bigger problem was salvaging the peace plan, which was then in danger of collapsing. There would only be progress on an agreement about assembly points if intense diplomatic efforts to keep the process afloat yielded success. He would let us know. I travelled to the HRC on the Thursday to coordinate measures with local activists who were acting as go-betweens between the guerrillas who wanted to report to the UN and us.

The wheels of diplomacy moved far more slowly than we had anticipated, however. The fighting continued and the harboured insurgent was becoming increasingly uneasy. As were we. The Terrorism Act remained in place (and would only be repealed a few months later with other discriminatory and repressive laws as part of the peace plan). Being party to harbouring an insurgent carried a five-year minimum term of imprisonment. When no word was heard from Thornberry about progress after two more days, our informal group met to decide on a course of action. Again, we felt let down by the UN. One of our group volunteered to transport the guerrilla to western Owambo near Ruacana for him to slip back to Angola and to let the others know that this would be the safer course. I then returned to Windhoek after these tense few days.

Our report did not find favour in all quarters. It received wide local coverage, together with one of my photos of the 21 corpses piled together at Ondeshifilwa, which was splashed across the pages of The Namibian. A few days later, a delegation of four leading members of the Swapo Youth League, prominent student activists and also friends, visited me at home to voice their concern about the report because it deviated from Swapo's official line, denying a breach of the ceasefire agreement, by asserting that all the guerrillas had merely gathered at 'temporary bases' to be monitored and observed by UNTAG. I explained that this version was contrary to the facts we encountered on the ground as we had reported. The guerrillas were not previously in the area and certainly did not have temporary bases there in any sense. All the evidence pointed to a large incursion, which was not only in violation of the ceasefire but seemed to be a massive military miscalculation with tragic consequences causing so much unnecessary loss of life and nearly the collapse of the peace plan.

Two of the group seemed to accept my explanation while the other two nevertheless forcefully urged me to retract that part of the report, which I declined to do.

Some of the local UN staff were disappointed with our criticism of their failure to be properly ready for the implementation of the peace plan at its outset. They were hopelessly understaffed on 1 April. Observers were only in place several days later. But Ahtisaari was big enough to acknowledge to me later that there were severe logistical challenges for his mission at the outset. He never showed any resentment at our criticism. On the contrary, his immensely professional and diplomatic approach characterised his dealings throughout the process. He plainly had appreciation for the role of civil society and a human rights organisation in raising our concerns.

Swapo brought an urgent court application calling upon the security forces to comply with the Inquest Act and exhume the bodies that had been dumped into mass graves.[74] This application was postponed and later became overtaken by diplomatic developments.

The intense diplomatic efforts took time to bear fruit. The western powers pressured the South African government (through its Foreign Minister, Pik Botha) to continue with the process and the frontline states in Luanda persuaded then Swapo President Nujoma to order all remaining PLAN troops inside Namibia to regroup and report in Angola.

It was agreed that the peace plan would continue. Nujoma's instruction to PLAN fighters to report in Angola was noted and Pik Botha

---

74   *The Namibian*, 6 April 1989.

promised Swapo guerrillas safe passage if they surrendered their arms to UNTAG at eight assembly points designated on the border and ten inside the country. This was too late for most surviving guerrillas, however. Most had already returned to Angola by then. Only seven had reported to assembly points by 17 April.[75] Importantly, all sides seemed satisfied that the process under the peace plan had been restored. Which it had, after this dangerous and tragic start.

It subsequently emerged that a high-level UN interview with the first two prisoners captured (at different places) on 1 April confirmed what was stated in our report. The captives both confirmed that they had received instructions to enter into Namibia and not to engage the security forces if they came across them because the ceasefire would come into effect on 1 April. Their orders included carrying all their arms with them, including RPGs, anti-tank and anti-aircraft devices. One of them said that, once in Namibia, they would receive orders from their commander about where to report to the UN. The other said he would receive instructions once in Namibia from his commander to establish a base that would be monitored by the UN. His task was also to observe whether South African forces were observing the ceasefire.[76]

The incursion, said by South Africa to involve about 1 200 PLAN fighters,[77] was a serious blunder. There was no provision in the peace plan for Swapo to establish military bases inside Namibia after the commencement of the ceasefire. On the contrary, it was a breach of its terms, costing so many lives unnecessarily. There has to date been no accountability on this issue on either side – neither by those who were party to the reckless blunder nor those who were party to the wholesale killings in the disproportionate response. Our early intervention, invoking legal and human rights principles, I believe helped to save some lives.

---

75 Thornberry, C. 2004. *A Nation Is Born*. Gamsberg Macmillan: Windhoek, p. 118.

76 Thornberry, C. 2004. *A Nation Is Born*. Gamsberg Macmillan: Windhoek, pp. 96–98.

77 *New York Times*, 4 April 1989.

After the stuttering and perilous start, the peace plan gradually picked up momentum as its key components were successfully completed at each stage, culminating in the elections and adoption of the Constitution. The LAC participated in certain of these, making representations on discriminatory laws to be repealed and commenting on draft legislation for the registration of voters and later for the election. A highlight for me was representing all of the prisoners in the political section in their application for release as political prisoners.

It was also heartwarming to witness the repatriation of about 40 000 Namibian refugees from exile. The UNHCR and its local partner, the CCN, excelled in this mammoth task.

The election itself was also a momentous occasion, smoothly conducted under UN supervision; in a miraculously short time, a fine Constitution was agreed upon by the Constituent Assembly with the required two-thirds majority.

Amidst these historic high points, there was tragedy of another kind entirely during the process. Anton Lubowski was assassinated outside his home on the night of 12 September 1989.

14

The assassination of Anton Lubowski

The prime eating spot in Windhoek in 1989 was Hotel Fürstenhof's dining room. On 12 September 1989, the implementation of the UN peace plan had reached an advanced stage, with the return of exiled Swapo leaders imminent and the elections less than two months away. Despite Windhoek teeming with observers and diplomats, the vice president of one of the LAC's principal funders, the Ford Foundation, had secured a booking at the Fürstenhof and invited me for dinner there. As the ornate plate covers were simultaneously removed with a flourish to reveal delectable offerings, one of the waiting staff briskly approached our table.

'Mr Smuts, you are wanted on the telephone.'

'Are you sure it's me they're looking for? I didn't mention to any-one I'd be here.'

'Yes, Mr Smuts, I'm very sure. I was told it's very urgent.'

It was approaching 8.30 pm. Andrew was on the line.

'I have terrible and shocking news. A few moments ago Anton was gunned down and killed outside his house as he was about to enter through the small gate.'

I gasped. 'What?'

'Yes, it's truly shocking. Michaela was inside the house at the time.

Heard the shots. She's unharmed, but in a severe state of shock. I am with her now and with Colonel Smit [of the police]. He says you must stay put until they arrive. Go back into the dining room. Don't go outside or attempt to go home. You must not move until the police arrive for you. And under no circumstances go home. Hold on a sec.'

He broke away for a moment and I heard another voice talking to him in the background.

'They should be there with you within 15 to 20 minutes.'

I was so shocked that I was only able to ask how he knew where to phone.

'I didn't. This is third place I've tried. Just wait for us and we'll brief you shortly.'

As I sank into my seat, I imparted the grim news to my host, engulfed in shock. I looked down at my plate, which would remain untouched, unable to speak and impatient to leave. We sat in silence until eventually Andrew motioned to me from the doorway. By then, a newsflash of Anton's killing had appeared on local TV and I could hear other diners talking animatedly about it. As I walked out, the steady din of diners' chatter gave way to a hush and whispering as their intense stares followed my every movement through the dining room.

Andrew said to follow him to his house, where he had just taken Michaela. Colonel Smit stressed that I must under no circumstances go home and that he would speak to me the following day. I called my friend Tony Figueira and asked him to join us at Andrew's. Tony agreed to let me spend that and the next night at his place.

A very shaken Michaela awaited me at Andrew's. Her body trembled as she wept quietly. She was inconsolable. A few more friends arrived to support her, all in disbelief at the tragic turn of events.

Michaela and I had become close friends after she joined the LAC upon its establishment in July 1988. Within a month or so she had met Anton, given our small social circle of like-minded people. They started going out and were soon in a committed and serious relationship. Anton was divorced. After meeting Michaela, he told me that he was ready to settle again although he sorely missed his children, who lived in Cape Town with their mother – who had insisted on very limited access by Anton in their acrimonious divorce, much to his intense frustration, as he doted on them.

Michaela and Anton were living together at the time. He had been held up that evening at the Swapo election offices and had called to ask her to be ready to join him for dinner with the Swapo election director, Hage Geingob. While waiting for him inside the house, she had heard a rapid series of bangs, which she thought could be firecrackers being thrown into the yard. Anton had parked in the street and was about to enter the pedestrian gate to collect Michaela, instead of driving into the motorised driveway gate, to save time. As he approached the gate, a hail of bullets struck him down from close quarters. Four of the bullets – in all, twelve spent cartridges were found there – struck Anton in the head. His death was instantaneous. The municipal streetlights in his street had, by strange coincidence, been turned off when he had been shot, but were later turned back on at the instance of the police after they had arrived at the crime scene.

One of their neighbours, hearing automatic gunfire, quickly came out to see a red Toyota Conquest speed off and discovered Anton's motionless body close to the pedestrian gate. He rushed to call his wife, a doctor, and also called the police, who were there within minutes. His wife pronounced Anton dead from the multiple bullet wounds to his head. A forensics expert estimated that they were fired at very close range – about six to nine metres. When the police broke the news to Michaela, the recent death threats that Anton and I had received were mentioned. The police decided to get hold of me. Andrew, who had been called to support Michaela, then tracked me down. It had all happened very fast. In his haste to collect Michaela, and given the darkness in the street, Anton most likely did not notice a nearby car approach – or, more probably, await – him in the darkness, conveying his assailants.

After Anton had started dating Michaela, I had seen him even more frequently than before as he was constantly in and out of our offices. He would always look in on me – often just to greet if in a rush, or sometimes to linger for a chat.

Anton and I had become friends in my first year at Stellenbosch University in 1973. We were in the same hostel and both had home addresses in Namibia. He hailed from Aus in southern Namibia. He had started at Stellenbosch the previous year and decided to switch to law, which meant that we were also classmates for three years. He was actually quite conservative politically at that time (but not a National Party supporter). He came from 'bloedsap' stock – supporters of the old United Party (of General Smuts), which opposed the excesses of the National Party. Anton's politics underwent a profound change after he moved to the University of Cape Town for his LLB upon completing his undergraduate degree with me at Stellenbosch. After completing his studies at UCT, he did his articles at Lorentz and Bone and became politically involved, holding a leadership position in the multiracial grouping called the Namibian National Front (NNF) that sought to provide a liberal, non-racial alternative to Pretoria's favoured ethnically based grouping, the DTA, and also to Swapo, seen by many as Marxist and communist.

A few years later, in March 1984, Anton joined Swapo. The press conference announcing this received wide coverage as Swapo now had a prominent white member. Except for the *Windhoek Observer*, the local media were vitriolic and antagonistic in their reporting of this. As an advocate in private practice, dependent on referrals from attorneys, all of whom except for Hosea were then white, his work almost dried up – only receiving some work from our firm. He became very active in politics and more prominent within Swapo's structures. He was a thorn in the side of the South African security establishment and their local backers, particularly *Die Republikein*, which was relentless in its attempts to ridicule and demonise him. He was detained by the security police six times after joining Swapo, but never once charged with any offence. In the run-up to the election, his stature within Swapo had grown considerably and he was appointed Deputy Director: Finance and Administration of the election campaign. He worked closely with the director, Hage Geingob, whom he much admired.

Our last serious discussion had been on the morning of 25 August. On the previous evening I had received an unsettling death threat. As I picked up the phone, a recording started to play – of a male voice with a slight Afrikaans accent menacingly saying in English, 'We know all about you. Sam is coming and we are going to get you.'

Towards the end of the recording, the sound of wailing and screaming women and children rose in the background and increased to a crescendo, to disturbing effect. The call was repeated. And followed by calls featuring wailing and screaming.

There had been some abusive and threatening calls in the past. At about the same time, there had been a crudely put together pamphlet made up photos of Gwen, me and John Liebenberg copied from the media with drawn-in targets superimposed on each of our faces and captions calling for us to be eliminated. There was a reference to Anton in the pamphlet (to the effect that I had prevented people like Anton from dying on the gallows.) These photocopied pamphlets had been strewn around the campus of the Academy.

However, this call seemed different. There was an immediacy to it, connected to the imminent return from exile of then Swapo president, Sam Nujoma, two or three weeks later. His homecoming was widely seen as one of the seminal moments in the peace plan. The call also seemed more professionally put together than the occasional abusive calls I had previously received.

I was alone at home at the time and received advice from Geoff Budlender to contact the Windhoek Police Station's charge office and ask them to record the threat in their occurrence register. About ten minutes later, a police lieutenant colonel was at my front door with a few uniformed policemen. He expressed concern for my security and left two armed guards overnight – one inside and the other outside the house. He returned in the morning. We agreed that the guards then be withdrawn as it was so intrusive.

I phoned Anton early that morning and suggested we meet. It was Friday, 25 August. He promptly came around to my office. To my surprise, he had not yet received a similar threat. He and Michaela had probably been out. I urged him to make sure that he answer the phone to avoid exposing Michaela to such a harrowing call, as I was certain he would receive one. Since joining Swapo, he had constantly been subjected to threats and abuse – far more than Gwen or I received. There had been an increase in these after the start of the peace plan. We turned to discuss current political developments and he spoke excitedly about the future and the prospect of a possible role in an elected Swapo government.

Geingob had mooted the idea of Attorney-General, a cabinet position, in a Swapo government. Anton discussed his intention to propose something different to Geingob – either in trade or tourism. But before doing so, he wanted to find out from me whether he could recommend me as Attorney-General as an alternative when making his proposal. He generously said that I was a better fit for that and that the law was ultimately not his true calling, adding that he badly wanted to work with me in a new government. I was committed to the LAC whose existence was then being challenged, and declined the idea of setting up a meeting with Geingob until after that was resolved and its position secured. I was also to embark on a ten-day camping trip to Kaokoveld immediately after the LAC case was heard on the following Monday (28 August).

We agreed to talk again upon my return. But that was not to be. He was gunned down on the second night after my return to town.

The day after Anton's killing, I was accompanied by heavily armed police to collect some clothing from my home. Colonel Smit interviewed me briefly about the recent threatening calls and, together with senior UN police observers, advised me to take immediate and elaborate measures to improve the security and not to stay at home until those were completed.

Cedric Thornberry also came to see me and, on behalf of Ahtisaari, strongly urged me to leave town until after the election for my own safety. The UN's intelligence had revealed that there remained a threat. He made a similar approach to Gwen. I left the next day but returned after five days for Anton's funeral, anxious to get back to work. On my return, Thornberry informed me that the UN insisted that I receive armed police guards at night and urged me to accept this arrangement. It remained in place until after the election results were announced. It was disruptive as the guards were on four-hour shifts, with the 2 am change always waking me up.

On the day after Anton's assassination, Col. Smit received a tip-off from a German-speaking couple about the suspicious conduct of an Irishman called Donald Acheson, who was a short-term tenant of their outside flat in Klein Windhoek. He had previously stayed there for a few nights at a time. He had returned on 10 September and had a hired car – a white Volkswagen Fox, which he exchanged for a red Toyota Conquest the next day. On the day of Anton's assassination, they saw him carrying an item that he appeared anxious to conceal. When he returned to his car later on, he carried a larger item covered up in a big hessian bag. It seemed heavy, and the size of an automatic rifle. This was also carried surreptitiously. They saw him noisily return later to ensure that he would be noticed. But he slipped out again later, climbing over a wall instead of using the path and gate so as not to be seen. And when he returned much later that night, he again scaled the wall to enter.

Acheson was arrested and held as a prohibited immigrant and on suspicion of murder. His hired vehicle had 'wonder glue' on the back number plate, consistent with using a false number plate.

A forensics officer also found that there were marks on the car roof matching those made by the butt of an automatic rifle resting on the roof when fired from close quarters at Anton.

After his arrest, Col. Smit left a pad and pen in Acheson's cell. Acheson obliged; some notes were subsequently found under his matress in his cell. They described meetings in Swaziland with Chappie Maree[78] after an initial approach by Ferdi Barnard.[79] The notes referred to receiving money and being sent to Windhoek. After returning to Johannesburg, there was mention of another meeting in Swaziland, more money, being told to return to Windhoek, and a rented car swapped for a red Toyota Conquest.

Col. Smit's breakthrough in the investigation came when he obtained a radio pager number from Acheson and was able to trace this number to Ferdi Barnard, a former policeman and convicted murderer in South Africa. During questioning, Acheson admitted that Barnard was his 'handler'.

Smit established from the Windhoek supplier that Barnard had hired the pager in the name of an alias he used.[80]

Smit turned his attention to Barnard and approached Brigadier Floris Mostert, who was investigating the murder of David Webster – a South African activist who, like Anton, had been gunned down outside his home in Johannesburg in May 1989 in what also appeared to be a political assassination.

Following Smit's approach and the evidence connecting Acheson to Barnard, Mostert moved against both Barnard and Calla Botha.

On 31 October 1989, Barnard was detained under security legis-

---

78   Known only to Acheson by his alias, Derek.
79   Referred to by his alias Harry van Staden.
80   (Harry van Staden).

lation, together with Botha. A few months beforehand, they had both been picked up by the police for their invasive and suspicious surveillance of the End Conscription Campaign[81] office in Johannesburg and one of its leading members, Bruce White. But they were released on the same day.

Barnard was formerly with the Brixton Murder and Robbery squad, which was well known for ruthless methods in investigating serious crime. Some of its members themselves turned to violent crime and turned out to be prime candidates for recruitment to a covert SADF unit called the Civil Cooperation Bureau (CCB), which engaged in killing opponents of the apartheid regime and other criminal behaviour to disrupt their activities and intimidate them.

In December 1984, Barnard had been sentenced to twenty years' imprisonment on two counts of murder, one of attempted murder and three of vehicle theft. After serving only three years, he was surprisingly released on parole in December 1987. Barnard was questioned by both Mostert and Smit and made two affidavits during his detention – the first on 27 November 1989 and a second to Smit on 21 December 1989.

In his affidavit, Barnard provided leads to Smit, linking the CCB to Acheson. Barnard admitted involvement in a 'military connected organisation' but professed ignorance of its name initially. Details of the CCB were later provided by Botha.

Barnard's first CCB handler was Lafras Luitingh, whose task was to recruit collaborators who would not be aware of the organisation.

In January 1989, Luitingh instructed Barnard to establish – through contacts with the security police in Windhoek – information about Anton, including where he lived and his position within Swapo. In March 1989, Luitingh told him to travel to Windhoek to ascertain the place of residence and his movements, and details of vehicles that

---

81   A leading anti-apartheid organisation, much hated by the military, which campaigned against compulsory conscription in South Africa.

Dan Tjongarero used, as well as his daily routine. Luitingh informed Barnard that the CCB wanted to drive a wedge between the external and internal wings of Swapo. Barnard suspected that Dan would become a target of the organisation. Barnard was to make contact with a certain 'Charles' in Windhoek (who turned out to be Charles Neelse) if he encountered any problems.

After returning to Windhoek, Barnard established Dan's home address through a journalist. After his return, he was told by Luitingh that Staal Burger[82] would deal further with him (and be his 'handler').

Barnard also disclosed that Acheson had been introduced to him after the latter's arrest for shoplifting. Acheson told Barnard that he had been a mercenary and was available as a 'hit man' if the pay was good enough. After reporting this meeting to Luitingh, Barnard was apparently paid off by Luitingh in June 1989. But this was not the end of his association with the CCB. A certain 'Chris' contacted him soon afterwards and offered him freelance work in Windhoek. This would include sabotaging minibus taxis used by Swapo and disrupting their meetings by various means, including using poisonous snakes.

Following Acheson's arrest, Barnard was contacted by Luitingh, who was concerned that no link should emerge between Acheson's arrest and the organisation. He was told to destroy his pager forthwith.

In Barnard's second statement on 21 December 1989, after a further interview with Smit (and no doubt after Botha's affidavit), he clarified Botha's role. He was told by Botha that Anton's murder was an approved (military) special forces 'operation' and that Chappie Maree had at the time been Acheson's handler.

Barnard did not, however, make a full disclosure and was untruthful in some respects. In his version, he was last in Windhoek in July 1989. But his vehicle was found at Windhoek airport on the day of

---

82   Referred to by his alias Nick Verbeek.

the murder. It had also picked up parking tickets during August 1989. And he omitted to disclose the surveillance upon Dan and Anton, which he had undertaken with Charles Neelse. Neelse subsequently gave evidence at the inquest into Anton's death in 1994; he had obtained a video camera and driven past Anton's house three times to take footage of his home and surroundings. Barnard had also given Neelse a list of Swapo vehicles to be sabotaged. Realising that a connection with Neelse was incriminating, Barnard sought to distance himself from Neelse by omitting these details.

Botha, too, made an affidavit during detention – on 12 December 1989. He had also been a policeman with the Brixton Murder and Robbery squad, which he left on 30 June 1988 together with his seniors, Lieutenant Colonel Staal Burger, Leon (Chappie) Maree and Lieutenant Abraham 'Slang' van Zyl. They were recruited together to join the CCB and given training by CCB head Joe Verster, Wouter Basson and another operative. Botha sketched details of CCB involvement in Namibia as well as CCB criminal conduct against activists in South Africa.

Botha was dispatched to Namibia in 1988 to assess Swapo's prospects of success in the election. His report predicted a Swapo victory. This did not go down well with Burger, Basson and Verster. Each member of his CCB cell was assigned two targets. His were Frank Chikane and Bruce White. Barnard worked for him after being dismissed by Luitingh. Botha confirmed their arrest while doing surveillance on White. He obtained Acheson's details and provided them to Burger, who informed him that Maree had become Acheson's handler.

After Acheson's arrest, Botha described a chaotic emergency CCB meeting convened at a Johannesburg hotel. Acheson's arrest had caused panic, particularly on the part of Burger and Maree. The meeting resolved that Maree should 'go away' and 'lie low'. After his arrest, Barnard was assured by Burger not to be concerned as 'it would be stopped from the top'.

During his detention Botha said he was visited by two brigadiers – Engelbrecht and Van Rensburg – and told by Engelbrecht that he must keep quiet.

Botha also stated that Namibia was a high priority for the CCB in 1989 and that Hidipo Hamutenya, then one of Swapo's foremost leaders who had returned from exile in 1989, was one of Burger's 'projects'.

Barnard and Botha's arrests occurred shortly after F.W. de Klerk was sworn in as state president of South Africa on 20 September 1989. The tide had eventually turned against P.W. Botha, who had been ousted from within South Africa's ruling National Party. In his inauguration, F.W. de Klerk promised reforms and relaxing the state of emergency.[83] Unlike his predecessor, he was not perceived to be part of the military or security force establishment.

A month after De Klerk assumed office, on 20 October 1989, the (South African) *Weekly Mail* broke the story of Butana Almond Nofemela, a former security policeman on death row who, within days of his scheduled execution, claimed that he was a member of a (police) security branch death squad, based at Vlakplaas, a farm near Pretoria. The death squad had assassinated several opponents of the apartheid state. These included the well-known Durban attorney, Griffiths Mxenge. Nofemela had been convicted of murdering a farmer, unconnected with his death squad activities. The fact that he was on death row for a brutal murder undermined the credibility of his claims. But he gave details of nine assassinations he claimed were carried out by that squad, providing the names of senior security police officers and the victims. These claims had a distinct ring of truth about them.

The breakthrough in exposing the Vlakplaas unit followed in early November 1989 by the recently established independent Afrikaans weekly *Die Vrye Weekblad*. Founded by editor Max du Preez and

---

83   *The New York Times*, 22 September 1989.

journalist Jacques Pauw, it soon earned a reputation for its fearless criticism of the apartheid state, incurring the wrath of the establishment in no time at all. Its exposés were exceptionally well researched. The authorities, plainly paranoid about its impact (and the truth it exposed), threw the book at them, prosecuting the paper and unleashing the power of the apartheid state against this courageous publication.

In early November, the *Vrye Weekblad* broke the story of Captain Dirk Coetzee, who had previously been in charge of the security police's Vlakplaas death squad and its deeply disturbing activities. He outlined a police unit bent upon assassinating apartheid's opponents both inside South Africa and outside its borders. The powerful story was written by Pauw, a truly outstanding investigative journalist who went on to expose not only the workings of that notorious unit but also the CCB and other state agencies engaging in extrajudicial killings and dirty tricks. He has meticulously documented the workings and operations of these state agents in two books.[84]

The leadership of the South African police vehemently rubbished Coetzee's claims, describing them as 'unfounded, untested and wild'. These reports rocked the South African establishment, but also reverberated through the region and in western capitals.[85]

Many of those involved in human rights work had for some time suspected state involvement in targeted killings of activists but proof and a will to investigate these crimes on the part of the police were lacking, as demonstrated by Shifidi's murder and its cover-up.

At about the time of these shocking revelations in the South African media came Smit's detective work, which linked Anton's assassi-

---

84   Pauw, J. 2017. *In the Heart of the Whore: The Story of Apartheid's Deatch Squads.* Jonathan Ball Publishers: Johannesburg; and Pauw, J. 2017. *Into the Heart of Darkness: Confessions of Apartheid's Assassins.* Jonathan Ball Publishers: Johannesburg.

85   *The New York Times*, 19 November 1989 and 23 November 1989; *The Boston Globe*, 22 November 1989.

nation through Acheson, to Barnard and Botha, to a covert military death squad (the CCB) which engaged in assassinating opponents of the apartheid state.

Pressure mounted on De Klerk to appoint a judicial enquiry. This he eventually did on 31 January 1990, announcing a commission of inquiry headed by Judge Louis Harms into 'murders and deeds of violence allegedly committed with political motives'.

Although the details of Barnard and Botha's affidavits were not in the public domain, the existence of a military hit squad would have been brought to the attention of the top echelons of the police in South Africa – and no doubt to De Klerk – prior to Harms's appointment.

Smit had also, on 2 February 1990, procured warrants for the arrests of Maree and Burger, implicated by Botha and Barnard, for complicity in Anton's murder. But unsurprisingly, they could not be located before Namibia became independent on 21 March 1990. The CCB connection to Anton's killing and news of those warrants would no doubt have been provided to (and troubled) the ultimate head of the CCB, Magnus Malan, Minister of Defence.

Within weeks, on 26 February 1990, Malan went on the offensive and announced in parliament:

> I want to disclose today that Lubowski was a paid agent of Military Intelligence. I am assured that he did good work for the SADF. The Chief of Staff Intelligence, General Rudolf Badenhorst would therefore never have approved actions against Lubowski.

There was widespread outrage at Anton's character being besmirched in this way – both in Namibia and South Africa. I certainly did not believe it. Nor did anyone else who had been close to Anton. It later became apparent that Malan's words were carefully selected. When the evidence about the CCB's structure and modus operandi emerged, Badenhorst was not part of the authorising chain of command for the CCB but the general officer in charge of Special Operations. He would not have approved CCB targets.

Malan referred to three deposits paid into an account Anton controlled. They were not in the name of military intelligence but from a company called Global Capital Investments.

In response to Malan's claim, F.W. de Klerk widened the terms of reference of Harms's inquiry to investigate whether Anton had worked for Military Intelligence, but not to establish whether a state death squad had been involved in his murder and attempts to disrupt the peace plan in Namibia. Harms took a very narrow view of his mandate and refused lawyers representing Anton's family from questioning witnesses about the involvement of the CCB in his killing because that had occurred outside South Africa – even though the murder conspiracy could have, and had, I believe, been formed in South Africa and was thus a crime in South Africa.

When evidence was given about payments to Anton at the commission, the military applied for it to be heard behind closed doors. Harms succumbed to that. Not even lawyers representing Anton's family were permitted to be present to challenge the evidence. On the strength of this one-sided self-serving testimony, Harms unfortunately concluded that Anton had been paid by Military Intelligence (MI).

I recall that Anton had, in his last months, mentioned being offered a share in commissions for purchasing houses on behalf of Swapo by an estate agent. I cautioned him against receiving any commissions or kickbacks whatsoever for any purchases. I was left with the distinct impression that he accepted my advice. He also spoke of dealings with a South African concern supplying furniture for the Swapo houses Anton had ordered. It was clear to me from our discussion that its agent had ingratiated himself with Anton. After his death, it was suggested that the three payments into the account controlled by Anton had its origin from those dealings and that the furniture concern was a MI front.[86] The payments were made by a company set up by MI through its lawyer. The amounts were paid into an account operated by a trust to fund bond instalments for a property in Hout Bay, Cape Town, acquired for Anton's divorced wife, where his children would be brought up.

I do not believe Anton knew about those payments made in June, July and August as his own personal and professional finances were generally disorganised. He often bemoaned that fact to me. And this was an account he would not have looked at regularly. Even if they did possibly amount to kickbacks for the furniture deal (which I very seriously doubt), I have no doubt that the actual origin of the funds (MI) was entirely unknown to Anton. It is likely that the MI operative in Windhoek involved with the furniture concern established from Anton the existence of this account by befriending him. Anton was outgoing and friendly, accessible to a fault, naïve and indiscriminate in permitting people to befriend him. This operative may then have caused the payments to be made so that it could subsequently be claimed that payments were made to him if it were ever suggested that MI or the military had any part in his assassination, which had been planned prior to those payments. And that is what happened, as it emerged at his inquest – his killing had been planned before the payments. The ultimate problem for Malan's claim and his credibility was that there was more than mere conjecture to support military involvement: there was a body of compelling evidence.

The timing of Malan's character assassination is highly suspicious in the context of facts that subsequently emerged, placing his much-tarnished reputation in an even worse light. His claim came amid mounting evidence of covert military activities by the time the Harms

---

86   Groenink, E. 2018. *Incorruptible: The Story of the Murders of Dulcie September, Anton Lubowski and Chris Hani.* ABC Press: Cape Town.

Commission commenced its work – and, more specifically, after Smit's warrants for the arrest of Burger and Maree on 2 February 1990 after he had obtained conclusive evidence connecting Acheson to Barnard, Botha and the CCB. Most significantly, only a few days before Malan's claim, on 20 February 1990, Slang van Zyl had come forward and made a lengthy statement to the police, explaining in detail how the CCB structure worked and his role within it. His statement was intended for the Harms inquiry and for Smit's murder investigation, firmly buttressing Smit's case implicating the CCB in Anton's murder. Malan would plainly have got wind of these dramatic revelations through MI and Smit's detective work directly linking the CCB to Anton's killing. Malan's outburst, coming only days after Van Zyl's damning statement, was no doubt a calculated and desperate attempt to mislead and deflect attention and blame from the military, as the minister responsible for it. In that capacity, he would have known of the CCB and its overall mandate and activities, even if he had not been fully briefed about each individual target.

Two days after Malan's announcement, investigators from the Harms Commission raided the CCB's secluded headquarters in a Pretoria suburb. Entry to the high-walled premises was refused and an investigator was obliged to scale the perimeter wall to find only secretarial staff there, with almost no documentation of the organisation. It had all been spirited away. The safe was empty. The Harms Commission's demands for documents were met with obfuscation as CCB leadership figures pointed fingers at one another. The result, obviously intended, was that no files were ever forthcoming. No coercive steps were taken by that Commission against these evasive witnesses to compel the documents, however.

The only incriminating evidence seized in the raid and ever obtained from the CCB was the diary of Wouter Basson, which provided convincing contemporaneous corroboration of CCB involvement in Anton's killing and other criminal conduct in Namibia.

Slang van Zyl made three further statements, including one to Smit on 22 March 1990 – the day after Namibia became independent.

In these most revealing statements, Van Zyl confirmed that he left the Brixton Murder and Robbery squad with Burger, Maree and Botha. In their training, it was inculcated in them that the CCB's credo was 'the maximal disruption of the enemies of the Republic of South Africa'. CCB's head, Verster, explained to them in training that when a 'project' entailed killing a person, it should afterwards appear that it was done with a criminal, and not a political, motive. It was stressed that nothing should be traced back to the government. This certainly explains why convicted criminals were sought-after recruits. Targets were accorded a priority ranking. The disruption of 'the enemy' could, according to Van Zyl, include anything from 'breaking a window to the killing of a person'. Targets were identified by the CCB itself and its members were involved in that task. Verster explained to CCB members that targets included those who endangered the safety of the state but enjoyed a high profile, making it difficult for the police to act against them.

The CCB, Van Zyl explained, was a unit under the division of Special Operations of the SADF. There was an 'inner' and 'outer' circle. Those in the inner circle were full-time SADF employees, known as the 'conscious' or 'aware' members. The outer circle comprised persons who were not full-time SADF employees and were indeed unaware that they worked for the SADF – the 'unconscious' members. The CCB was divided into cells, each with a coordinator who was the link to the managing director – Verster. Cells formed part of a region, headed by a regional manager. There were eight regions, including one in Namibia. Regional managers liaised directly with the managing director (Verster) and the chairman, who was a member of the general staff of the SADF in charge of special operations. He had oversight of the CCB and approved its projects.

It came as huge shock to me when it later emerged that the CCB chairman at the time of Anton's death was Major-General Eddie Webb, whom I had known well during my conscription. He had taken over at the beginning of 1989 from Major-General A.J.M. Joubert.

Van Zyl also spelt out that each member made use of at least one or more aliases or code names. Each member was to formulate what was termed a 'blue plan' – a seemingly legitimate business in the private sphere unconnected to the SADF. They would simultaneously have a 'red plan' – their actual, lethal, CCB activities conducted under the cover of their 'blue plan'. They were told to ensure that nothing should be traced back to the SADF.

Although the CCB's focus was largely outside South Africa, with only one of its eight regions (region 6) being South Africa, both Van Zyl and Botha's evidence was that region 6, to which they were attached, was – together with the region for Namibia and another region – focused full-time on Namibia in 1989 to pursue the CCB objective of 'maximal disruption of the enemy' (Swapo) including assassinations and criminal 'dirty tricks' such as sabotage.

Region 6 of the CCB comprised Staal Burger as regional manager and Wouter Basson as coordinator. Its cell members were Van Zyl, Maree and Botha. Within a region, members would propose 'projects' in detail to the regional manager, who would take the proposal to the managing director for approval. A 'project' would detail the target, a motivation for the selection of the target and the method of execution. A budget would accompany a proposal.

When proposals were finally presented, only the motivating member, the coordinator and regional manager would attend, with the managing director, Verster. This was known as the 'in-house presentation'.

According to Basson's subsequent evidence at the Webster inquest, a presentation was preceded by a preliminary study plan, involving a collection of facts and evaluation. If approved at the 'in-house' meeting, it would be presented to the chairman and thereafter executed.

Van Zyl's evidence was thus crucial in prosecuting CCB members for Anton's murder as it coherently set out the CCB's structure and its modus operandi. It is small wonder that Magnus Malan wanted to deflect attention from this covert SADF unit.

After a few postponements in custody, Acheson appeared in the High Court on 18 April 1990, charged with the murder of Anton. Ismail Mohamed, brought in as an acting judge (and one of South Africa's most brilliant counsel, who later served as Chief Justice of both South Africa and Namibia) presided. The Prosecutor-General applied for a postponement of the trial. This was opposed by Acheson's counsel. Smit testified in support of the postponement. The arrest warrants for Burger and Maree issued on 2 February had not resulted in their arrests. After independence, Burger's position was that he was not amenable to court processes from Namibia as a foreign state. Ferdi Barnard informed Smit that he was no longer prepared to testify as a witness. Nor were Van Zyl and Botha. Smit testified that the only way Van Zyl, Botha and Barnard's presence could be secured would be through diplomatic channels. The court postponed the trial to 8 May to enable the prosecution to pursue diplomatic initiatives to procure the attendance of those witnesses. When the case resumed on 8 May, the prosecution provided no evidence of any diplomatic initiatives and instead withdrew the charge of murder against Acheson. The approach of the Prosecutor-General, Hans Heyman, was subsequently trenchantly criticised for this by Judge Levy, who presided over the inquest into Anton's death.

Acheson was then free to go and left Namibia. Some months after his release, Acheson gave a statement to the Brixton Murder and Robbery squad in Johannesburg. It provided more incriminating detail than he had earlier disclosed to Smit. After his arrest for shop-lifting in 1989, a police sergeant sounded him out about going to South West Africa to monitor Swapo, given his military background in Rhodesia. He was then put in touch with Barnard, who also asked if he would go to Windhoek to monitor the elections and observe certain people – and if he would be willing to kill. He was later contacted by his new controller, Chappie Maree (whom he only knew by his alias).[87] He then received his first payment. They subsequently met at the Royal Ascot Hotel in Johannesburg. He agreed to go to Namibia and, after his return, met Maree in Swaziland and also in Johannesburg. He returned again to Windhoek, after receiving another payment from Maree.

Maree called upon him at his rented flat in suburban Windhoek and tasked him with sabotaging Swapo vehicles. He handed explosive devices to him to give to an operative called Taxi (possibly Neelse). Maree gave him Anton's vehicle registration number, and told him to keep a lookout for it. The instruction was also to establish Gwen's vehicle's registration number.

In early September, Maree instructed Acheson to travel to Swaziland to obtain more funds. Maree met him there and again tasked him to return to Windhoek, arriving on 10 September. He had another meeting with Maree in Windhoek and received instructions to hire a car and also to poison Gwen. Not happy with the VW Fox he had hired, he discussed this with Maree as well as difficulties with the plan to poison Gwen. He changed the car for a red Toyota Conquest. Acheson received an AK-47 at his flat, which Maree directed him to take to the Kalahari Sands Hotel on the evening of the murder. But Acheson said he could not deliver it because of a heavy police presence. Instead, he drove out of town on the airport road and buried it there. He returned to his flat, saw newsflashes announcing Anton's murder on TV, and received a call from Maree to lie low for a few days, and then to go to Lusaka where Maree would meet him.

After his release from custody on 7 May 1990, Acheson said he was paid R20 000 in cash and subsequently travelled to Athens where

---

87   Derek.

he received a further US$4 000. He suspected that his legal fees were also paid by the CCB.

The murder investigation by Smit stalled after Acheson's release and the reluctance of both Burger and Maree as accused and Van Zyl, Barnard and Botha as witnesses to attend proceedings in Windhoek.

The Namibian government has never disclosed which steps, if any, it took to secure their presence to face justice in Namibia. No formal extradition proceedings were ever pursued, despite the overwhelming case against them. When this hiatus continued for a few years, a judicial inquest was convened into Anton's death. The formal statutory purpose is to determine whether his death was brought about 'by any act or omission *prima facie* involving or amounting to an offence on the part of any person'. The broader purpose is to have an open inquiry to promote public confidence in the administration of justice and ensure that those responsible for deaths from unnatural causes properly account for what happened and, as far as possible, be brought to justice.[88] The inquest was presided over by Judge Harold Levy. Evidence was heard in April, May and early June 1994; Levy's detailed findings were provided on 23 June 1994.

The Legal Assistance Centre agreed to represent the Lubowski family at the proceedings as there was no longer funding available for private practitioners to do work of that nature, as had been the case in previous years. In 1992, Andrew had taken over from me as director of the LAC and I had returned to private practice. He asked me to assist. He had secured the services of Colin Kahanovitz of the Cape Bar to work full time on the inquest. Colin had worked as an attorney for the LAC for a few years and had just started out at the bar. He would do the research and much of the preparatory work and I would come in, led by the exceptionally fine senior counsel, Wim Trengove of Johannesburg, for the cross-examination of Smit and key

---

88   See *Marais NO v Tiley* 1990 (2) SA 899 (A) at 901.

CCB witnesses. I would also present argument at the conclusion of the inquiry. Wim kindly offered to assist without charge. This plan worked perfectly. Colin conducted a thorough and penetrating analysis of all available material from the Harms Commission of 1990, the Webster inquest in 1992 and all the statements in possession of Smit. All this material served before Judge Levy.

I have already referred to the main features of Barnard, Botha and Van Zyl's statements. Basson was subjected to extensive cross-examination at the Harms inquiry and Webster inquest concerning entries made in his 1989 diary recovered in the raid on the CCB offices. Those entries were revealing. The pages for crucial dates had been torn out of the diary, including the date of Anton's killing and a number of days preceding it. Although some of the diary entries were abbreviated or expressed in cryptic terms, several self-evidently had a direct bearing upon Namibian targets and suspicious activities in Namibia. Much of this was conceded or not disputed by Basson in cross-examination. The first reference to a Namibian target in his diary was in an entry made on 25 April 1989 in which Niko Bessinger, a prominent Swapo leader, was mentioned.

It emerged in evidence at our inquest that CCB operatives Neelse and Niemoller had made a video recording of Anton's home on 8 May. There is a corresponding diary entry on that date referring to making a 'preliminary study of priority targets'. The same date has a reference to targets allocated to operatives, with Van Zyl coupled to a project relating to 'Swapo' and that Staal Burger was allocated Von Finkelstein, bearing a close resemblance to the name of my friend Bjorn (Finky) von Finkenstein, a prominent white Swapo member who became mayor of Windhoek some years after independence.

Namibia featured frequently in entries after 1 July, confirming Van Zyl's evidence of a greater focus by the CCB upon Namibia from that time. There is an entry on 10 July making mention of 'Namibian Taxi Services', 32 vehicles to be 'disrupted', and then 'disrupt Swapo meetings, disrupt Swapo loudspeakers', 'get hold of snakes' and disseminate disease in 'camps' (with reference to an attempt to introduce cholera bacteria at a Swapo refugee returnee camp, which fortunately failed to cause any damage).

On the following day, entries confirmed Van Zyl's evidence of CCB's region 6 being deployed in Namibia, referring to Swapo activities – including social gatherings and recruiting members for 'Swapo underground'. Burger is specifically mentioned. Under cross-examination, Basson conceded that the focus on Namibia was under the direct orders of Verster, the CCB's head. This entry was followed up by another on 14 July, identifying Swapo taxis and indirect references to sabotage and arson of those vehicles. There was another reference to monitoring and disrupting political gatherings and further entries about 'water, power and loudspeakers' below that. Another entry spoke of 'drinking places' and getting hold of 'medicine' (possibly referring to poison at watering holes with a reference to Namibia by Night, a popular bar and nightclub in Katutura at the time, apparently frequented by Hidipo Hamutenya.

On 27 July, Niko, Dan and Hamutenya are specifically referred to, as well as 'monitor client 2', calling for proposals concerning the latter. Our inference was that Anton was client 2 because surveillance by Barnard and Neelse came at roughly that time in the form of another video of his home. This entry closely relates to that of 3 August where the following is stated:

Bepaal opsies rondom kliënt 2
– vriende
– bewegings
– amptelike program
– sos bedrywighede

Opsies

1. Toordokter

2. Medies

3. Karbom

4. Naby aksies

5. Afstand aksie?

Kliënt no 1 voor einde Aug

2 middel Sept

Kliënte saam ondersoek? Jack bespreek.

This translates as:

Determine options around client 2

– friends

– movements

– official programme

– social activities

Options:

1. Witch doctor

2. Medical

3. Car bomb

4. Nearby actions

5. Distant action?

Client no 1 before end of Aug

2 middle Sept

Investigate clients together? Discuss with Jack.

This entry speaks for itself, discussing options in respect of client 2 whom we inferred was Anton. 'Witch doctor' and 'medical' no doubt referred to some form of poisoning or chemical attack. 'Nearby' and 'distant' would suggest the options of shooting at close range or from a distance. The reference to Jack is to Verster. The inference that Anton was client 2 is supported by the reference to mid-September, as Anton was killed on 12 September.

These entries tied in with Van Zyl's evidence of an 'in-house' presentation on 1 September to Verster (and the need for his approval) and where Maree told Van Zyl that he was to present on Anton. Van Zyl and Botha were then asked to leave the room. It is no coincidence that the top third of the page of Basson's diary for 1 September (the day of the presentation) was torn out – as were the pages for 2, 3 and 4 September, as well as for 12 September. Basson's explanation for removing these pages was devoid of any credibility, saying he needed pages to make notes on. The entry for 12 September was forensically reconstructed by police experts from indentations as follows:

'Vermom. Nie bel, kleredrag verander, nuwe klere, slegs volgens plan optree, nie pager gebruik, nie persoonlike kontak na job, alibi om na Zambië te gaan, langer agterbly, twee dae, versterking nie by adres gewees nie.' ('Disguise. No phoning, change clothing, new clothes, don't use pager, no personal contact after job, alibi to go to Zambia, stay behind longer, two days, reinforcement should not be at address.')

Basson conceded in cross-examination that this entry was in the form of instructions to someone after a task was completed and looked like the type of instructions given to an assassin after completing an assignment. This also tied in with Acheson's affidavit that he was told to go to Lusaka after waiting at the flat for two days. It would seem that these instructions were probably given to Acheson's handler, Maree, on 12 September. Significantly, there was an absence of entries after 15 September having any bearing on members of CCB's region 6.

This fits in with Van Zyl's evidence of the emergency meeting after Acheson's arrest, where members were worried about Acheson being connected to them and resolved to scale down activities for the time being.

The diary entries also confirmed the evidence of other CCB activities in the run-up to the election – intelligence gathering on 'targets'. Given Botha's evidence of Hamutenya being an approved project that Burger was obliged to cancel, it would seem that he was probably client number 1. There are discernible indications of other persons receiving CCB attention, such as Dan, Gwen and Niko and others who were not referred to by name.

There was also other evidence of admissions made by CCB operatives that Anton was a CCB 'project'. Brigadier Mostert, who investigated Webster's killing, said that Verster had admitted to him that the CCB was responsible for Anton's assassination. The deputy head of criminal investigation of the South African police, General Jakob Joubert, said his abiding impression after a meeting with Lieutenant-General Badenhorst, head of Military Intelligence, and Major-General Eddie Webb, chairman of the CCB and head of Special Operations in the SADF, was that Anton had been a CCB 'project'.

Another CCB operative, Pieter Botes, is said to have informed General Joubert that Anton had been a CCB project.

Smit also provided a detailed account of CCB involvement in Namibia in his statement and evidence in the inquest into Anton's death before Judge Levy when it eventually got under way in April 1994. With the exclusion of Barnard, Botha and Van Zyl, most of the witnesses who had made statements to him were called and testified, including two other CCB operatives, Neelse and Niemoller.

Shortly before the inquest, Neelse had changed his name to Wildschut. He was an 'unconscious' member of the CCB. His initial handler was Johan Niemoller, who also gave evidence at the inquest. After being employed by Niemoller from early 1989 to May 1989,

Burger became his handler, known only to Neelse by his alias. During his employment with Niemoller, he acquired photographic equipment with money provided by Niemoller, who also bought him a car. His mandate from Niemoller was to observe Swapo meetings and conduct surveillance of specified buildings and installations. He subsequently assisted Niemoller in making a video of Anton's home.

Neelse had made three affidavits to Smit, but in his oral testimony he tried to retract some components, such as Niemoller referring to Anton as the 'bliksem' and that he had met Burger through Niemoller. Significantly, Neelse had returned to Niemoller's employ after making his statements to Smit. This may have had something to do with his sudden amnesia about prior incriminating statements concerning his boss. He was coincidentally represented by the same attorney as Niemoller at the inquest and had travelled on Niemoller's private aircraft to attend the proceedings. In Wim's cross-examination, he soon admitted discussing aspects of the inquest with Niemoller and that it was after those discussions that he had sought to make 'corrections' to his affidavits.

When he switched employment to Burger in May 1989, his instructions were to continue as before. Burger had said to him that he wanted Dan and Anton's 'testicles on the table'. He sought to deny this in his oral testimony, only later to concede its correctness. Burger also gave him R15 000 to buy a taxi to use between Rehoboth and Windhoek and informed him that he would deal with someone else afterwards. Neelse was then put in touch with Barnard, who instructed him to buy pagers for them both, confirming the transcripts of those pagers. He hired a video camera, which he and Barnard used to video Anton's home. He also accompanied Barnard when a journalist wearing a disguise identified Dan and Anton's homes. Barnard later informed him that he had to cancel 'everything around' Dan and Anton and that Burger would be further involved. This statement was also denied at the inquest.

Neelse also confirmed that he had spoken to Chief Inspector Terblanche of the police in Windhoek about the identity of one of the killers of a UN guard at Outjo – a crime thought at the time to have been committed by right-wing extremists bent upon disrupting the election process, but which, with hindsight, could have been part of covert operations. He also informed Terblanche that he had instructions from Barnard and Burger to sabotage Swapo vehicles and silence prominent Swapo leaders. He mentioned the aliases used by Barnard and Burger. Under cross-examination, he conceded that silencing meant killing them. Terblanche was called to testify, acknowledged what was said, and said he had informed the head of the security police, Brig. Badenhorst, who in turn denied Terblanche told him that. No one ever did anything about that tip-off.

During his cross-examination, Neelse admitted that, despite having Barnard's pager number – one of those involved in the conspiracy to kill Anton – he had not gone to the police. His diary for 1989 also had pages excised. He conceded that these would have included contact details for Burger and Barnard and a certain Frik of the Namibian region of the CCB (whose identity to this date remains a mystery) as well as their instructions to him, including relating to the murder of Anton.

Niemoller also gave evidence after making two statements to Smit. He was a former member of the crack 5 Recce (Reconnaissance) Batallion of the SADF. His uncle, Joe Verster, had engaged him as a member of the CCB. He was supplied with ample capital (presumably from CCB funds) to set up a cover business (blue plan) in Upington involving manufacturing camouflage uniforms. He knew that the CCB formed part of the Special Operations division of the SADF. His instructions came from Frik, regional manager of the CCB in Namibia, and someone known to him as Hannes Coetzee. He used his cover as a businessman and farmer to obtain access to Anton and Swapo officials. He had three meetings with Anton – the first in

Johannesburg, and the following two at the Swapo offices – about mining rights in Namibia and a legal issue. He reported these contacts to the CCB.

His instructions were to make video recordings. He eventually conceded under Wim's rigorous cross-examination that he had made a video of Anton's home. Wim's brilliant cross-examination – the best I have witnessed in my years of practice – had him conceding that the video recording was made with the view to identify targets as part of reconnaissance of a CCB target, with reference to Anton's home. He eventually conceded that it would not look good for him to admit to having made a video of Anton's home, as doing so could indicate that he had a hand in Anton's killing.

In his first affidavit, he said he expressed criticism about Anton's slaying to one of his handlers, Hannes Coetzee. When questioned about that, he was extremely evasive.

Niemoller corroborated Neelse concerning the video made of Anton's home and his 'blue plan' employment and use of Neelse. Niemoller confirmed that he had stayed at the Safari Hotel's caravan park, where acidic substances intended for the sabotaging of Swapo vehicles were later discovered by Smit.

At the conclusion of evidence, we argued that his evasive and untruthful answers concerning the CCB and his role within it indicated a guilty state of mind. He had deliberately tried to conceal as much as possible concerning the CCB and refused to provide anyone's identity, except Verster's, although he conceded he knew Lafras Luitingh. His reasons for failing to give Smit Hannes or Frik's contact details were evasive and not credible.

The evidence implicating the CCB and its operatives in Anton's murder (from the initial statements to evidence before the Harms and Webster inquiries and in our inquest) overwhelmingly established that Anton had been assassinated by the CCB. It would not have been a CCB operation without some obfuscation, however – even if belatedly and ineptly attempted. A new line of inquiry emerged in May 1993 when *The Namibian* ran a leading story of sensational claims of local police involvement in Anton's killing. Willem Rooinasie, a former member of the Task Force unit of the pre-independence police, asserted that there had been a conspiracy among local police and the military to murder Anton and that his former supervisor, Warrant Officer Riaan White, had pulled the trigger. The newly appointed head of the Namibian police, General Andima, appointed Warrant Officer Saunderson and Sergeant Neumbo to conduct an investigation into these claims because Rooinasie had implicated Smit in the conspiracy. These policemen found another witness, Romanus Munango, who also made claims of a similar conspiracy, although material differences between the two accounts emerged.

Rooinasie was serving twenty years in prison for robbery, attempted murder, housebreaking, theft and arson at the time. His first statement was not only internally inconsistent but implausible in its own terms. Worse was to follow as his two further statements contradicted each other and the first. Furthermore, it emerged that he had a motive to get at White, who had reported him for fraud and other transgressions while he had been in the police. He gave evidence at the inquest and was comprehensively discredited; Levy found him to have fabricated his account. His version was rejected in its entirety, as was Munango's described by Levy as a 'pack of lies'.

This utterly inept attempt to distract from the real evidence, which conclusively established CCB involvement in Anton's murder, was baffling. Pauw makes the point that it was ineptitude, after all, that characterised much of CCB's conduct, with reference to a string of examples like the botched attempt to contaminate the water at the Döbra refugee camp.[89]

---

89   Pauw, J. 2017. *Into the Heart of Darkness: Confessions of Apartheid's Assassins*. Jonathan Ball Publishers: Johannesburg, pp. 229–230.

After the conclusion of all the evidence at the inquest, we argued for a finding that members of the CCB, a unit of the SADF's Special Operations, together with others hired by them had formed a common purpose to murder Anton. We argued that following the persons associated themselves with the CCB's common purpose to murder Anton: Maree, Burger, Barnard, Botha, Van Zyl, Acheson, Wildschut (Neelse), Basson, Verster, Niemoller and such further CCB members whose identity could not be determined in the inquest. It was clear to us that all the evidence conclusively pointed that way.

Levy returned a finding that, prima facie, Acheson had shot and murdered Anton; and that his murder had been initiated by and involved the CCB, listing Barnard, Maree, Burger, Basson, Niemoller, Botha, Verster, Van Zyl and Wildschut as accomplices. We agreed with the latter portion of the finding but did not consider the finding that Acheson had actually fired the shots to be supported by the evidence. That was also not our suspicion, even though the evidence certainly pointed to his involvement and his having a common purpose with others to have committed the murder.

We deplored the failure of the police to act upon the tip-off they had received about the planned killing. As far as I know, no disciplinary action resulted from this gross dereliction of duty. Although Smit deserved credit for making the breakthrough in linking the CCB to Acheson, we argued that there had been a failure to investigate local involvement in the CCB vigorously. We called for further investigation to establish the identities and activities of other CCB members, such as Hannes Coetzee and Frik, with a view to prosecutions. That, as far as I know, never took place. There is every reason to believe that there was some local complicity in Anton's murder. At the very least, Neelse had implicated the unidentified Frik and Hannes Coetzee, and they were local. Aside from Neelse, there were no doubt other members of Frik and Hannes's cell in Namibia, as well as some 'unconscious' members whom they paid and used – members who also proposed targets and projects of their own, and engaged in disruption of Swapo's election campaign.

Unanswered questions remain.

Some time after the David Webster inquest, Barnard was charged with – and, in 1998, convicted of – his murder. He was also convicted of another murder, the attempted murder of Dullah Omar, defeating the ends of justice and unlawful possession of firearms. He was sentenced to two life sentences and an additional 63 years' imprisonment. His former wife testified (for the state at his trial) that Barnard admitted to working for the CCB and that a hitlist he kept at home included Anton – as well as Winnie Madikizela-Mandela, Archbishop Desmond Tutu and Chris Hani. Barnard was released on parole on 2 April 2019. In the report, it was stated that Staal Burger welcomed this development and added that Barnard's release 'was long overdue'.[90]

It was not difficult to speculate why Anton had been a target. Although he was not within the top leadership of Swapo, he was its leading white member and destined for a senior and probably cabinet position in a Swapo government. Looking at the mindset of CCB members who identified and proposed and targets for approval, Anton would have been high on their list. Elements within the security establishment were often racist and vilified whites as betrayers when they identified themselves with and supported the liberation of the country. Their racism often caused them to inflate the importance of whites in the resistance, because their views of racial superiority meant that blacks would be incapable of achieving much without whites being involved. It would seem that Anton was client number 2 and that Hamutenya, then a very senior member of Swapo leadership, was client number 1. According to the evidence of

---

90   Wiener, M. 2019. 'He loved to be feared' – A reminder of who apartheid hitman Ferdi Barnard is. News24, 7 March 2019. Available at https://www.news24.com/Columnists/Mandy_Wiener/he-loved-to-be-feared-a-reminder-of-who-apartheid-hitman-ferdi-barnard-is-20190307.

CCB operatives, Dan Tjongarero was another leading target. It was clear from these sources that he had been selected in a bid to drive a schism between the 'internal' and 'external' wings of Swapo. The notion of a fundamental division between these factions was driven by baseless security force propaganda and repeatedly given prominence by *Die Republikein*. It was a tactic employed to sow discord and division where it did not essentially exist. CCB members who proposed their targets would have been influenced by, and probably believed, this propaganda – and may also have been swayed by *Die Republikein's* constant vilification of Anton. That hate speech certainly created a toxic climate of antagonism against Anton, but he remained undeterred; to his credit, he took every opportunity to build bridges between the white community and Swapo.

The street where Anton's home was located and where he was slain was renamed Anton Lubowski Street a year or two after the inquest. In the first year of his presidency in 2015, Hage Geingob decided to accord Anton a state funeral, and his remains were reburied at Heroes' Acre. I was honoured when asked to pay tribute to Anton on that fitting occasion.

15

Swapo's detainees

No book about human rights and Namibia in the 1980s would be complete without reference to the Swapo detainee issue.

In the second half of 1985, allegations started to surface concerning detentions and abuse of detainees at the hands of Swapo in Angola, and in Zambia before that. Sean Cleary, the suave, media-savvy operative in the AG's office who tirelessly promoted the recently installed IG, latched onto these. The timing of the allegations suited the South African cause. Much was made of the bill of rights in the IG's empowering proclamation, then juxtaposed with the allegations emerging about Swapo's human rights abuses.

At first, there was no reliable confirmation. But the allegations became more specific, from more sources, and gained in credence. They needed to be taken seriously.

I approached Bishop James about them. Swapo had briefed him and a few other church leaders travelling abroad that there were detainees who had infiltrated Swapo to spy for South Africa. 'Confessions' to this effect, recorded on video tape, were shown to him and other church leaders. Bishop James, like many of us, was aware of South Africa's infiltration of progressive organisations. He felt reassured by the Swapo presentation. I was less convinced about the reliability of the 'confessions' extracted from those in detention. I had learnt that these were inherently untrustworthy, especially when detainees had been isolated and abused, and that detainees could be coerced or worn down by their tormentors and torture to say what the latter wanted to hear.

My own concerns did not go away. Instead, they were heightened when rumours surfaced of the death of Tauno Hatuikilipi, apparently by suicide, after being detained as an alleged spy. He had gone into exile after serving as director of the Christian Centre, the forerunner of the CCN. Although I did not know him well because he had gone into exile just before I had started to practise, he was impressive in that capacity and certainly did not strike me as spy material – but rather as future Swapo leadership material. I similarly doubted the spy label that was later also pinned on student leaders I knew better, and who had gone into exile, landed in detention and not returned.

Hatuikilipi's death was confirmed in February 1986 when Swapo held a press briefing in London. At that occasion, Hidipo Hamutenya, then Swapo's information secretary, accused South Africa of 'recruiting, training and infiltrating agents'[91] into Swapo ranks. Swapo's foreign secretary, Theo-Ben Gurirab, confirmed in that briefing that approximately 100 people were being held by Swapo for spying activities and would not be brought to trial. He complained that Swapo cadres had died 'because of information transmitted to the enemy by these people'. He acknowledged that there were concerns about the well-being and rights of detainees, but said that Swapo was in a war situation and could not be 'opened up for scrutiny'.[92]

I raised the matter with Gwen and felt the need for an editorial in *The Namibian* to call for fair trials and procedural rights for those accused of spying. Following the news of Hatuikilipi's apparent

91   *The Namibian*, 21 February 1986.
92   *The Namibian*, 21 February 1986.

suicide, I became deeply sceptical that all the detainees were spies and felt the need for safeguards. After some persuasion, Gwen let me prepare an editorial calling upon Swapo to provide for fair trials and afford the opportunity to those accused 'to answer to the alleged crimes in courts in Zambia and Angola and for international observers to be permitted to attend the trials'. I added:

> To deny those accused of serious crimes the right to a fair trial, the right to legal representation and the right to defend themselves is to move into the shady moral area currently occupied by the South African Government itself when dealing with its political opponents.

Gwen agreed to place the editorial in the same edition that carried a report on the London briefing by Hamutenya and Gurirab.[93]

The issue continued to resurface from time to time with fresh allegations of abuse or a new voice added to those calling for accountability.

As I was about to leave for London to address an Anti-Apartheid Movement (AAM) seminar in October the following year on the effect of the apartheid state's policies and actions on children, Anton contacted me. He had been approached the day before by a family in Tsumeb that was deeply concerned about the well-being of their daughter, Bience Gawanas, who was said to have been detained by Swapo. Anton asked me to raise her plight with Hidipo Hamutenya, who was also scheduled speak at the event. My response to Anton was that it may have more impact if he were to raise the matter, given his standing within Swapo – he had joined a few years before and was growing in stature there. His star was on the rise within the movement. He resisted that suggestion: doing so would impede his prospects within Swapo. He felt that this concern would not apply

---

93   *The Namibian*, 21 February 1986.

to me, not being a Swapo member and, unlike him, not seeing my future in politics. He also felt that it would count for more if I raised the matter, as a human rights lawyer with credibility. I was not sure about that, but agreed to raise the matter of Bience's detention. It was the first time I had been approached, albeit indirectly, by a family to raise a matter of this nature with Swapo.

I had heard of Bience. She had gone into exile while pursuing legal studies at the University of the Western Cape and had later successfully completed her law degree in England. I had represented one of her brothers, Alex, when he had been arrested and charged during student unrest. (The charges were later dropped.)

At the time, the terrorism trial against Andreas Heita and his co-accused was running. The presiding judge kindly agreed not to sit on the Friday to enable me to travel to London for the weekend to speak at the seminar.

At the very start of the proceedings on the Saturday, I approached Hamutenya about meeting in private. We hurriedly slipped out to have lunch at a nearby pub, instead of at the venue, so that we could talk confidentially. At his instance, he was accompanied by Swapo's chief representative in London, Shapwa Kaukungwa, whom I knew. I introduced the topic I wanted to raise. Hamutenya was taken aback and immediately cut me short. He would prefer to have that conversation one on one with me. There was no time for that, I said, because my flight home was straight after lunch the next day. He proposed a breakfast meeting the following morning at the hotel where we were both staying. He supplied his room number at my request. Our conversation then turned to other topics.

He did not appear at our agreed time the next morning at the hotel's breakfast area. After about 30 minutes I called his room repeatedly. No reply. I had my breakfast and returned to my room. I tried again and again to call him. Still no reply. I continued at intervals to try to reach him without success until I went downstairs for a lunch with Archbishop Trevor Huddleston, the president of the AAM, and other leadership figures from the organisation. Hamutenya was also invited to the lunch. He failed to show up for that too.

My departure to the airport was directly after the lunch. Before leaving, I asked the archbishop if we could have a private word. I told him of Bience's detention and her family's concerns about her well-being. I requested him and the AAM to raise Bience's detention with Swapo, seeing that Hamutenya had deliberately denied me that opportunity. He was visibly shaken by this news and my request. He knew Bience from her time in England and assured me he would do so. I knew that my action would adversely affect my relationship with Hamutenya, which it did.

I was not sure when I would have the opportunity to travel and raise the issue again, and was heartened by the archbishop's steadfast determination to do so. (My concerns about future travel were well founded. After my return, my passport expired. I applied for a new one. After some weeks, the eventual response to my repeated enquiries to the Civic Affairs office, which issued passports, was that my application had been referred to the AG. After several more weeks – and, no doubt, Helen Suzman's very kind intervention – an official in the AG's office called to say that it had been decided to grant me a renewal and that my new passport could be collected at the Civic Affairs office the next day. Instead of the usual five-year renewal, mine was only granted for a year; I was told I would in future need to apply annually.)

Upon my return from the AAM seminar, I decided to send a short fax to the Swapo London office for Kaukungwa, simply referring to the issue I had raised and requesting that it be urgently looked into. I did so without mentioning any names or specifics, for obvious reasons. A few months later, an AAM activist visiting Windhoek in 1988 called upon me and said I would understand the cryptic message she was requested by Swapo to relay to me. It was that my request had been acceded to. The next day, it was the turn of an upbeat Anton to call on me to say that an immensely relieved family had received word of Bience's release from detention.

I met and befriended Bience in 1989 when she returned to Namibia from exile. Bience later joined the LAC until she was appointed as one of the first Public Service Commissioners at the instance of the first prime minister, Hage Geingob. She was later to serve as Namibia's Ombudswoman and still later had the distinction of being appointed as a Commissioner of the African Union in Addis Ababa.

In early 1989, with the implementation of the UN peace plan approaching, Swapo acknowledged that it was holding 201 'South African Spies' who would be released in terms of Resolution 435.[94] One of the express terms of the Resolution included the release of political prisoners by both sides to the conflict.

On 4 July 1989, a group of 153 former Swapo detainees were repatriated to Windhoek on a UN transport plane. Shortly before repatriation, some of them had formed the Political Consultative Committee (PCC) to campaign for the release of other detainees still being held, publicise abuses perpetrated by their Swapo minders and campaign against Swapo in the upcoming election for the Constituent Assembly.

Straight after their arrival, they called a press conference. They graphically described egregious abuses, torture and detention in appalling conditions in what they called dungeons, which were pits underground. Some stripped down to display the scars of torture. These were plain to see. They also claimed an ethnic bias to decisions to detain directed at non-Owambo Swapo members, as well as a bias against educated Owambo members from the cities. The PCC also claimed, at that press conference and at subsequent ones, that Swapo

94   Human Rights Watch. 1992. *Accountability in Namibia: Human rights and the transition to democracy. An Africa Watch report.* Human Rights Watch: New York, p. 92.

was still holding several hundred more detainees. Many members of the PCC actively took part in election campaigns.

Several parties opposing Swapo in the forthcoming election courted former detainees and used their accounts of ill-treatment in their election campaigns against Swapo. Their accounts no doubt damaged Swapo's campaign.

Some other former detainees returned separately as part of Swapo's repatriation. Still others escaped from detention and returned under their own steam. And many never returned at all.

I met with some of the former detainees, who told me about their experiences.

Several of them put pressure on Mr Ahtisaari to ensure that all Swapo detainees be returned to Namibia. The PCC vocally took up the issue, supported by a group known as the Parents' Committee (PC), which had, for a few years by then, been campaigning for the release of Swapo detainees.

In response to this mounting pressure, supported by several overseas NGOs, Mr Ahtisaari appointed a mission comprising senior UNTAG officials to visit Swapo camps in Angola and Zambia to determine whether any Swapo detainees were still being held at those locations. The camps in question had been identified by PCC members in their submissions. The PCC and other individuals also provided the UN with lists of persons who had allegedly been detained and not returned in 1989.

The UNTAG mission was headed by Ambassador B.A. Clark of Nigeria, the UNTAG representative in Angola, and included several senior UNTAG officials. The mission compiled a list of 1 110 names from those supplied to it. The mission visited the designated camps and bases in September 1989. In its report, the mission said that most facilities had been abandoned and stripped of building materials. It found that the 'geographical locations as well as the physical layouts of sites visited corresponded in the main with the original information' provided by the PCC and others. Holding cells, including some at the Etale Camp, were 'partly sunken into the ground'.[95]

Their report was released on 11 October 1989. They found that all the camps and facilities were abandoned or had closed several weeks before, and that there was 'no evidence that any persons were being held against their will at any of these locations'.[96] The mission concluded that 'the majority [of the 1 110 names] have been repatriated or accounted for'. The mission found, however, that 315 persons on the list were unaccounted for. Of the total number provided to it, the mission found that 914 persons had been incarcerated. Of these, 484 were said to have been released or repatriated, 71 had not in fact been detained, 115 were reported to have died, 52 could not be identified because of insufficient details supplied, and 315 remained unaccounted for. According to the Human Rights Watch report,[97] several former detainees pointed out inaccuracies and inconsistencies with this breakdown in the mission's report, supported by references to specific former detainees wrongly categorised or not properly dealt with.

Following these revelations and the accounts of former detainees, a committee of progressive European NGOs requested Bishop James and me to approach Theo-Ben Gurirab about the issue. These NGOs had supported and funded activities against the apartheid regime, both inside and outside the country, especially in channelling EU funding to Namibian initiatives and partnering with the Namibian Development Trust that I had co-founded. We were asked to convey to him that they considered that future NGO support and funding for an independent Namibia would be dependent upon Swapo providing some form of accountability on the Swapo detainee issue. Bishop James declined to get involved in the issue but I agreed to

---

95   Human Rights Watch, p. 100.
96   Human Rights Watch, p. 100.
97   Human Rights Watch, pp. 100–101.

convey their sentiments and their quest for an undertaking to address the issue to Gurirab.

At our meeting, he listened stern-faced, then bluntly responded: 'We'll not be blackmailed by the promise of future aid by foreign NGOs. Swapo will make its own choices on what to do on that issue without their interference or prescription. Please convey that to those who sent you.'

I scrupulously noted down his message and responded: 'I understand your position as spokesperson. But on a personal note, your response seems completely at odds with the Ben I met and came to know since 1982 – humane and concerned with human rights.'

He nodded and took a deep breath, then slowly continued: 'I gave you our official position as an organisation. That is what you came for and that's what I gave in terms of my mandate. But how do you think I feel when I face my dear sister in Usakos? Two children she brought up did not return. Do you not think I know and understand the pain as well as the concerns people like you have on this issue?'

All I could say as I got up to leave was that I felt deeply for his sister and their entire family. He warmly embraced me as I left.

Shortly after this meeting, Swapo gained a comfortable majority in the November election, although not the required two-thirds to adopt a constitution on its own. This meant the need for a spirit of compromise so that a constitution could be prepared and passed with the requisite majority. The Constituent Assembly formed a Constitutional Committee headed by Hage Geingob, who later became the first prime minister (and, in 2014, was elected to the Presidency). Compromise from all sides characterised the work of that committee. He in particular, as chairman, as well as the DTA's Dirk Mudge, played constructive roles that eventually led to the final draft being unanimously adopted – no mean feat, given the prior distrust and enmity and the pressure of a very tight deadline. The Constituent Assembly had taken office in late November 1989 and, under Geingob's deft leadership, on 9 February 1990 had remarkably formally adopted the Constitution, rightly hailed internationally as one of the world's finest. Credit should also go to the three experts appointed as a drafting committee, headed by Arthur Chaskalson. They skilfully drafted what had been agreed upon by the Constitutional Committee under Geingob's stewardship. I had strongly recommended Arthur's appointment as Swapo's nominee to Hartmut, who was a member of the Constitutional Committee and became the first Attorney-General of the independent Namibia. Hartmut and Vekuii Reinhard Rukoro (the latter then of the Namibia National Front or NNF) tirelessly toiled as the link between the Constitutional Committee (on which they both served) and Arthur's drafting committee.

Human rights protection is a prominent feature of Namibia's fine constitution. The parties had previously committed themselves to a list of principles in an addendum to the UN peace plan (known as the 1982 principles). The Constitution, however, goes further than those principles in its protection of human rights.

The right-giving Constitution and the incoming president's commitment to a policy of national reconciliation gave rise to a widespread feeling of optimism for the future in building our new nation. As part of the policy of national reconciliation, it was made clear that there would be no prosecutions for abuses by either side to the conflict.

As a practical matter, prosecutions would have been difficult. The AG's eleventh-hour amnesty in breathtakingly wide terms was directed at preventing prosecution for those on the South African side, most of whom had returned to that separate sovereign state and would have needed to be extradited. But there were many in Koevoet and other security force structures who had been born in Namibia, or had remained there. They had mostly not occupied leadership positions. They, too, were covered by the amnesty. On Swapo's side, there was a widely worded amnesty for those who returned from exile.

Although I certainly would have preferred prosecutions for the most egregious abuses on both sides, I accepted that this would be difficult and only possible upon successfully challenging the AG's amnesty directive. I also accepted that wholesale prosecutions could be damaging and divisive, and place the hard-won peace under strain. There was nonetheless a compelling need for some form of accountability. Past abuses needed to be investigated so that victims and their families could obtain the truth about what had happened and those involved in gross human rights abuses could be identified and sanctioned, even if no prosecutions were to take place. At a minimum, they should be disqualified from occupying public office and positions of power.

Instead of appointing an inquiry or a commission – as many, including me, called for – in October 1990, a mere six months after independence, the new government announced the appointment of Solomon 'Jesus' Hawala as chief of the army, the third-highest position in the Namibian Defence Force. Hawala had been in charge of the Swapo detention camps and of Swapo security, and had featured prominently in most accounts of abuses in those camps. This appointment was widely condemned by the Council of Churches through its respected leader, Dr Abisai Shejavali, and by Gay McDougall, Amnesty International and the LAC. The government strongly defended his appointment, with Hidipo Hamutenya unsurprisingly at the forefront, accusing critics of 'selective morality' in 'singling out' Hawala.[98]

Despite the extensive criticism, the appointment went ahead.

At a human rights workshop in Swakopmund in February 1991 organised by the Raoul Wallenberg Institute and the local Swedish Embassy, I was asked to address the topic 'Namibia and Human Rights: Are we on track?' While acknowledging with pride how far we had progressed, I raised a few items of concern and the need for

---

98   Human Rights Watch; *The Namibian*, 25 October 1990.

robust debate and critical assessment – as opposed to the culture of silence that seemed to have set in, restraining society from criticism. There seemed to be a widely held perception of adverse consequences if one spoke out. In a country where the state and parastatals employ about half of those in formal employment and where some sectors of the economy are dependent upon access to state resources such as in mining and fishing, and where tendering for state contracts plays a significant role in the economy, perceived adverse consequences had the potential to take on considerable proportions, given the system of patronage starting to take shape.

I specifically singled out the sensitive issue of past human rights abuses by all sides to the conflict. Many of my clients had disappeared in the night, never to be seen again. Koevoet was no doubt responsible for several of those disappearances. But other elements of the security forces also had much to answer for. My clients and their families thirsted for answers. I also referred to abuses in detention on the part of the liberation movement. I quoted the internationally accepted standards embraced by Human Rights Watch in an earlier publication,[99] stressing that accountability for past human rights abuses meant making known all that could be reliably established concerning gross human rights abuses, their nature and extent, and the identity of victims and perpetrators – including those who devised and implemented policies resulting in gross abuses.

Accepting that prosecutions would be legally difficult as a result of the AG's amnesty and possibly counterproductive in the context of the government policy of national reconciliation, I stressed that it was also important to understand what the concept of reconciliation properly presupposed. It could not mean that the past should be merely brushed aside or forgotten: people could only forgive or become reconciled if they knew what they were forgiving or reconciling themselves

---

99   Melander, G. 1991. Report No 9, Human Rights Workshop, Namibia, 18–24 February 1991. Raoul Wallenberg Institute: Lund.

to. While war trials and tribunals may thus not be legally appropriate, thorough investigations should nevertheless be undertaken for the sake of the victims and their families and in the interest of the country as a whole. The lingering uncertainty concerning the fate of those who went missing or did not return should end, I said, and those involved in serious abuses should be exposed. This should happen if the government took rights seriously, stressing the adage of the need to learn from an honest assessment of our past in order to avoid the same path in our future.

I turned to Hawala's appointment and the repeated allegations of his centrality to so many extremely grave abuses and the fact that he had not publicly refuted the persistent allegations to that effect. Until and unless his name was cleared in an investigation, his appointment amounted to a serious blemish on an independent Namibia's human rights record. I stressed that anyone who had committed serious human rights abuses was simply unfit to hold a position of authority. The same would, of course, apply to former Koevoet members and security policemen.

I concluded that an inability to address past abuses undermined my ability to express unqualified confidence in the future protection of human rights.

Unfortunately, there was no commission or investigation into past abuses – not even a limited one to establish the identity of those who had disappeared or had not returned, and the circumstances of their disappearances. Instead, the wound caused by these abuses has continued to fester. Families have not been able to obtain any form of closure. Gross abusers of human rights have continued to hold office. Many former detainees who returned were still labelled as spies and continued to endure that awful epithet. In many instances, they were consciously or indirectly discriminated against in employment as a consequence – in most cases, unjustifiably. Despite that stigma and their scars, many have been able to overcome these disadvantages and the odds, to play meaningful roles in our democracy over the past 28 years. Bience is a prime example. But the issue remains un-addressed.

There were a number of attempts by opposition members in Parliament to bring about some form of accountability for Swapo detainees. In November 1990, the National Assembly passed a resolution calling upon the Chief Justice to approach the ICRC to investigate the status of those who had disappeared during the war and who were still unaccounted for.

In the following month, the ICRC Head of Delegation responded that, under ICRC's mandate, it could only deal with the government of Namibia and not one its separate branches, such the legislative branch. It would, in principle, be prepared to assist if the government approached it. It would initially take up unresolved cases already referred to it and then decide, on the basis of results, whether it would be able to deal with new requests from families.

For several months, the process stalled.

No approach by the government was forthcoming. In April 1991, an opposition MP, Moses Katjiuongua, reintroduced a motion calling for the establishment of a judicial commission of inquiry, stating that the ICRC was not the 'appropriate instrument' to investigate the matter. (This was because it was limited to tracing those who had gone missing in conflict, and could not determine any accountability.) On 28 May 1991, his motion was defeated after a bitter debate. On the following day, Hartmut, as Attorney-General, introduced a motion requesting the prime minister to inform the ICRC of the government's acceptance of its conditions. It was unanimously passed on 31 May 1991. During the following month, the ICRC was duly approached by the prime minister in accordance with this motion.

The tracing work of the ICRC faced a lack of cooperation from the governments of South Africa, Zambia and Botswana (although Zambia subsequently changed its stance). Swapo appointed a liaison officer to handle tracing requests. His response was tardy. In August

1991, 70 requests were sent; in February 1992, only 28 of those had been answered. In the meantime, it was announced that the ICRC would close its delegation in Namibia by the end of June 1992.

Shortly before its closure, the ICRC announced that it had received a further 1 710 new tracing requests following its public appeal to families with missing relatives to file requests. Most of the new cases concerned missing PLAN fighters, the overwhelming majority of whom were thought to have died in combat.

By the end of June 1992, the ICRC had received 170 replies from Swapo. Thirty of the persons were stated as having been 'last seen in detention' and were reported to have succumbed to disease.

Following the closure of the ICRC delegation in Namibia, the tracing of missing persons ground to a halt. No significant steps have been taken since.

In 1996, the publication of a book about the issue – *Namibia: The Wall of Silence* by Rev. Siegfried Groth,[100] a German pastor – was denounced by President Nujoma as a 'false history' written to 'smear Swapo and open up old wounds which were about to heal'. President Nujoma did not deal with the allegations in Groth's book, however. Nor were the wounds then about to heal. They have not been healed since.[101] Sadly, many families have not received any further word on the fate of their missing loved ones. No statement at all as to the fate of those who never returned. Not a word of regret. Not a single word. Nor have those responsible for abuses been identified, or faced any consequences, barring their consciences. The failure of any form of accountability whatsoever for past abuses on both sides remains a blot that tarnishes Namibia's human rights record.

---

100 English translation from German by Hugh Beyer (Peter Hammer Verlag, Wuppertal, Germany, 1995), distributed in Southern Africa by David Philip Publishers.

101 This is clear from an articulate account by a former detainee recently published. Oiva Angula's *SWAPO Captive: A Comrade's Experience of Betrayal and Torture* (Zebra Press, Cape Town, 2018) graphically describes both the conditions of detention and the circumstances that led to detentions by Swapo.

Epilogue

For years, the apartheid state created the illusion of scrupulously following and upholding the law, even laws that facilitated harsh state
action against subjects. These included laws that authorised forced
removals and detention without trial, restricted movement on grounds
of race, conscripted people to serve in its army and made interracial
love a crime. There was a fastidious enforcement of these noxious laws.

Under P.W. Botha, an assiduous militarisation of the apartheid state
brought about a discernible shift in the approach to the law. The end
would justify the means – no matter how unlawful and objectionable
the means were, and became. When stifling dissent or dealing with
opponents could no longer fit comfortably within the omnipotent
battery of draconian laws, or where the military engaged in excesses,
the law was to be overridden by indemnity provisions or simply
breached with impunity. The shockingly wide indemnity powers in
section 103 ter of the Defence Act were invoked to prevent the courts
from adjudicating the court challenge to military detentions for six
years without trial, and later to thwart the murder trials of those
charged with bludgeoning Frans Uapota to death and those to be held
responsible for Immanuel Shifidi's death.

The end justifying the means also meant routine torture of

detainees. Koevoet was established and operated upon that principle too. The means employed by that unit resulted in countless deaths and disappearances. That count remains unmeasured, because so many victims landed in shallow and anonymous graves. It is no coincidence that the notorious Vlakplaas death squad that emerged in South Africa in the 1980s was headed by Eugene de Kock, who cut his teeth in callous illegal conduct as a company commander of Koevoet from 1979 to 1983. A unit that prided itself on its 'kill rate', rewarded its members handsomely in financial terms for each kill of an alleged insurgent before or after capture, and included alleged collaborators speaks of a state that had abandoned any vestiges of a moral compass.

The descent into lawless conduct extended beyond military and paramilitary matters and the combatting of insurgency. The power of the state was also unleashed upon political opponents of the regime and upon lawful political activity not favoured by the military. There was the inevitable slide into the opaque world of covert units that engaged in extrajudicial killings. This trend is amply demonstrated by the murder of Shifidi when the military disrupted a legal Swapo meeting, and culminated in the calculated killing of Anton in 1989.

The incremental militarisation and the resultant undermining of the law during the dark days of the 1980s placed heavy demands on my approach to practising law, premised upon and driven by a belief in the value of law as means to bring about justice. Amid harsh laws, the invocation of indemnities to avoid scrutiny and security force lawlessness and terror, holding the state and its agents to account became increasingly difficult. But it also became ever more compelling to do so. What was crucial was maintaining a belief in the law and rights – by assisting those caught up in, and endeavouring to take every opportunity to challenge these methods, practices and injustices by invoking the law and seeking to vindicate legal standards. This ultimately meant having to leave private practice to tackle these challenges more systematically by establishing the LAC and using the media to expose human rights abuses.

Circumstances dictated the development of a different kind of practice. But it took brave clients to risk the brunt of further security force action to stand up against the ruthless regime. Often they did so at grave personal risk, especially when in isolated, far-flung communities without means of communication and where the reach of the law was tenuous and its protection marginal – factors exploited by Koevoet and the military. This resilience is personified in Victoria Mweuhanga's refusal to accept the cover-up of her husband's murder and to mount a challenge that South Africa's State President P.W. Botha himself was obliged to answer. Another was Josef Katofa, whose committed activism enabled us to challenge the Mariental detentions – ultimately at the cost of his own liberty. Few of these clients received recognition for their fearless contributions after independence. They have my abiding respect, undiminished by the passage of time, which has been a motivating factor for writing this book – out of respect for their selfless contributions in showing how the law was used and abused during those years.

As for those who featured in the cases I have discussed, Josef Katofa courageously continued his activism until independence. Had it not been for a controversy reported in the media concerning a pastor at a funeral at the ELCIN church at Eengolo requiring mourners to remove a Swapo flag from a coffin in September 2009, his death would have passed almost unnoticed by everyone except for members of the community in that area. Katofa's name was only mentioned in passing in the report in *The Namibian* as a 'well-known Swapo veteran' from the area whose funeral had caused the commotion. The thrust of the report centred on the banning of party flags at ELCIN funerals. Apart from this terse and coincidental reference, there followed no tribute or acknowledgement of his life and part in the liberation struggle – in that publication or elsewhere. I felt compelled to pen a short tribute, which was later published in the monthly journal *Insight*. I referred to his courageous and crucial role in the Mariental case, his incarceration for that, and his importance as a symbol of defiance in the western part of Owambo before independence. His legacy lives on in the law reports because of the groundbreaking principle established in his case. Like many others who had taken huge risks and demonstrated great courage during those years, his contribution went largely unnoticed and without any official recognition after independence. I concluded my tribute:

> The controversy at his funeral should never have arisen. Indeed, his coffin should have been draped in the National colours and a national honour accorded to him.

Upon independence, Dan was appointed a deputy minister in the first cabinet in the Ministry of Information, hardly harnessing his skills or recognising his role. His ill health plagued him. When he died a few years later, his immense contribution went largely unrecognised by those in power. Niko was appointed Minister of Environment in the first government. He, too, died relatively early, after serving a single term. *The Namibian* continued to flourish under Gwen's skilful stewardship until she stood down a few years ago to make way for Tangeni Amupadhi's appointment as editor. It continues its fearless reporting.

To my mind, the single most significant leadership role played in the struggle for human rights and human dignity within Namibia during the 1980s was that of Bishop James. His quiet and unassuming role was decisive in uniting the churches and the communities they served against the abuse of human rights during those years. His massive contribution to the liberation struggle likewise received little official recognition. But that mattered not to those whose lives he touched. Their tribute at his memorial service was as striking as it was dignified and fitting. The small Anglican cathedral in Windhoek was packed, as was the adjacent hall and all seats and standing room outside, where the service was relayed. At the conclusion of the service, we inside the cathedral were asked to remain seated while those who had been standing and sitting outside and in the adjacent hall could first file past the coffin to pay their respects. For more than an hour and an half, the steady stream of people passing in deferent silence through the church to pay their respects for his contribution seemed never-ending. There could be no more fitting and moving tribute.

Dr Shejavali was moved to deliver a powerful sermon at Bishop James's memorial service about being let down by independence's not having delivered more in terms of tackling inequality, uplifting people from poverty and restoring human dignity after the ravages of colonialism. Dr Shejavali continues in his retirement to provide moral leadership on compelling social and ethical issues.

Samson continues to speak out for those who were detained by Swapo and on other issues of injustice.

After distinguishing himself in private practice, Hosea recently took up the newly created position of Deputy Judge-President of the High Court, a position he occupies with distinction. Harmut was Namibia's first Attorney-General and acquitted himself well in that office. He served a single term, making an unheralded constructive contribution to the development of the law during those crucial years. After a brief period in private practice as an advocate, Michaela returned to the LAC to set up the Aids Law Project there. After groundbreaking work in the field, she was appointed to head a regional structure coordinating that work in the region. She continues to occupy the position. Andrew is now in practice as a senior counsel. Karel Ndoroma serves within the management cadre of the Ministry of Regional and Local Government and Housing. Wilfried Emvula of the LAC's Walvis Bay Advice Office and Nico Kaiyamo of the Nomstoub Advice Office in Tsumeb were elected to their respective Regional Councils in 1992 and from there to the National Council. Emvula was appointed a deputy minister and later ambassador to France and Ethiopia, and is now retired. Ambrosius Haingura of the Rundu Advice Office was made Governor of the Kavango Region. He died some years back. Petrus Bernadinus Shekutumbah, former political prisoner, was also elected to the Regional Council (for Omusati) and served on it for seventeen years, including a five-year stint as a member of the National Council. Andreas Heita joined the Namibian Defence Force after independence and sadly died suddenly in recent years when visiting Angola. The cause is thought to have been a form of food poisoning.

Magnus Malan, who cast that scurrilous slur upon Anton's name, was not required during his lifetime to properly account for the crimes committed by the SADF's CCB and other covert units – or for other war crimes, for that matter, while at the helm of the SADF – although he provided brief unsatisfactory testimony to the South African Truth and Reconciliation Commission. His central role in undermining the rule of law has received little attention. Hans Dreyer died of cancer a few years back. He was not held to any form of account either for any of the crimes perpetrated by Koevoet.

Die Republikein is now a different newspaper in independent Namibia, with balanced reporting. Its former leadership under Des Erasmus continued in the early years of independence and never once expressed regret or remorse for the venomous maligning of opponents of the apartheid state, even after they had died, or for how the newspaper had distorted the truth. But those elements in the newspaper have themselves passed on or moved on, and long since been replaced by a more even-handed mindset. In fact, the first note of congratulations I received on my appointment to the High Court came from its then editor, Estelle de Bruyn.

As for me, I have never given up on my belief in the value of law as a positive force for bringing about justice and effecting social change. This still remains my guiding principle. Since independence, our right-giving Constitution has provided a far more favourable environment for pursuing these ends. It was my privilege during practice to assert constitutional rights in many cases in seeking to hold the state to the promises contained in our Constitution. And at times I acted for the state in claims made against it. After several years in private practice, I have been fortunate to have received the opportunity to apply this guiding principle of fidelity to the law and the Constitution on the bench to the best of my ability, first at the High Court and, for the past few years, at the Supreme Court of Namibia.

And as for the cases described in this book, it was my very great privilege to serve the clients and communities involved in and affected by them.

ACKNOWLEDGEMENTS

Many of my friends encouraged me to write this. They include Hilary Charlesworth in Australia, Edwin Cameron, Susannah Cowen and Karen Collett in South Africa and many in Namibia – Hosea Angula, Tangeni Amupadhi, Immanuel (JK) Shovaleka, Ginger Mauney, Mindy Burrell, Norman Tjombe and Esi Schimming Chase. I am most grateful to Hilary and Edwin for suggesting that I apply for a writing residency from the Rockefeller Foundation at that magnificent venue, Bellagio on Lake Como in northern Italy and then supporting that application. In that beautiful and stimulating environment, I was able to complete about a third of the book. I am grateful to the Rockefeller Foundation and to my fellow residents there during that time who were supportive and made many useful suggestions. In particular, my warm thanks to Pilar Palacia of the Foundation.

I am also deeply grateful to Peter Orton for reading much of the manuscript and providing invaluable advice and very helpful suggestions to my great benefit and of the book. I am also grateful to my sisters Margie and Sarah Joseph for reading the manuscript and their advice and very useful comments and my other friends who read part of the manuscript and imparted their valued input, including Mindy, Hosea, Tangeni, Emily Schlink and Nelson Nagenda. And to Margie for preparing a map for the book.

There are also those who kindly agreed to be interviewed about events of those times or about people who featured in them. They include Samson Ndeikwila, Gwen Lister, Michaela Clayton, Paul Iipumbu, Karl Ndoroma, Hosea Angula, Hartmut Ruppel, Helao Shituwete, Mike and Dee-Dee Yates, Andrew Corbett, Theo Frank, Bernadinus Shekutambah and Frans Angula. Henry Shimwetukeni and Kemanya Amkongo very kindly helped with legal and historical research. Ms Dorkas Ekandjo of the High Court was extremely helpful in locating records of proceedings in the court's archives.

I am greatly indebted to my efficient personal assistant, Liz Basson, who patiently helped me in pulling things together in her free time and maintained her enthusiasm throughout the process.

I have already mentioned my sister, Margie's indefatiguable assistance which exemplified the unequivocal support I received throughout those years from my close family for the work I did covered by this book – my late parents, Margie and my brother Tony and sister-in-law, Jackie Bourn and also from Maria Kazapua, and from Sacky Kefas and Paavo Uutako during the writing of this book.

343

I am also grateful to the writers' group started by Peter Orton in Windhoek who have generously commented on the two chapters submitted to them – Rémy, Emily, Colletta, Susannah, Mutaleni, Kavena, Pancho and Cecil.

The Namibian has also generously permitted the reprinting material from their archives. A special word of thanks to Mirzia Van Heerden for her assistance in that regard.

Gina Figueira very kindly granted permission to print some of Tony's wonderful images and so kindly assisted in selecting them. The cover photographs and some others featured elsewhere are his. It is fitting that some of his photos adorn the book, given his warm friendship during those years – and afterwards – and his unwavering support for the work.

I am also indebted to Jacques Pauw for his excellent research which went into his two books which I consulted on the chapter on Anton Lubowski's assassination as well as to Colin Kahanowitz for his meticulous notes on the Webster Inquest and Harms Commission which he prepared for us for the inquest into Anton's death.

I am grateful to my colleagues in the judiciary for their support and encouragement in writing this, especially Chief Justice Peter Shivute and Deputy Chief Justice Petrus Damaseb.

My gratitude also goes to Angela Voges appointed by my publishers to edit the book and to the publisher, Erika Oosthuysen together with Sonwabiso Ngcowa, for their professionalism and ever helpful support during the publication process and to Jean Pieters as publicist.

Finally, there is my huge debt of gratitude to all those I was privileged to work alongside during the years covered by this book – learning so much from the fine lawyers it was my great fortune to work with and especially the many clients whom I was privileged to serve in these cases and who at the time were prepared to put their faith and trust in this young and inexperienced lawyer. Many are sadly no longer alive but would know of my deep respect and admiration for their selfless and principled resistance and defiance.

DAVID SMUTS, Windhoek, 2019.

INDEX

101 Battalion (SWATF) 187, 191-192, 195, 197, 199, 202-205, 208, 210, 214, 237

Abrahams, Kenneth 228-230
Accountability in Namibia: Human Rights and the Transition to Democracy 28, 325
Acheson, Donald 292-296, 299, 302, 304-307, 311-312, 316-317
Ackerman, MF 213
African National Congress (ANC) 13, 62, 164
African Union 325
AG 8 of 1980 8, 260
Agony of Truth, The 38
Ahtisaari, Martti 278-279, 281, 283, 292, 326
Aids Law Project 339
Akweenda, John 93, 100, 259, 263
Akweenda, Martin 93, 96, 98, 106, 119, 259, 263
Akweenda, Thomas 93-94, 97-98, 118, 259, 263
Allgemeine Zeitung 164
Amadhila, Solly 227-229
amnesty 215, 329-331
Amnesty International 78, 330
Amukwaya, Immanuel 199
Amupadhi, Tangeni 338
Amutenya, Dominic 49-51
Amutenya, Willy 50-51
Andima, General 316
Angelu, Nikolau 146-148, 154, 157

Angula, Frans 95, 120, 178, 180
Angula, Hosea 27, 36-37, 39, 41-42, 44-47, 51-52, 56, 73, 76-78, 81, 95, 102-103, 105-106, 130, 132-137, 139, 149, 152, 157, 189, 202-203, 207-208, 211, 218-219, 221-222, 225-227, 240, 243-245, 265-266, 289, 339
Angula, Kondja 85
Angula, Oiva 334
Angula, Ono 274
Angula terrorism trial 107, 118, 120, 178, 180
Anti-Apartheid Movement (AAM) 322, 324
Anton Piller order 263-265, 269
apartheid 3-5, 12-15, 22-25, 30, 34, 60, 68, 79, 82-83, 108, 124, 134, 148, 161-165, 169-172, 176, 180-181, 184, 188, 205, 224, 228, 236, 238, 240-241, 243, 251, 267, 294, 297-299, 316, 318, 322, 327, 335, 340
Apocalypse Now 139
Ausfiku, Ben 245, 249

Badenhorst, Brigadier 314
Badenhorst, Rudolf 299, 300, 312
Ballach, Frans 105, 110-111, 113-119, 119, 126-127, 130, 142
Barnard, Attie 265-266
Barnard, Ferdi 293-297, 299, 301-302, 305-306, 308-309, 312-314, 316-318
Basson, Wouter 296, 302, 304, 308-309, 311, 316-317

345

ABOUT THE AUTHOR

DAVID SMUTS has been a Judge of the Supreme Court of Namibia since 2015. From 2011 to 2014 he served as Judge of the High Court of Namibia, before which he was in private practice in Windhoek as senior counsel.

Since 2011, Justice Smuts has delivered over 200 judgments in matters ranging from constitutional challenges to organised crime legislation to motor vehicle accident fund legislation (on equality grounds), freedom of the press raised in defamation proceedings, sexual harassment in the workplace, the need for exemplary sentences for perpetrators of domestic violence, the need to reform legislation protecting endangered species and striking down inordinately long prison sentences as unconstitutional, and an action for damages for adultery.

In June 1988, Smuts founded the Legal Assistance Centre of Namibia and served as founder director from 1988 to 1992. Before that, he practised as an attorney in Windhoek, starting his articles in 1980 and interrupting his practice to complete an LLM at Harvard Law School in 1983. His practice focused primarily on work related to human rights.

Smuts argued for the political status of political prisoners and their release as part of implementation of UN peace plan in 1989, and provided representations to the UN Special Representative during the implementation of the peace plan. He was also a member of the legal team, led by Wim Trengove, SC, that represented family of the late Anton Lubowski at the inquest into his death.

In 1990, he received an award as a Human Rights Monitor from Human Rights Watch, New York. He was elected an Orville H. Schell, Jr. Fellow at the Yale Law School in 1990 and a member of the American Academy of Arts and Sciences in April 2019.

Prior to his appointment as a judge, he served as (non-executive) chair of the Board of Standard Bank Namibia. He co-founded *The Namibian* newspaper in 1985. During his practice, he served terms as President of the Society of Advocates of Namibia; from 2000 to 2009, he was a member of the Judicial Service Commission of Namibia upon nomination by the Law Society of Namibia.

Death, Detention and Disappearance is his first book.

He lives in Windhoek.

www.ingramcontent.com/pod-product-compliance
Lightning Source LLC
Chambersburg PA
CBHW032146080426
42735CB00008B/605